Converting to Islam

Amy Melissa Guimond

Converting to Islam

Understanding the Experiences
of White American Females

Amy Melissa Guimond
Hollywood, Florida, USA

ISBN 978-3-319-54249-2   ISBN 978-3-319-54250-8 (eBook)
DOI 10.1007/978-3-319-54250-8

Library of Congress Control Number: 2017939862

Cover illustration © Cameran Ashraf / GettyImages

Printed on acid-free paper

This Palgrave Macmillan imprint is published by Springer Nature
The registered company is Springer International Publishing AG
The registered company address is: Gewerbestrasse 11, 6330 Cham, Switzerland

This book is dedicated to the Caucasian female American converts to Islam who are currently living in the United States and abroad. Without these women, and the women in this study, gathering this knowledge would have been impossible. Not only did these amazing women help me to better understand the phenomenon in question, but they also provided the support and reassurance that was necessary through this arduous writing process. I greatly respect each of these women as women first, then as friends. Furthermore, I would like to acknowledge that the writing of this manuscript may be mine, but the experiences discussed within are entirely theirs. For me, this study was less about contributing to the much needed discourse that includes female American converts to Islam, and more about giving these women the opportunity to feel validated and empowered by giving them the platform to share their stories.

ACKNOWLEDGMENTS

The writing of a book is much like running a distance race – it is far easier to do when you have people out there supporting you and cheering you on. I know a little bit about running distance races, and I know how important those cheerleaders are! To my number one cheerleader, my dear husband Ray, who understood the importance of this study from day one and who supported me along the way by providing comfort, motivation, and encouragement. Thank you. I love you every day that ends with Y. To my parents and the rest of my family for having faith in me when I struggled with having faith in myself, I can't thank you enough.

To Dr. Claire Michele Rice, Dr. Robin Cooper, and Dr. Evan Hoffman, a thank you beyond words. You were the experts who pushed me to excel over the years by providing various valuable insights on feminist research, methodologies, prejudice and equality, privilege and hatred, and cultural conflict. I would not have been successful in this journey without your guidance, tutelage, and generosity of your time.

To my dearest colleagues and friends: Dr. Heather Wellman, Dr. Cade Resnick, and Dr. Nikki Incorvia: thank you for those late night existential dialogues. You have been amazing counterparts over the years. With you all, I have shared laughter and tears, and I am forever thankful for the encouragement and support that you have provided along the way.

To my running community, thank you for providing the escape that I needed, if only one step at a time. I owe immense gratitude for reading my early drafts and helping to guide me through the analysis process to my insightful friend Theresa Corbin.

CONTENTS

LIST OF FIGURES

LIST OF TABLES

A Social Urgency

Islam is believed to be the fastest growing religion in the world, and it has been estimated that by 2025, approximately 30% of the world's population will be practicing Muslims.[1] The Pew Research Center has a slightly more conservative projection, estimating that by 2030, 26.4% of the world's population will be adhering to Islam.[2] These numbers indicate that there will soon be an estimated 2.2 billion Muslim practitioners worldwide.

Due to federal regulations against asking about religious affiliation during the US Census, the precise number of Muslims living within the United States is unknown; however, the Muslim American population has been estimated by a number of demographers who have suggested that on the low end, the Muslim American population is 2.35 million,[3] and at the high end approximately 6–7 million.[4] In the United States, it is anticipated that if current trends continue, the Muslim American population will increase by more than double in the next 20 years.[5] A recent study published by The Association of Statisticians of American Religious Bodies (which tracks religions through a study every 10 years) found that Islam is the second largest religion in 20 American states,[6] most of which are in the Southern and Midwest regions, though there are large pockets of Muslims throughout the country based on county.[7]

Some demographers believe that Islam may have surpassed Judaism as the second largest faith in the United States.[8] Alternately, the Pew Research Center indicates that while the margins between the Jewish and Muslim populations have decreased, practitioners of Islam have not

© The Author(s) 2017
A.M. Guimond, *Converting to Islam*,
DOI 10.1007/978-3-319-54250-8_1

yet surpassed practitioners of Judaism.[9] It has been estimated that between 1990 and 2001, the Muslim American population grew by 200%.[10] Whether this increase was through immigration, increased birth rates, or conversion was not noted. A more recent study suggests that the Muslim population has grown by 1 million in the decade between 2000 and 2010.[11] In 2008, it was believed that there were over 1,209 active mosques in the United States,[12] and as of 2004, there were 300 ethnic Muslim associations, 200 Muslim student groups, 200 Islamic schools, 100 Muslim community media outlets, and 50 Muslim social service groups which operated within the United States,[13] numbers which continue to grow. While it may be the fastest growing religion in the United States, scholars are actively questioning whether Islam could soon become the fastest shrinking religious demographic in the United States due to intermarriage and assimilation.[14]

The American Muslim community can be separated into two parts: (1) immigrant and (2) American-born (or indigenous).[15] Morey and Yaqin suggest that there are actually three categories of Muslims living in the United States: (1) Muslim immigrants, (2) descendants of African slaves, and (3) white Muslim converts.[16] Contrary to commonly held beliefs, indigenous Muslims and converts actually make up the largest population of Muslims who live in the United States.[17] In reality, Arab-born Muslims make up only an estimated 20% of the Muslim population living in America, though many Americans still incorrectly assume that to be Arab is to be Muslim and that to be Muslim is to be Arab.[18] This assumption about what it means to be Muslim and Arab was highlighted by Abdo who argued that Muslim Americans "live in the heart of America but they are often defined solely by Americans' perceptions of Muslims abroad, whether they are insurgents in Iraq or Saudi oil tycoons in Riyadh."[19]

Amongst the indigenous Muslim population in the United States, the largest group based on race is African-American, but Hispanic and Anglo percentages are increasing.[20] Because societally we focus so much on physical traits (skin and facial features) for categorizational purposes, we frame Muslims as *other* outsiders and as part of diaspora communities.[21] This leaves white converts to be overlooked. Caucasian-American conversion makes up approximately 3% of all American conversion rates, and this rate is increasing.[22]

Although Islam was present in the United States prior to September 11, 2001, most of the American population never paid attention to Muslims until after the terrorist attacks, and similarly many Muslim Americans pre-9/11 also did not feel as if they had to think about their Americanness.[23] As Gaskew indicated,

> The terrorist attacks of September 11, 2001 served as a turn in the road for many Muslims in The United States, allowing various latent social conflicts to surface and challenge the current discourse on what it means to be a Muslim American in a post-9/11 world.[24]

Many Muslims feel that their religion was hijacked along with the four passenger planes during the terrorist attacks of September 11, 2001,[25] which (in the words of Gaskew) leaves Muslims being "torn between the realities of September 11, 2001, the incredible loss of human life and suffering, and the accusations that Muslims and their religion of Islam were responsible for this act of violence."[26]

It should be noted that although Muslims and Arabs were targeted after other world events involving the United States – the Iranian Hostage Crisis (1971–1981), the World Trade Center bombing of 1993, the Gulf War, the USS Cole bombing in 2000[27] – September 11, 2001 finds the most prominent position in the American collective consciousness because it had the highest level of destruction and was most shocking to the American collective psyche. Huddy, Feldman, Lahav, and Taber found that after September 11, health researchers noted significant increases of depression, anxiety, and post-traumatic stress disorder amongst Americans, regardless of religious affiliation.[28] For this reason, the September 11, 2001 terrorist attacks are the primary starting point used in this book to mark a shift toward widespread social acceptance for Islamophobia.

Since the September 11, 2001 terrorist attacks, there has been a dramatic increase in anti-Muslim sentiment, as society has been marred by Islamophobia. Islamophobia has been defined by Morey and Yaqin as a "view of Muslim Cultures as monolithic, isolationist, threatening, prone to violence and inherently hostile to the west."[29] For the purpose of clarity, this book defines the term Islamophobia in a broad all-encompassing sense, encapsulating a social fear, distrust, and dislike of those who are perceived to be Muslim and a generalized rejection of all things and people associated with Islam,[30] as well as the fear that leads to hostility, discrimination, and hatred of not only those who are Muslim, but also those who are perceived as being Muslim.[31]

Many people in the United States have adopted a mutually exclusive attitude when it comes to being American and being Muslim, and this sentiment only seems to be growing. In 2003, 25% of the American population said that Islam is more likely to promote violence than other religions, and this number increased to 50% the following year.[32] In her book *Mecca and Main Street*, Abdo found that marginalization, discrimination, and an increase of stress were all common recurring themes for Muslim Americans, and that these commonalities followed a similar trajectory as other marginalized cultural, ethnic, racial, or religious groups in the United States.[33]

Acceptance of Muslim immigrants in the United States also followed similar patterns of other immigrant groups prior to 9/11, while post-9/11 immigration and assimilation issues were only exacerbated and highlighted as there was a post-9/11 backlash against Muslims.[34] Compounding the problem is government-sanctioned surveillance on entire communities and familial networks. Morey and Yaqin indicate that "Western nations have employed a complex and precise set of surveillance systems designed to profile, track, and when necessary exclude the problematic Muslim other."[35] Examples of well-known overt profiling and tracking include the NSEERS program (National Security Entry-Exit Registration System) and the Uniting and Strengthening America by Providing Appropriate Tools Required to Intercept and Obstruct Terrorist act of 2001 (USA PATRIOT) Act.

It has been argued that USA PATRIOT has damaged relationships between Muslims and law enforcement in a top-down manner, affecting all people in the law enforcement spectrum including state and local officers.[36] Muslims have reported being targeted and harassed by law enforcement, including reports that Muslims have been subjected to traffic stops without cause which resulted in all passengers in the vehicle being required to prove their US Citizenship.[37] Muslim Americans who have been subjected to inquiry through the USA PATRIOT Act have been marred by "deep feelings of shame, guilt and humiliation that they were forced to endure from what many perceived as an Islamophobic social environment."[38]

Problematic is the demand on Muslims that they continually prove their Americanness if they want to have an allegiance to Islam. Generally, the social context in post-9/11 America is one of mutual exclusion where Muslims and Americans cannot share identities, and where increased backlash toward Muslims leave many wondering about whether it is possible to claim both the status of Muslim and American. Abdo noted that in the wake of 9/11, "mainstream America had imposed a stark choice on Muslim believers everywhere: Disavow key aspects of your faith and culture, or risk being lumped together with the September 11 militants."[39]

Research has shown that while there has been an increase in anti-Muslim sentiment, very few Americans actually know much about Islam or its history.[40] In 2004, only 25% of the American population had positive thoughts about Islam, and 46% incorrectly believed that Islam is the most likely religion to encourage violence.[41] In the span of 1 year, the American population who believed that Islam is the most likely religion to encourage violence had grown from 46% to 60%, and this number has continued to rise.[42] The presidential race of 2015–2016 illustrated that not much had changed.

In the 9 months immediately after 9/11, The Council on American Islamic Relations (CAIR) indicated that Muslims (or perceived Muslims) were victimized in 1,715 incidents of hate crimes, discrimination, and profiling, including 303 reports of actual violence.[43] Similarly, the Federal Bureau of Investigations (FBI) Hate Crimes Unit recorded a rise in physical attacks on Muslims from 28 attacks in 2000 to 481 attacks in 2001.[44]

It is clear that hate crimes and anti-Muslim backlash (against those perceived to be Muslim or Arab) is on the incline since 9/11, yet many believe that hate crimes and violence are still being underreported.[45] It is possible that Muslims are underreporting their victimization as a direct result of the lack of trust and the breakdown in relationships between Muslims and law enforcement that resulted after USA PATRIOT was passed and NSEERS was put in place.[46] Since September 11, 2001, there has been a dramatic shift in popular understanding of Muslims and Arabs, whether American or not, toward one where they are denied due process and are instead treated as if they are guilty until proven innocent. In the 3 years after September 11, 2001, 44% of interviewed Americans believed that it was acceptable to infringe on the civil liberties of Muslim Americans, 26% said that it was acceptable for the federal government to keep a close eye on mosques, and 29% said that undercover federal agents should investigate Muslim civic organizations.[47]

Fourteen years after September 11, during the 4 months between the Parisian Terrorist Attacks on November 13, 2015 and the middle of February 2016, there were 38 isolated hate crimes throughout the United States, the majority happening before New Year 2016.[48] Nearly 15 years after 9/11, in the aftermath of the mass shooting and attempted bombing in San Bernadino California on December 2, 2015, the then Republican presidential hopeful Donald Trump publicly called for a "total and complete shutdown" of the United States to Muslims. It was unclear to many whether this was a ban only on immigration, or if he was also suggesting that American Muslims traveling abroad (including Muslims who are deployed members of the US Military) should be denied reentry to the United States. At the time, studies showed that 45% of respondents supported a ban on Muslims, and 3 months later, a survey by YouGov found that this support had increased to 51%.[49] Rather than a complete ban, the then Republican presidential hopeful Ted Cruz called for heightened surveillance and patrols of Muslim American neighborhoods. Surveys in March 2016 indicated that 45% of respondents support "securing Muslim neighborhoods."[50] What to do about the *Muslim problem* became a frequent talking point and a full-fledged political platform throughout the 2015–2016 political season.

Women and men who have made a decision to present themselves in ways which identify themselves as part of this religious group (such as the hijab for women or the kufi for men) are at increased risk for being targets of Islamophobia-related backlash. Morey and Yaqin indicate that women who cover via hijab "are made to carry the burden of representation, symbolizing far more than their male counterparts,"[51] as they are more readily recognizable and so frequently depicted, represented, and viewed as brainwashed underprivileged victims of abusive men. It was this kind of misconception about the rights and role of women in Islam that fueled the then presidential hopeful Donald Trump's verbal assault on Gold Star Mother Ghazala Khan for not vocally participating in a speech about her late son Captain Humayun Khan during the Democratic National Convention in July 2016.[52] While many Americans quickly admonished Mr. Trump for targeting this woman, online discourse focused on how her status as a Gold Star Mother should make her off-limits to verbal assault, yet there was very little discussion about how these specific allegations were fueled by inappropriate and incorrect assumptions about the role of women in Islam.

Pew Research Center found that 22% of Muslim-identifying women fear wearing hijab or participating in other outward identifiers of faith, because they are specifically afraid of the increasing intolerance toward Muslims as exhibited in American culture.[53] It is possible that this fear of wearing the hijab comes from an acute realization on the part of these women that while wearing their headscarves, they themselves become symbolic of Islam (and representative of all things Muslim), which can be a precarious position when in a non-Muslim Islamophobic country.[54] The cost of wearing the hijab can be high (particularly for those seeking work) and although it is a personal choice rather than a religious obligation, Muslim women find that they must both defend themselves (from non-Muslims) if they choose to veil, and defend themselves (from other Muslims) if they choose not to veil.[55]

Since September 11, 2001, there has been an influx of conversions to Islam, both globally and in the United States.[56] Three months after September 11, 2001, Chairman of CAIR, Nihad Awad, told a Saudi newspaper that approximately 34,000 Americans had converted to Islam,[57] but there are issues with the veracity of such numbers because conversion records are neither created nor maintained in Islam.[58] Malhotra estimated that between the mid-1990s and 2002, approximately 20,000 Americans had converted to Islam, including 14,000 African-Americans, 4,000 whites, and 1,200 who were of Hispanic descent.[59] Approximately 7,000 female Americans (of a variety of racial demographics) convert to Islam every year,[60] making up approximately 46% of the conversion narratives.[61]

And yet, the conversion experiences to reflect these numbers are not adequately represented in the academic literature. According to Muhammad, the significant underrepresentation in the literature can be alarming as Muslim women struggle to find their place within society. She wrote:

> I could not find myself in the history books. Where were the in-depth stories of American Muslims? Where were the detailed histories, the women's views, the studies of difficult intercultural exchanges, the accounts of activists and the coming-of-age stories that put a human face on the religion's adherents, effectively not leaving them vulnerable and alone in times of crisis? How can anyone understand your plights if they do not know who you are?[62]

It is this absence of the representations of female converts to Islam that this research was aimed to explore and contribute to.

WHY ME?

In qualitative research, one must remain aware that the researcher is the instrument and that the researcher's life experiences can never fully be separated from the research itself.[63] For this reason, it becomes paramount to this research that my own life experiences, particularly those which shaped my interest in this topic, be articulated.

My mother was the first daughter of a Jewish man who had, in his early life, studied at the Chabad to become an Orthodox Rabbi. After the death of a dear childhood friend, and later serving in WWII and being involved with both the first storm of Normandy and the liberation of a small Nazi concentration camp, he drifted from his religious upbringings. Although no longer actively practicing, he wanted his children to have a religious faith. He always found Orthodox Judaism to be too stifling and chose for his children to be raised within the Conservative movement.

After my parents were married in a Conservative Synagogue, they moved to rural New Hampshire where the synagogue of convenience was Reform. My mother, having been a professionally trained vocalist, became the Cantoral Soloist at this small Reform synagogue and they quickly found their religious home. By the time they adopted me at the age of five, they were well established within this religious community, although my father was not as active in religious life.

I was born to an unwed, nonpracticing Catholic mother who was incapable of raising me due to a series of health issues. In my very early life, she did her best to raise me with the help of her deeply religious Catholic parents, but I was soon placed into foster care. I was baptized Catholic as a baby but did not attend religious services or learn any religious doctrine during my years in foster care.

After being adopted, I regularly attended religious services with my adoptive mother. At religious services and at religious preschool, I learned the lessons of the Torah. At home, my mother did her best to teach me the stories from the New Testament so that I could understand various religious teachings. By the time I was six, I was presented with a choice of which religious faith I would like to pursue. I chose to convert to Judaism, probably less for the doctrine and more for the fact that it would bring a closer bond between me and the two people I loved more than anything, my parents. At the time, my grandfather feared that at some point later in life, others would try to revoke my status as a Jew or claim that my conversion was null,[64] and he asked my parents to have me converted through an Orthodox ceremony, thus making me Orthodox according to Jewish law.

While I remember parts of visiting the *Mikvah* and having my conversion to Orthodoxy, at the time, I did not have the processing skills to really understand what was happening. After my conversion, my family returned to the Reform synagogue that my mother was clergy at, and I received years of religious training, which culminated in my Bat Mitzvah at age 13, which signified that I was an adult Jewish woman with all rights and responsibilities within the Jewish faith.

My faith wavered in high school and I began to explore alternate religions. None of these religions resonated with me, but Judaism did not appear to resonate with me anymore either. Compounding my disillusionment with Judaism was that when I was a senior in high school, I was attacked by three girls while getting off of the school bus, and for the duration of the attack, they screamed crude religious slurs and sexual epithets at me. This was before much of the hate crime legislation as we now know it, but should this type of assault take place in today's era, there is no doubt it could have been prosecuted as a hate crime. After the assault, my faith was considerably shaken.

During my undergraduate studies at the University of Rhode Island, I identified as a nonpracticing Jew. I worked at the university chapter of Hillel, but I felt as if I was drifting further and further away from religion. At one point during my sophomore year, I was approached by some new friends who invited me to go to a coffee shop with them and other members of one of the campus Christian organizations. After that night out, I began spending more and more time with members of this organization, and they began to share more personal testimonies of their religious faith and encouraged me to do some Bible study. Over time, I began to feel as if I was being called to convert to Christianity, although in retrospect, I realize that I was struggling in my faith, but starving for friendship more. I asked to be baptized on more than one occasion, but no matter what arrangements that we made for my baptism, plans never panned out.

I returned from Rhode Island believing that I was destined to live the life of a "good Christian woman" (whatever that meant) and was startled to learn that my mother (who had always supported my exploration into other spiritual avenues) was less than thrilled. She indicated that she would support me in whatever choice I ultimately made, but I could tell that she was hurting for my spiritual well-being. She asked me to attend a weekly

Torah study with the Rabbi and some other members of the congregation I was raised in. Not wanting to hurt her further, I agreed. With time, and some very direct conversations with this study group, I began to realize that there were always aspects of the Christian doctrine that I had not fully believed. After much soul searching, I further realized that it had not been Christianity itself that I had been drawn to, but rather the idea that I could have regular fellowship with a large group of people who each had such a strong moral compass. As my religious studies continued, I realized that my religious faith was Judaism and I found that this was indeed my spiritual home.

Meanwhile, my adult life was continuing to be shaped by a political structure marred by what the 43rd president of the United States was calling a *War on Terror*. Ten days before my 21st birthday, while I was still a senior in college, four airplanes were hijacked and flown into World Trade Center 1 and 2, The Pentagon, and a field in Pennsylvania, in what would be the largest terrorist attack to take place on American soil. Prior to the September 11 terrorist attacks, I had been planning to join the Peace Corps, but after 9/11, my priorities shifted and I felt an urge to pursue a dream of working in law enforcement. After my graduation from college, I worked in various federal national security and law enforcement capacities.

Over time, I became increasingly weary of the antiterrorism initiatives and the frequent bombardment of terrorism fueled rhetoric that was ever present in federal law enforcement culture. Eventually (and for some-what unrelated reasons), I left what could have been a career in law enforcement and returned to school to work on a Master's degree in Conflict Analysis and Resolution. While there, I became increasingly interested in conflict within religious groups, and although never desir-ing to be a religious scholar, I began to research various religious texts for the purpose of understanding the variances between them. I also became keenly attuned to the intersectionality of religious conflict and culture, prejudice, discrimination, hate crimes, and segregation. I became acutely aware that although I was in a leading program in Conflict Analysis and Resolution, as students, we all contributed in the greater system in minute ways such as the way we organized our seats in class, who we chose to work on assignments with, and how we communicated with one another. I was concerned that the Muslim and Middle Eastern students in my class were being marginalized, particularly the females who chose to cover themselves by donning hijab.

I tested this theory for myself by wearing hijab for 28 days and chronicled my thoughts and experiences on a YouTube channel dedicated to this personal project. My experience was wonderful. While trying at times, challenging my own thoughts about modesty and feminism was eye opening. The responses that I got through my YouTube channel were mixed, with some people being supportive and others being abusive, vulgar, and disturbing. Since then, I have become increasingly interested in the apparent mutual exclusivity for those who are Muslim American, particularly white converts to Islam.

During the early phase of researching for this manuscript, I began to run as a way to release emotional tension and offset the negative impact that researching hate crimes, ethno-violence, prejudice, and discrimination has had in my daily life. Originally from New England, I had always watched the Boston Marathon on television and in 2013, being a new half marathon runner, I was very excited to tune in to watch the proceedings and look for friends who were competing. I was horrified when at 2:49 pm, two bombs exploded on Boylston Street, meters before the finish line. I quickly felt as if my worlds were colliding and knew that the first people who would be blamed were those with ties to either the Middle East or Muslim extremism.

I became glued to the television over the next several days as a city that I loved looked like a ghost town. I feared for friends and family who lived in the city. I hoped that this was not going to be blamed on Muslims and fuel the already Muslim-hostile American social climate.

When the suspects were finally identified and located, the media became engrossed with the story of Dzhokhar Tsarnaev and his Caucasian-American wife, Katherine Russell-Tsarnaev. Russell-Tsarnaev was raised in Rhode Island by her Protestant family and had converted to Islam in college while courting with Tsarnaev. In the aftermath, I frequently overheard people indicating that she had been involved with this heinous terrorist attack, for no reason other than because she was a white American who had converted to Islam. The metamessages in this discourse indicate that to convert to Islam as an American is to have nefarious ulterior motives, to convert to Islam as an American is to be a traitor to one's country of origin, and to convert to Islam as an American is to have some type of mental defect or disorder. All of these allegations are things that this research is designed to investigate.

What's the Problem?

In the current academic literature, while the experience of discrimination based on gender, race, ethnicity, or other marginalized religious group have all been explored, there is a recognized void of research on the post-9/11 shared lived experiences of Muslims (or those perceived to be Muslim or Arab).[65] That also means that there is subsequently a dearth in the literature exploring the shared lived experiences of what it means to be a white female American converted to Islam in post-9/11 America. This research was designed not only to look at the ways of conflict that exists between white female American converts to Islam and their non-Muslim American counterparts, but also at the conflicts that they face within themselves as they navigate a successful integration of various aspects of their identities.

To date, the experiences of Caucasian female Americans who have converted to Islam since September 11, 2001 have been noticeably absent from the literature, and with the increasingly hostile social temperature toward Muslims, there is a social urgency in both exploring and understanding their shared experiences, including how they integrate, incorporate, and juxtapose the various aspects of their identities.

The lack of representation of these women in the literature meant that a thorough literature review prior to beginning this research included a systemic triangulation of literature already available regarding the individual identity statuses first. I recognize and accept that by speaking about what Muslim women need in terms of freedom from oppression – by discussing issues of grave importance to those who appear to be oppressed yet never inviting them to join the dialogue – Western feminists are violating a basic tenet of feminism itself.[66] For this reason, this research was conducted in a respectful feminist-forward way so as not to further marginalize those who had already been on the receiving end of marginalization. This feminist-forward, feminist-driven methodology included identifying the specific needs of the demographic being studied and empowering them to join the conversion about their outcomes.

What's the Point?

The purpose of this phenomenological study was to describe and understand the experience of Caucasian female Americans who have converted to Islam in post-9/11 America. Currently, the Caucasian female American convert to Islam is defined as a white female living in the United States who practiced any religion other than Islam but who has converted to Islam. Here, the term post-9/11 America referred to not only the physical location of the United States, but also the cultural climate and attitudes that have taken hold since the September 11 terrorist attacks. The sample size for this research included eight participants who met the criteria of inclusion in this phenomenological study in that they were all Caucasian-American females over the age of 18 who had converted to Islam since September 11, 2001, who were over the age of 18 at the time of their conversion, and who were raised in the United States. The sample population included female participants who varied in age from 26 to 59 years old, who represented three different geographic categories (urban, suburban, and rural living). No state was represented more than once, and the areas of the Pacific Northwest, the West Coast, the American Southwest, Alaska, and the Hawaiian Islands were not represented.

To that end, the central and secondary research questions were formulated as follows:

- RQ_1: What is the shared lived experience of Caucasian female American converts to Islam in post-9/11 America?
- RQ_2: What impact does the increasingly hostile social climate towards Muslim Americans have on the spiritual, social, physical, and mental integration of the participants?
- RQ_3: How is conflict experienced between Caucasian female American converts to Islam and those around them?
- RQ_4: How is conflict experienced within the selves of Caucasian female American converts to Islam in post-9/11 America?

WHAT'S THE POTENTIAL IMPACT?

According to Wilmot and Hocker, conflict is defined as "an expressed struggle between at least two interdependent parties who perceive incompatible goals, scarce resources, and interference from others in achieving their goals."[67] Perception is ultimately at the crux of all conflict and for the conflict analyst, the goal is to be able to decipher what is perception and what is an accurate representation of the experiences of those who are at the epicenter of the conflict.[68] This study aimed to better understand the experiences of Caucasian female Americans who have converted to Islam since September 11, 2001 and bring forth new knowledge regarding this population's experiences, perception, and lived reality with interpersonal, intrapersonal, and cultural conflict, which have been previously neglected in the literature.

Although conflict is experienced differently from person to person, conflict is an inevitable part of the human experience. Conflict can be positive and help to shape a new positive discourse, or it can be derisive and cause chaos and destruction.[69] Although some may aim to eliminate conflict altogether, it would not be advisable to do so as conflict is frequently the catalyst for positive social change.[70]

The experiences of Caucasian female Americans who have converted to Islam since September 11, 2001 illustrate a twofold conflict in that these women experience the effects of both expressive conflict and instrumental conflict. According to Augsburger,

> expressive conflicts arise from a desire to release tension, to express frustration, and to discharge emotion and are usually generated from hostile or negative feelings. Instrumental conflicts arise from a difference in pathways or goals: they are directed toward actual ends and press for visible outcomes.[71]

This study aims to better understand how this destructive conflict is experienced by Caucasian female Americans who have converted to Islam in post-9/11 America. For the purposes of this text, I have adopted Augsburger's explanation of destructive conflict as

> Characterized by four tendencies. In this case, the individuals or groups tend to: (1) expand the number of issues, participants, negative attitudes, and self-justifications; (2) emancipate the conflict from its initiating causes so it can continue after these are irrelevant or forgotten; (3) escalate into strategies of power and tactics of threat, coercion, and deception; and (4) polarize into uniform opinions behind single-minded and militant leadership.[72]

This destructive conflict as experienced by Caucasian female Americans who have converted to Islam in post-9/11 America is fueled in whole by a system and industry of Islamophobia that has been socially accepted in the

United States, as well as in varying locations globally. For Caucasian American women who have converted to Islam, the conflict regarding Islamophobia is one that not only speaks to religious conflict and interpersonal conflict with the surrounding community, but also one that is deeply intertwined with their conceptualization of the self, the formulation of identity, and the importance of personal choice.

Finally, because it is generally understood in the current discourse on genocide that there are eight stages in the process of genocide (classification, symbolization, dehumanization, organization, polarization, preparation, extermination, and denial),[73] it would not be negligent to posit that if this conflict is left unaddressed, the mistreatment of Muslim Americans by mainstream non-Muslim Americans has the potential to erupt into a widespread movement which could culminate in the deaths of upward of 6–7 million people.

NOTES

1. Samuel P. Huntington, *The Clash of Civilization and the Remaking of the New World Order* (New York: Touchstone, 1996).
2. "America's Changing Religious Landscape," *Pew Research Center,* May 12, 2015, http://pewrsr.ch/1FhDslC.
3. Lori Peek, *Behind the Backlash: Muslim Americans After 9/11* (Philadelphia, PA: Temple University Press, 2011).
4. Geneive Abdo, *Mecca and the Main Street* (New York, NY: Oxford University Press, 2006); Peter Morey and Amina Yaqin, *Framing Muslims: Stereotyping and Representation after 9/11* (Cambridge, MA: Harvard University Press, 2011); Lori Peek, *Behind the Backlash.*
5. "Future of the Global Muslim Population," *Pew Research Center,* January 27, 2011, http://pewrsr.ch/1hUQ1qG.
6. "Islam the 2nd Largest Religion in 20 States," *OnIslam,* June 5, 2014, http://bit.ly/2aD3Wmb.
7. Reid Wilson, "The Second Largest Religion in Each State," *The Washington Post,* June 4, 2014, http://wapo.st/UcWdB5.
8. Geneive Abdo, *Mecca and the Main Street*; Carol L. Anway, *Daughters of Another Path* (Lee's Summit, MO: Yawna Publications, 1996); Debra L. Dirks, "Introduction: America and Islam in the 21st Century: Welcome to the Sisterhood," in *Islam Our Choice: Portraits of Modern American Muslim Women,* ed. Debra L. Dirks and Stephanie Parlove (Beltsville, MD: Amana Publications, 2003), p. 1–16.
9. "America's Changing Religious Landscape," *Pew Research Center.*

10. Debra L. Dirks, "Introduction: America and Islam."
11. Reid Wilson "The second-largest religion in each state," The Washington Post, June 4, 2014, http://wapo.st/2ow9OqL.
12. Najwa Raouda, *The Feminine Voice of Islam: Muslim Women in America* (South Bend, IN: The Victoria Press, 2008).
13. Mohamed Nimer, "Muslims in the American Body Politic."
14. Omar Khalidi, "Living as a Muslim in a Pluralistic Society and State: Theory and Experience," in *Muslims' Place in the American Public Square: Hope, Fears and Aspirations,* ed. Zahid H. Bukhari, Sulayman S. Nyang, Mumtaz Ahmad, and John L. Esposito (Walnut Creek, CA: AltaMira Press, 2004), p. 38–72.
15. Tony Gaskew, "Confronting Political Islam: An Ethnographic Representation of Muslim Americans in the Aftermath of 9/11" (doctoral dissertation, Nova Southeastern University, 2007); "America's Changing Religious Landscape," *Pew Research Center.*
16. Peter Morey and Amina Yaqin, *Framing Muslims.*
17. Tony Gaskew, "Confronting Political Islam."
18. Asma Gull Hasan, *Why I am a Muslim: An American Odyssey* (London: Element, 2004).
19. Geneive Abdo, *Mecca and the Main Street*, p. 3.
20. Geneive Abdo, *Mecca and the Main Street*; Tony Gaskew, "Confronting Political Islam."
21. Peter Morey and Amina Yaqin, *Framing Muslims.*
22. Tony Gaskew, "Confronting Political Islam."
23. Ibid.
24. Ibid., p. xiii
25. Geneive Abdo, *Mecca and the Main Street*; Tony Gaskew, "Confronting Political Islam;" Lori Peek, *Behind the Backlash.*
26. Tony Gaskew, "Confronting Political Islam." p. 76.
27. Brigitte L. Nacos and Oscar Torres-Reyna, "Framing Muslim-Americans Before and After 9/11," in *Framing Terrorism: The News Media, the Government and the Public,* ed. Pippa Norris, Montague Kern, and Marion Just (New York, NY: Routledge, 203), p. 133–157.
28. Leonie Huddy, Stanley Feldman, Gallya Lahav, and Charles Taber, "Fear and Terrorism: Psychological Reactions to 9/11," in *Framing Terrorism: The News Media, the Government and the Public,* ed. Pippa Norris, Montague Kern, and Marion Just (New York, NY: Routledge, 203), p. 255–278.
29. Peter Morey and Amina Yaqin, *Framing Muslims,* p. 49.
30. Barry van Driel, Introduction to *Confronting Islamophobia in Educational Practice,* ed. Barry van Driel (Staffordshire, England: Trentham Books Limited, 2004).
31. Nathan Lean, *The Islamophobia Industry* (London: Pluto Books, 2012).

32. Geneive Abdo, *Mecca and the Main Street.*
33. Ibid.
34. Tony Gaskew, "Confronting Political Islam."
35. Peter Morey and Amina Yaqin, *Framing Muslims.*
36. Tony Gaskew, "Confronting Political Islam."
37. Ibid.
38. Ibid., p. 179.
39. Geneive Abdo, *Mecca and the Main Street*, p. 114.
40. Carol L. Anway, *Daughters of Another Path.*
41. Nathan Lean, *The Islamophobia Industry.*
42. Ibid.
43. Geneive Abdo, *Mecca and the Main Street.*
44. Ibid.
45. Tony Gaskew, "Confronting Political Islam;" Lori Peek, *Behind the Backlash.*
46. Tony Gaskew, "Confronting Political Islam."
47. Lori Peek, *Behind the Backlash.*
48. Liam Stack, "American Muslims Under Attack," *The New York Times,* February 15, 2016, http://nyti.ms/28PT2vo.
49. Peter Moore, "Divide on Muslim Neighborhood Patrols but Majority Now Back Muslim Travel Ban," *YouGov,* March 16, 2016, http://bit.ly/1VTHqIN.
50. Ibid.
51. Peter Morey and Amina Yaqin, *Framing Muslims,* p. 40.
52. Captain Humayun Khan, United States Army, 1st Division 2000–2004, K.I. A. near Baqubah, Iraq (9/9/1976–6/8/2004), Posthumously awarded The Bronze Star Medal and The Purple Heart.
53. "Muslim Americans: Middle Class and Mostly Mainstream," *Pew Research Center,* May 22, 2007, http://pewrsr.ch/2aLExGR.
54. Geneive Abdo, *Mecca and the Main Street.*
55. Stefano Allievi, "The Shifting Significance of the Halal/Haram Frontier: Narratives on the Hijab and Other Issues," in *Women Embracing Islam: Gender and Conversion in the West,* ed. Karin van Nieuwkerk (Austin, TX: University of Texas Press, 2006), p. 120–149.
56. Geneive Abdo, *Mecca and the Main Street;* Yvonne Yazbeck Haddad, "The Quest for Peace in Submission;" Willy Jansen, "Conversion and Gender, Two Contested Concepts," in *Women Embracing Islam: Gender and Conversion in the West,* ed. Karin van Nieuwkerk (Austin, TX: University of Texas Press, 2006), p. IX–XII; Peter Morey and Amina Yaqin, *Framing Muslims;* Lori Peek, *Behind the Backlash;* Karin van Nieuwkerk, Introduction to *Women Embracing Islam: Gender and Conversion in the West,* ed. Karin van Nieuwkerk (Austin, TX: University of Texas Press,

2006), p. 1–16; Monika Wohlrab-Sahr, "Symbolizing Distance: Conversion to Islam in Germany and the United States," in *Women Embracing Islam: Gender and Conversion in the West,* ed. Karin van Nieuwkerk (Austin, TX: University of Texas Press, 2006), p. 71–92.

57. Geneive Abdo, *Mecca and the Main Street.*

58. Monika Wohlrab-Sahr, "Symbolizing Distance."

59. Priya Malhotra, "Islam's Female Converts," in *Religion in Politics and Society,* ed. Michael Kelly and Lynn M. Messina (New York: H.W. Wilson, 2002), p. 172–175.

60. Ibid.

61. Reid Wilson, "The second-largest religion in each state," The Washington Post, June 4, 2014, http://wapo.st/2ow9OqL.

62. Precious R. Muhammad, "To be Young, Gifted, Black, American, Muslim, and Woman," in *Living Islam Outloud: American Muslim Women Speak,* ed. Saleemah Abdul-Ghafur (Boston, MA: Beacon Press, 2005), p. 37.

63. Clark Moustakas, *Phenomenological Research Methods* (London: SAGE, 1994); Jerry W. Willis, Muktha Jost, and Rema Nilakanta, *Foundations for Qualitative Research: Interpretive and Critical Approaches* (London: SAGE, 2007).

64. Orthodox Judaism is the only officially recognized movement in Israel for a variety of activities. While the conversion process for those converting via Conservative and Orthodox avenues, *who* performs (and who officially witnesses) the conversion appears to be the main point of contention. Because Orthodox Jews do not recognize the validity of non-Orthodox conversions this has become a source of relatively latent conflict both in Israel and elsewhere. Anticipating an increase in this conflict over who is *really Jewish*, my grandfather had fears that as an adult, I would not be recognized as Jewish and would not be entitled to the life cycle rituals within the faith.

65. Geneive Abdo, *Mecca and the Main Street*; Muninder K Ahluwalia and Laura Pellettiere, "Sikh Men Post-9/11: Misidentification, Discrimination, and Coping," *Asian American Journal of Psychology* 1, no 4 (2010); Ben K. Beiten and Katherine R. Allen, "Relisiance in Arab American Couples After September 11, 2001: A Systems Perspective," *Journal of Marital and Family Therapy* 31, no 3 (2005); Peter Morey and Amina Yaqin, *Framing Muslims*; Lori Peek, *Behind the Backlash.*

66. Peter Morey and Amina Yaqin, *Framing Muslims.*

67. William W. Wilmot and Joyce L. Hocker, *Interpersonal Conflict (7th ed.)* (New York, NY: McGraw-Hill, 2007), p. 9.

68. Ibid.

69. David W. Augsburger, *Conflict Mediation Across Cultures* (Louisville, KY: Westminster John Knox Press, 1992); William W. Wilmot and Joyce L. Hocker, *Interpersonal Conflict.*

70. David W. Augsburger, *Conflict Mediation Across Cultures;* William W. Wilmot and Joyce L. Hocker, *Interpersonal Conflict.*
71. David W. Augsburger, *Conflict Mediation Across Cultures*, p. 29.
72. Ibid., p. 47.
73. Gregory H. Stanton, "The Eight Stages of Genocide," *Genocide Watch,* March 16, 2016, http://bit.ly/1jEhWKd.

CHAPTER 2

An Intersectionality of Islam, Women, and Conversion

The neglect of Muslim Americans in social science literature is alarming due to increasing hostilities toward the Muslim American population since September 11, 2001. In the wake of September 11, 2001, Arab American couples have felt "pressured to decide whether they are Arabs or Americans, with little room in between, resulting in feelings of frustration, confusion and anger,"[1] yet no research has specifically focused on this identity fracture in the nonimmigrant community, the conversion community, or at the intersectionality of those with being white and female. Similarly, no research has specifically focused on developing a theory which explains or describes the identity integration and juxtaposition faced by female Americans who have converted to Islam since 9/11. In recent years, it has become increasingly obvious that there is a social urgency in researching the experiences of Muslim Americans in general, but particularly those with multiple minority statuses.

ISLAM AND THE BASICS

Although the US Government is prohibited from collecting information regarding religious identity, it is estimated that there are 1–7 million American citizens who practice Islam, with some Muslim groups claiming that the numbers fall at the higher end of this span.[2] Although Islam in America is experiencing rapid growth, few Americans know about Islamic doctrine or about the history of Islam.[3] American Muslims recognize that they need to be more vocal in educating their non-Muslim counterparts

© The Author(s) 2017
A.M. Guimond, *Converting to Islam*,
DOI 10.1007/978-3-319-54250-8_2

about their faith because they understand that as long as the understanding of Islam is presented from a Western Lens, the misinterpretation and the negative judgments will continue.[4]

There are many misconceptions about Islam: that it does not share common values with other religions, that it is inferior to the religions of the West, that it is irrational and barbaric, that it supports violence and terrorism, that it was a political ideology that has morphed into a religious faith, and that it is archaic and unable to keep up with the changing times. The following section provides a very brief overview of the religious foundations of Islam in order to lead to discussion of the misconceptions and stereotypes that dominate American discourse on Muslims. This is not intended to be all-inclusive or comprehensive.[5]

The Basics of Islam

At the most basic level, the religion is called Islam and the people who follow the religion are called Muslims. Arabic is a language based on root words and the root of the word *Islam* is *Salam* – meaning peace. The religion calls for a peaceful existence with one creator which is why Muslims will frequently use the phrase "religion of peace." Islam has also been translated in a nonliteral way meaning submission, subservience, or surrender to the creator.

Although stereotypes suggest some homogeneity amongst Muslims, this is not the case. Because Islam has been married with local customs in differing regions, there is a spectrum of different practices amongst the Muslim community. The religious text remains the same, but there are various different cultural factors that influence how the faith is practiced.[6] Although there are a number of different sects within Islam, the two sects that the majority of Muslims identify with are Sunni and Shia. Sunnis make up approximately 84–94% of the Muslim population worldwide, and Shia make up approximately 10–16% of the population worldwide.[7] These percentages are also reflected amongst American Muslims as well.[8]

Regardless of which branch of Islam that the individual identifies with, all Muslims believe in the same five tenets. These five tenets, also known as the *Pillars of Islam*, are (1) *the shahada*, also known as the declaration of faith which states that the observer must say and believe the statement that "there is only one God (*Allah*) and Muhammad is the messenger of God"; (2) *Salat*, the five times daily prayer; (3) *Siya*, the fasting which occurs during the holy month of *Ramadan*; (4) *Zakat*, the annual welfare contributions for the poor and ailing that are usually given during the holy month of *Ramadan*; and (5) *Hajj*, the obligatory pilgrimage to Mecca that all Muslims must embark on once during their lifetime should they have the health and means to do so.[9]

Islam provides a Muslim with a direct relationship with God and there is no centralized mouthpiece for Muslims or the Muslim community.[10] Within the Sunni *Ummah* (the religious community), there are no formal clergy. Alternately, the Shia Ummah believes that clergy is acceptable and Imams serve as heads of the religious community.[11] Although Imams lead in terms of the business aspects of the Muslim organization and as religious scholars, the Qur'an teaches that no Muslim voice is more powerful than others.[12]

Islam shares similar values to other religions that are practiced in the United States: charity for the less fortunate, active engagement within the community, a desire to better the religious community and surrounding community, working hard, participation in the political system, reducing racial and gender inequality, and more. It is important to note that Muslims also believe in pluralism, freedom of religion, democracy, and a respect for all is part of their core values.[13]

Islam's Relationship with Other Religions

Though commonly believed to be at odds with Christianity or Judaism, based on the Qur'anic texts, Islam does not have a problem with either of these faiths and considers them equally as cousins and fellow *People of the Book*.[14] In other words, contrary to commonly held stereotypes of Islam, this religion respects – and God accepts – other religions based on justice and morals. The commonly misused term *infidel* actually means "nonbelievers of God as a singular being" and was never intended to be used to describe Jews or Christians.[15]

Islam is a diverse religion in practice, but Muslims also hold personal diversity in high esteem. Islam is thought to cross various cultural barriers and serves to level the playing field between race, language, gender, and socioeconomic class.[16] Although Muslims believe in unity and brotherhood within the Ummah, racial and ethnic tensions (as well as class and gender partitioning within the population) have shown that it is not a perfect process of brotherhood with complete unity and equality.[17]

Islam's Relationship with Violence

Popular misconceptions lead the non-Muslim population to believe that Islam is more directly associated with violence and terrorism than other religions, but simply put, this is not the case. Part of the confusion seems to revolve around the word *Jihad*. While the idea of Jihad is conceptualized by Muslims as a personal struggle rooted in a peaceful introspection of an individual's own self-centered and self-serving goals,[18] the idea of Jijad is terrifying for many non-Muslims because it has been mistranslated over the years to mean "holy war" and has been used by powerful people to suggest that Muslims are perpetually engaging in a religious war against the West. In reality, within Islam, violence toward others as an offensive attack is severely verboten.[19] The Qur'an does permit violence but only to be used as a means to protect oneself or their family.

In recent years, "honor killings" and female genital mutilation have been falsely attributed to religious practice, when in actuality these practices are condemned within the teachings of Islam. There is also an extensive list of members of the Orthodox Islamic community that condemn murder and terrorism, despite the current dominant discourse.[20] Similarly, the Qur'an opposes domination or oppressing others, and though Muslims claim that participation in their religious community makes them morally superior to those who don't participate, the idea of using this superiority to oppress or subjugate others has been condemned.[21]

In stark contrast of the stereotype of Muslims being set on perpetuating violence, the doctrine of the Qur'an leads itself to negotiation, compromise, and peaceful forms of conflict resolution.[22] This could be an explanation of why there is a high rate of conversion amongst inmates in the American penal system and how Islam became viewed as a *jail house religion*. The rates of conversion amongst American inmates are seen as a testament to the reconciliatory nature of the religious doctrine, in that not only can it help inmates reframe their interpersonal dynamics, but it can also have immense success with helping inmates to interpret and understand their own personal challenges, including understanding poverty and race relations, and their trajectory through the criminal justice and corrections system.[23]

Islam's Concept of Fitrah

Islam teaches the concept of *fitrah*, in which it is believed that all people are born Muslim, meaning: they are submissive toward God and are born innocent, they know the difference between what is right and wrong, and fitrah is there whether a person ever identified with being Muslim or not.[24] This concept suggests that during a person's life, they may be exposed to other religions (through culture and through socialization), and they then identify with these other religions. For this reason, when a person converts to Islam, the Muslim community will frequently call it a "reversion" instead of a "conversion." For the purposes of this study, these terms are used interchangeably.

WOMEN IN ISLAM

In the United States, the number of Muslim American women is uncertain, but the available data show that Muslim American women are more educated and more financially stable than their non-Muslim American counterparts.[25] Peek noted that

> Muslim American women are one of the most highly educated female religious groups, second only to Jewish American women. Muslim Americans also have the highest degree of economic gender parity, meaning that men and women tend to be on "equal footing" in terms of earnings of any religious group in the United States.[26]

It is also worthy to note that of the 3–6 million Muslim Americans in the USA, over 50% earn an annual income of $50,000.00 per year and 58% have college, graduate, or postgraduate degrees.[27] This suggests that there is a great deal of value placed on the education and upward mobility of Muslim American women, contrary to the belief that these women are voiceless and subjugated.

Since September 11, 2001, more Muslim women have been taking a visible and active role in the American Muslim diaspora, whether it be through working outside the home, politics, or advocacy. Since the war on terrorism, Muslim women have also been taking a far more active role in opposing war.[28] Some Muslim feminists argue that the Muslim woman's place in the public sphere and increasing participation in social action has done much for redefining what it means to be a female Muslim in the United States.[29] Although Muslim women are encouraged to be active and engaged in the public sphere, as understood by most Muslim communities, Muslim women are restricted from being chaplains at prisons, universities, colleges, hospitals, or as general Imams at their local Mosque.[30]

Feminism in Islam

Though many cultures limit the rights of women, claiming that these limitations are founded in Islam, we must remember that Islam itself dictates that women be equal to men and affords women the same right as men. It is through this politicization of Islam and the patriarchal manipulation of the teachings of the Qur'an that stereotypes and myths about the role of women flourish.[31] The way that Islam is discussed is itself an engendered process due to the fact that the images of Muslim men and women are each part of a twofold equation which cannot survive without their counterpart.[32] According to Hammer, in this equation:

> The image of the oppressed and silenced Muslim woman is only second to the even more pervasive image of the violent Muslim extremist male and its association to terrorism. These negative images are complementary and interdependent in their assumption that the violent and oppressive nature of Muslim men necessitates and produces the silent, victimized and oppressed Muslim woman.[33]

The commonly held perception of Muslim women relegates them to always following behind their husbands and being treated as little more than chattel personal, but this has no basis in Islam. On the contrary, feminism actually flourishes in the Qur'an itself, but because Sharia law is taken from interpretations of the scriptures and *Hadiths* (interpretations of the scriptures by respected Islamic scholars) by jurists, we see women being oppressed in predominantly Muslim countries.[34] This is the influence of people on religion rather than the influence of religion on people.[35] Feminists within the Muslim community are working hard to highlight the differences between the Qur'anic doctrine that emphasizes equality (including that for all genders) and patriarchal cultural practices.[36] It is through this work that they are hoping to erode generations of androcentric attitudes.

In popular culture, it appears that Islam is indelibly linked to oppression of women and it is rare for non-Muslims to consider that it is the patriarchal culture – rather than religion – that is enforcing the oppression. In general, we turn a blind eye to the way that women are oppressed in Western cultures including oppression through discriminatory pay practices, the novelty at the possibility of the first female president, a constant bombardment of legislation aimed at limiting women's reproductive rights, rape culture and other difficulties in prosecuting rape and sexual harassment, and a glass ceiling for women in the work place – yet rarely is this seen by feminists to be as big a threat to women as Islam.[37]

Many Americans are concerned about Muslim countries where violence against women is prolific, yet they turn a blind eye to the fact that in every 9 seconds, there is an American woman being abused by either a partner or a date.[38] There is a constant outcry over the idea that in some Muslim communities around the world, it is common practice to perform honor killings, acid attacks, genital mutilation, and abuse associated with polygamy, but it should be remembered that these behaviors are not prolific.[39] There are indeed cultures where female circumcision is performed under the false claim that to do so is Qur'anically based, but these sensationalist stories are not the norm.[40] Further, while many in the West see Muslim women as being abused and oppressed within Muslim marriages, this is not the case, and indeed the rates of abuse and domineering relationships within Muslim pairings are no higher than they are for people who practice other religions![41]

Due to misinformation, many non-Muslims incorrectly believe that feminism has no place in Islam; however, Raouda noted that Muslim traditions are inherently feminist, albeit a different interpretation of feminism – one that is rooted in the Qur'an.[42] This can leave Muslim women in the West feeling as if they are precariously balancing the two slightly differing definitions of feminism. The Muslim interpretation of feminism aims to redefine religious teachings that have been misinterpreted and manipulated to serve patriarchal purposes. The reality of the Muslim feminism movement is that the attention is always focused on Western organizations that are fighting to liberate and rescue oppressed communities where women are being abused, instead of focusing on the solidarity of indigenous women and activist groups founded and maintained by women in these areas.[43] In turn, the problem becomes cyclical in nature and thus perpetuates the myth that Muslim women need to be liberated and rescued by feminists of the West. Ultimately *saving brown women* (a thought process which began during the early orientalist thought and which has stood the test of time)[44] remains an important concept which is deeply embedded in the minds of the majority of Western women.

Orientalist Definitions of the Role of Women in Islam

The orientalist thought process is deeply entrenched in the way that the West views women and their role in Islam. Prior to the nineteenth century, there was little research on Muslims in general, but when there was, it had been conducted by European men who had no actual access to women within the Muslim communities that they were working with. This left researchers making unsubstantiated claims about how women were being tyrannized at the hands of their male counterparts.[45] This orientalist thinking – particularly that toward women within Islam, which came from a feigned objectivity toward Islam and was founded in deep seated xenophobia – was based on pure assumption and conjecture, yet it has stood the test of time.[46]

Like their non-Muslim counterparts, Muslim women who have been victimized in the home are less likely to report their victimization at the hands of their partners due to a variety of factors. Research that has focused on violence within Muslim families has found that there are additional factors leading to a failure to report such acts.[47] This includes the increased tension between the Muslim/Arab communities and local law enforcement that has arisen after September 11, where Muslim women fear being stereotyped or marginalized for their status specifically *as* Muslim women.[48] Muslims recognize that, for the most part, they are being excluded from discussions relating to their community, and they are frequently excluded from task forces that are specifically designed to address violence against women.[49] How ironic that the stifling of Muslim women's voices perpetually relegates their narratives to the background during the very discussions that are designed to empower them to bring their voices to the foreground!

Her Hijab, Her Choice

American Muslim women are faced with challenges about what it means to be at the intersection of their American identity, their Muslim identity, and their female identity,[50] particularly when choosing to wear modest, traditionally Muslim, attire. Hughes argues that there is still some concern within the religionist part of academia and scholarship regarding whether the veil and hijab are a part of religious doctrine, or whether this has been a cultural practice, misinterpreted throughout the years, which has been transmitted transgenerationally under the claim of being religiously founded.[51] Throughout history, the hijab was mostly seen as a symbol of socioeconomic status amongst the elite classes, but in the past 100–150 years, the practice has undergone a revival amongst all socioeconomic groups within Muslim society.[52] Though the interpretations of religious text vary about whether it is obligatory to cover or not, many women who choose to cover indicate that it is less about what they believe that Muslim women *should* do, and more about how they express themselves as Muslim women and how they represent their faith.[53]

Though there are many assumptions about the practice of veiling, women who choose to wear it say that it allows them to be faithful to the ideals of Islam as well as serves as a way to be less objectified as women.[54] Addressing how adopting the hijab made her feel, Yousuf-Sadiq wrote:

> I became equally as secure with my hijab and I felt something I'd never felt before: control. Without hijab, society's standards of beauty dictated how I presented myself to the world and, by extension, how I thought of myself when I didn't measure up. When following the Islamic dress code, I had control over who did and didn't look at me, who did and didn't touch me. I had a greater sense of authority over how people viewed me because for the first time, people were not seeing my outer appearance – they were seeing *me*.[55]

For many, the choice to cover is one that is complex and conflict laden. The majority of Muslim women in the West choose not to wear conservative and traditional Islamic dress for many reasons, among those being that they do not want to be seen as targets, they did not adopt the style of dress prior to immigrating or converting, they are not ready for the adult responsibilities and role that comes with adherence to this type of dress, or they believe that modesty does not necessarily translate to wearing hijab.[56] Twenty-two percent of Muslim-American-identifying women have reported that they are fearful of wearing hijab or participating in other outward identifiers of faith because they are afraid of the increasing intolerance toward Muslims as exhibited in American culture.[57] Although some woman chose to remove their hijabs immediately after the September 11 terrorist attacks due to fear, in the years since, more American Muslim women have joined the covering movement.[58]

Some converts to Islam have indicated that the choice of changing to more modest dress after their conversion, including an increased proclivity toward wearing the hijab, can increase friction with family and friends, as well as in the workplace.[59] In the current American social context, "the hijab is no longer seen as an innocent mark of a woman intent on maintaining her cultural and religious identity, but as a threatening symbol of a pathologically anti-western ideology,"[60] and this perception of threat can lead to intense interpersonal conflict.

Although it is illegal in American employment practices, hijab has kept Muslim women from getting jobs or advancing in the workplace.[61] Bosses and superiors fear that Muslim women wearing hijab will be distracting to customers and many do not allow head coverings as part of their uniforms.[62] In the US Military, the wearing of hijab for women while in uniform is still being discussed though some commanding officers have chosen to allow this practice on a case-by-case basis.

When it comes to the discussion of women and their modest dress, many Muslim women in the West are tired of the exhaustive discussion of hijab and having their identities boiled down to whether they choose to cover their hair.[63]

Voice

Above all, American Muslim women want to ensure that instead of being seen as women in headscarves, their voices are being heard and that they are equally dedicated to their faiths and nationality.[64] Hammer noted that women in Islam are "not spoken to, but rather spoken about, a common feature of much of the Islamophobic discourse as we have seen it reincarnate in various forms over the last decade."[65] Again, this boils down to the very people who could help construct the alternative discourse to Islamophobia are the very ones being excluded from the conversation.

Inviting Muslim women to participate in the dialogue would "entail a shift in terms of discussion: instead of being portrayed as voiceless victims, Muslim women would become actors capable of changing their own circumstances [if they choose]."[66] According to Ernst, "Muslim women, whose voices are rarely sought out are both attacked in anti-Muslim hate crimes and viewed with pity as victims who need to be saved from their own religion."[67] By perceiving covered women as no more than "silent dummies unable to speak for themselves, needing outsiders to speak for them, and to interpret the meaning of their traditions for them,"[68] feminists are undermining the inherent feminist concept that women should be uplifted, empowered, and have their voices be heard.

RELIGIOUS CONVERSION

Religious affiliation and strong religious community can provide a framework for a healthy life, including strengthening family bonds, fostering personal integrity and growth, encouraging trust, reducing depression and anxiety, providing support and guidance, building conflict resolution skills, and giving hope for a positive future.[69] Religions are socially constructed from the time we are children, and conformity to the culture and roles of our parents is what leads us to turn "tribal rituals into personal habits."[70]

Approximately two-thirds of all children rebel against the religious teachings of their parents, half doing so before the age of 16 years.[71] Allport recognized that this stage can also come for people who are in periods of intense crisis and noted that

> It is in the critical periods of life, when desire is more intense, that religious consciousness is acute. Many people are religious only in moments of crisis; the rest of the time they rub along comfortably and godlessly, content to let their religious sentiment lie dormant.[72]

Searching for a religious identity is not only limited to those who are in personal crisis, but even the happiest of people may search for religious explanations to help process the complexities that they are surrounded by societally.[73]

Conversion to any religion other than that of one's parents is a complex, nuanced, context-laden, and driven process that is difficult to analyze from an academic perspective because it is a process frequently based on the individual's personal lived experiences.[74] Most countries do not track religion in their census data, therefore statistics on the religion of practice vs. the religion of rearing are hard to come by.[75] Although difficult to track statistically, the study of conversion is of utmost importance because these changes of religion (and the change of perspective that frequently accompanies this change) can help resolve both interpersonal and intrapersonal conflict.[76]

Religious conversion must be conceptualized as a process, rather than a singular moment in a person's life. According to van Nieuwkerk:

> Conversion does not stop at the moment of embracing Islam, and it is not solely a mental activity of accepting a new belief. It requires embodiment of

new social and religious practices. Within this process of embodiment and learning new practices, new ideas and insights are created that can generate new discourses and receptivity to other voices of Islamic discourse . . . the approach to studying conversion as a process of embodying new practices brings to the fore the realization that identities and discourses are implicated in each other.[77]

Because of the contextual nuances of an individual's religious conversion, it can be difficult to discern what the intellectual process is for those who convert. It is paramount that anyone studying religious conversion be aware that conversion stories are all reflective, in that they happen after the conversion has taken place and after the individual's life experiences are reinterpreted to fit into specific conversion narrative molds.[78]

There are no singular precursors or causes for conversion but instead that it is always based on a combination of physiological, environmental, or socio-logical factors which cannot be precisely pinpointed.[79] Beyond the multitude of personal issues that a person considering conversion grapple with as they go through their decision-making process, in places where the dominant social discourse leads people to believe that there is a mutual exclusivity of being both feminist and Muslim, women who contemplate conversion to Islam face intense personal strife as they are forced to reconcile what they believe and what others in the greater community believe. There is no straightforward answer to why women convert to Islam, and the issues are a complex, context-driven set of circumstances that are deeply intertwined with their personal identities and their own understanding of social discourse.[80]

Single mothers, students, and women who are considering marrying Muslim men are amongst the most rapidly increasing demographic of converts to Islam in the United States.[81] American conversion to Islam does not follow any specific regional or educational patterns, but it reso-nates with women through personal, social, spiritual, and intellectual ways.[82] Some researchers have argued that there are three models for conversion to Islam: (1) marriage – either because of marriage or in order to marry; (2) relational – meeting Muslims and having exposure to the Muslim experience; and (3) rationale – intellectually based through reading and other academic exploration.[83] Anway included a fourth model for conversion which includes travels (or extended visits) to Muslim or predominantly Muslim countries.[84] Although religious revivalism and coercive conversion have been included in some models of conversion,[85] neither of these types of conversion are considered part of this study as revival entails a return to a more orthodox practice of the same religion, and Islamic doctrine does not advocate for compulsory conversion.

While dominant discourse would lead us to believe that the American women who are converting to Islam come from undereducated social classes, Islam appears to be resonating with the intellect of educated women – regardless of official educational achievements.[86] For many converts, conversion itself was not the initial purpose of investigating Islam and neither was the desire to marry a partner from the Muslim faith.[87] It should be noted that Islamic Law does not mandate that Jewish or Christian women convert in order to marry Muslim Men, and most women who make the decision to convert to Islam through the marriage avenue do so because of a desire to share at least a basic understanding of their spouse's faith – which in turn leads to personal introspection which causes the faith to resonate.[88]

Indeed, women explore Islam for a number of reasons – a curiosity and desire for knowledge, a desire to better proselytize to Muslims about converting to other faiths, a desire to fulfill their own spiritual needs – and the decision to convert was a happy side effect of their increased understanding of Islam. There is difficulty in determining whether individuals from specific religions are more likely to convert to Islam.[89]

Religious Conversion as a Process

According to van Nieuwkerk, "conversion is a multi-layered, continuous process in which new identities and discourses are produced and reproduced. Some individuals can become susceptible to conversion through personal trajectories and biological experiences, yet the new message must be plausible."[90] Converts frequently describe their conversion as a process, rather than a specific time and space oriented moment,[91] and this process can be complex, taking many forms.

The personal introspection that converts to Islam face can easily be explained by the four-stage model developed by A.H. Baker in his book *Extremists in our Midst: Confronting terror.*[92] In this model, individual enters into the conversion process at the founding phase where they explore aspects of the faith, ideas and concepts resonate, and they make the actual conversion.[93] This would be the stage where the *shahada* is taken, and the individual might begin calling themselves a Muslim. From there, converts move into the youthful and formative phase where the individual continues to explore the ideology and the teachings, and when they may become overzealous and idealistic.[94] The third stage of the process is the adult phase which is usually marked by an exploratory process that may include a broadening of understanding of both positive and negative teachings of the faith, and where the foundations for ongoing religious observance are created.[95] The final phase of the conversion, labeled the "mature phase," is marked by reflective inquiry into the self and how the religion and the self interact.[96]

Roald simplified the stages of conversion to include only three distinct stages: (1) love; (2) disappointment; and (3) maturity.[97] In the first stage, also known as the love stage or the convertitis stage, new converts become virtually obsessed with the faith, learning about and practicing the new faith as often as possible. In the disappointment stage, the individual may find discrepancies in the behaviors and ideas of indigenous Muslims, and they become jaded about the faith. In the maturity stage, new Muslims are able to rectify the discrepancies that they found in the disappointment stage, and they are able to return to themselves, while repairing the fractures that happened during the disappointment stage so that they can reintegrate and develop new identities within the faith.[98]

It should be noted that regardless of which conversion model is used, it is accepted that contextualization and understanding of the faith, the role that the religion will play within the individual, and the role that the individual will play within the faith community is not a linear process.[99] Individuals may move both backward and forward in their processes, at various points in their lives.[100]

Conversion to Islam as Conflict Resolver for Women

For female converts, conversion to Islam can solve three discrepancies within other faiths: (1) the discrepancy between sexuality and gender relations; (2) the problem of poor social mobility; and (3) the struggles between understanding the categories of nationality and ethnicity.[101] Because Islam is a religion that is strongly rooted in diversity, and because it teaches that all humans are equal in the eyes of Allah, it is appealing to those who have been part of oppressed groups.[102] Islam answers the question of how we move on after making mistakes or having significant flaws because Islam teaches that only Allah can be flawless and be perfect, it allows for the individual to better accept their own perceived or actual imperfections.[103]

For female converts to Islam, Islam can solve the seventh-century issue of female infanticide and the maltreatment of women (and the poor) in that the Qur'an gives women rights to own property, gain an inheritance, get a dowry, and both choose and gather support (emotionally and financially) from her husband.[104] Further, Muhammad advocated partici- pation in politics by women, keeping of the maiden names so as to break traditions of females being treated as property, the idea that females should sign prenuptial agreements to protect themselves in the case of divorce, and educational rights for women.[105] Anway indicated that women who have converted to Islam:

> Believe that Allah, through the Qur'an 1400 years ago, set in place rights for women that have never at any time, been equaled in the spiritual, intellec- tual, political, social, and economic areas of life. Some of these rights… [include] maintenance and kindly treatment, education and a career, and being regarded as an equal with man before God but with roles that are somewhat different in their responsibilities.[106]

Though each individual comes to their religious identities by following different trajectories and makes the choice to covert for different reasons, it must be noted that American women are converting to Islam at high rates.[107] Although there is a plethora of literature available on general religious conversion, the academy contains very little information regard- ing conversion to Islam.[108]

Due to the fact that the Western stereotypes of Muslim women are that of oppression and maltreatment, there can alternately be an increase of identity conflicts within women who have converted. New converts to Islam must shift their identities (within their self-conceptualization) because Islam values being a Muslim first, all other identifiers coming as secondary.[109] Bullock highlighted this when she wrote:

> I felt the same, but I was often treated with contempt, I was not treated as I had been as a white, middle-class woman. It was my first personal experience of discrimination and racism, and made me see my previous privileged position in a way that I had never before properly understood.[110]

Female converts to Islam must face the harsh reality that they are choosing to leave a position of privilege for a new position within a marginalized population, a shift which can ignite or fuel previously developed conflicts within the self and others.

Conflict with Members from Religion of Departure

It is not uncommon for religious converts to face increased interpersonal conflict with members from the religious group that they are leaving. Some religious groups attach an intense stigma to religious apostate and treat them as if they are dangerous.[111] People within religious groups frequently talk about faith in terms of absolutes where there is a zero-sum conflict between "divinity" and "evil." Those who are perceived to have turned their backs on their faith (which is interpreted as being aligned with "divinity") are perceived as choosing "evil."[112] According to Jansen:

> The deserted religion will reject and punish any apostates, and denounce the calls made by other religions. Punishments for apostasy may range from calling names – with negative connotations such as renegade, apostate, backslider, or turncoat – or ostracism, forfeiture of inheritance rights, loss of guardianship of children, loss of conjugal rights, or even death. Conversion therefore always has a double face, from the perspective of receiving and of the departed religious group.[113]

For converts to Islam, those who return home to families and friends who are not Muslim can see an increase in familial tension.[114] One study found that female converts to Islam who had returned home to their non-Muslim husbands and families saw an increase in tension, particularly related to their modest choice of dress, a possible newfound rejection of alcohol, and changes to the way that meals are prepared in the home.[115] In some cases, converts say that their nonconverting families saw their conversion to Islam as an alliance to terrorism.[116] The perceived rejection that converts experience within their families post-conversion falls along two trajectories: (1) the lack of familial understanding of the choice; and (2) an abject refusal to understand the choice.[117] Why Western women would choose Islam has proven to be problematic for many Americans because they mistakenly view Islam as antifeminist.[118]

In a German study of female conversion experiences, it was found that converts to Islam experienced othering and exclusion from relationships that had existed prior to their conversions,[119] and it is believed that German conversion experiences may mirror those of Americans. New converts to Islam may be surprised to find "suspicion from both the majority and minority group, and new kinds of discrimination of which they were previously unaware."[120] Supportive relationships were required for longevity and strength of religious resolve for the recent converts in Germany.

Americans who convert or the children of converts may face a breakdown in relationships with non-Muslim family and friends, and this is more likely to be experienced by Caucasian converts than black or Latino converts.[121] Religious conversion, particularly in social climates where there is a negative political charge toward the chosen religion – including a mutual exclusivity between identifying as members of that religion and the dominant culture – can result in immense conflicts. In Dutch society, recent Caucasian converts reported feeling as if they were moved from a position of privilege to one where they are viewed as "symbolic migrants."[122]

Conflict with Members of Religion of Arrival

Recent converts to Islam are met with two typical responses by born-Muslims: (1) skepticism of those who are not highly educated on doctrine; and (2) admiration of those who become obsessed with all things of Islam.[123] New converts are frequently expected to know all doctrine and follow all Islamic practices immediately on their conversion, which can lead the recent convert to become obsessive about learning new doctrine and following it to the word.[124] It is not unusual for recent converts to be seen as spokespersons for Islam, taking on roles of leadership within the Muslim community and serving as facilitators for interfaith dialogues because they may have a firm enough grasp of the doctrine in multiple faiths that they can be perceived as less of threat and can help bridge the gaps.[125]

But although they may take on leadership roles, converts to Islam deal with emotional and psychological isolation, which can make the conversion process even more difficult.[126] Recent converts frequently act not only as both defenders of their choice to convert but also as defenders of their newly established Muslim identity.[127] All that is needed to formally convert to Islam is a public declaration of the *shahada*, and it is then assumed that the convert will immediately begin living their lives under Islamic rules[128] but ongoing support in religious study seems to be missing. It is important for new converts to have strong support systems within their new religious community to guide them along their religious paths. Poor post-conversion support (and a low acceptance by born-Muslims) has combined to cause approximately 50% of recent converts to eventually leave Islam in pursuit of other religious paths.[129] According to Anway, "disillusionment, confusion, unanswered questions – these describe the early religious experience of many women. However in spite of frustration, their stories show their devotion, of being in 'search mode' and looking for stability in their religious life."[130]

Born-Muslims may not understand that Muslim converts have differing spiritual and social needs. Being born and raised Muslim implies an ingrained sense of history of the plight of Muslim people,[131] something that recent converts must juggle as they find their new place not only within the religious community but also with society as a whole. Some converts have claimed that there is a cliquishness of the immigrant community comprised of people who appear to always be judging to see if they are making ritualistic mistakes or for holding too tightly to one particular group's practices.[132] While Islam aims at leveling social, racial, and gender inequalities, there are a variety of social hierarchies that converts to Islam must navigate.[133]

Some immigrant groups believe that the hijab is a religious requirement, and this can cause tension for female Muslim converts as they decide whether they wish to adopt this practice. Uddin highlighted this tension when speaking about the "Hijab Cult" which was made up by mostly immigrant Muslims saying:

> This group ostracized women who didn't wear hijab, making them feel like lesser Muslims, somehow weaker in their faith than those who wore it. Even though members of this cult were backbiting and constantly judging others' actions according to their personal rubric of proper Islam, they were still elevated as a symbol for all of those "immodest" women to emulate.[134]

For converts, feeling as if they are being judged or being ousted as other within the Muslim community can be more common if the convert is unwed, female, and white.[135] Language barriers between recent converts and the immigrant Muslim community can also create problems for integration within the community, but this is where having a sponsoring Muslim family or having a potential spouse within the community can be of great benefit.[136]

It can be difficult for recent converts to discern which practices are those which are cultural and which of those practices are religious. Navigating and interpreting the cultural differences of how the faith is practiced can be problematic for the recently converted because immigrant and born-Muslims frequently want converts to follow the cultural practices already established in their particular Muslim community.[137] Many new converts may choose the path of least resistance and adopt specific cultural understandings of the faith.[138]

Many recent female converts have symbolic name changes, a practice which is encouraged in various Muslim dominated cultures, however, is not obligatory based on the Qur'an.[139] Other female converts change their attire to one of more modesty, adopting the hijab. For some, donning the hijab is comforting because they feel as if they are no longer being judged based on Western perceptions of beauty, but for others, this can create more interpersonal issues and conflict with family than the actual conversion because it is seen as too intense of a personal transformation.[140]

Both the processes of name changing and altering the physical appearance are symbolic of the individual's choice to leave the non-Muslim life behind and begin a new life as a Muslim. These and similar rituals are important to religious life, as they can help set a new tone for a person's religious identity, as well as reinforce their confidence in the religious decisions that they have made.[141] Ultimately, the conversion process is one of many transitions and personal transformations where converts travel to places of "confusion to peace, from conflict to resolution, from adrift to coherence, from emptiness to fulfillment, from loneliness to belonging to a community where one is embraced and celebrated."[142]

The internet can play an integral role in the conversion and role integration process for females who have recently converted to Islam and because of the plethora of chat rooms, list serves, and websites for the new convert to turn when she needs support, it has proven invaluable.[143] In some cases, female converts who have sought online support through the conversion process report that they feel closer to their online friends who support their conversion than they do to their own families.[144] Online opportunities for support frequently take two forms: (1) a discussion and testimonial of how the individual came to choose Islam as a religious affiliation; and (2) a discussion and testimonial of the difficulty of telling their families of their conversion decision, where many people reported experiencing societal and familial alienation.[145]

Despite rejection and other negative experiences both with immigrant Muslims and with their pre-conversion relationships, the available literature indicates that new female converts have had overall positive experiences with the conversion process and post-conversion life.[146] Haddad indicated that "for the most part converts report that they are very happy with their decision and accept their role as agents of harmonization between Islam and an often skeptical American society."[147]

NOTES

1. Ben K. Beiten and Katherine R. Allen, "Resilience in Arab American Couples," p. 263.
2. Brigitte L. Nacos and Oscar Torres-Reyna, "Framing Muslim-Americans."
3. Carol L. Anway, *Daughters of Another Path*; Lori Peek, *Behind the Backlash*.
4. Geneive Abdo, *Mecca and the Main Street*.
5. For better understanding of the tenets and beliefs taught within Islam, it would be advisable to seek out Muslim religious scholars and leaders. The most comprehensive web based information source that I have found is www.whyislam.org and they also suggest that discussions with local Muslim leadership are advised.
6. Deepa Kumar, *Islamophobia and the Politics of Empire* (Chicago: Haymarket Books, 2012).
7. Asma Gull Hasan, *American Muslims: The New Generation* (New York: Continuum, 2000).
8. Asma Gull Hasan, *American Muslims*.
9. Carol L. Anway, *Daughters of Another Path*.
10. Claude Salhani, *Islam Without a Veil* (Washington, DC: Potomac Books, Inc., 2011).
11. Asma Gull Hasan, *Why I am a Muslim*.
12. Asma Gull Hasan, *Why I am a Muslim*.
13. Louay Safi, "Truth and Vanity Shape Anti-Americanism and Islamophobia," in *Islamophobia and Anti-Americanism: Causes and Remedies*, ed. Mohamed Nimer (Beltsville, MD: Amana Publications, 2007), p. 21–26.
14. Asma Gull Hasan, *Why I am a Muslim*.
15. Kirk Heriot, *Understanding Each Other After 9/11: What Everyone Should Know about the Religions of the World* (Fort Bragg, CA: Lost Coast Press, 2012).
16. Joe L. Kincheloe and Shirley R. Steinberg, "Why Teach Against Islamophobia? Striking the Empire Back," in *Teaching Against Islamophobia*, ed. Joe L. Kincheloe, Shirley R. Steinberg, and Christopher D. Stonebanks (New York, NY: Peter Lang Publishing, 2010), p. 3–27; Khurrum Mirza and Naved Bakali, "Islam: The Fundamentals Every Teacher Should Know," in *Teaching Against Islamophobia*, ed. Joe L. Kincheloe, Shirley R. Steinberg,

and Christopher D. Stonebanks (New York, NY: Peter Lang Publishing, 2010), p. 49–64.

17. Jamillah Karim, *American Muslim Women: Negotiating Race, Class, and Gender within the Ummah* (New York: New York University Press, 2009).

18. Amber Hague, "Islamophobia in North America: Confronting the Menace," in *Confronting Islamophobia in Educational Practice*, ed. Barry van Driel (Staffordshire, England: Trentham Books Limited, 2004), p. 1–18.

19. Kirk Heriot, *Understanding Each Other*.

20. Hassan A. Mian, "What is Islam? A Conversation with the Magisterial Intellectuals of the Past," in *Teaching Against Islamophobia*, ed. Joe L. Kincheloe, Shirley R. Steinberg, and Christopher D. Stonebanks (New York, NY: Peter Lang Publishing, 2010), p. 65–76.

21. Scott C. Alexander, "We Should Deconstruct Our Supremacist Master Narratives," in *Islamophobia and Anti-Americanism: Causes and Remedies*, ed. Mohamed Nimer (Beltsville, MD: Amana Publications, 2007), p. 15–20.

22. Frederick M. Denny, "Islam and Peacebuilding: Continuities and Transitions," in *Religion and Peacebuilding*, ed. Harold Coward and Gordon S. Smith (Albany, NY: State University of New York Press, 2004), p. 129–146.

23. Ibid.

24. Asma Gull Hasan, *Why I am a Muslim*.

25. Saleemah Abdul-Ghafur, Introduction to *Living Islam Outloud: American Muslim Women Speak*, ed. Saleemah Abdul-Ghafur (Boston, MA: Beacon Press, 2005).

26. Lori Peek, *Behind the Backlash*, p. 12.

27. Amber Hague, "Confronting the Menace."

28. Narzanin Massoumi, "Beyond Personal Belief? The Role of Religious Identities Among Muslim Women Respect Activists," in *Women and Islam*, ed. Zayn R. Kassam (Santa Barbara, CA: Praeger, 2010), p. 63–92.

29. Yvonne Yazbeck Haddad, Jane I. Smith, and Kathleen M. Moore, *Muslim Women in North America: The Challenge of Islamic Identity Today* (New York, NY: Oxford University Press, 2006).

30. Yvonne Yazbeck Haddad, Jane I. Smith, and Kathleen M. Moore, *Muslim Women in North America*.

31. Khurrum Mirza and Naved Bakali, "Islam: The Fundamentals."

32. Carl W. Ernst, Introduction to *Islamophobia in America: The Anatomy of Intolerance*, ed. Carl W. Ernst (New York, NY: Palgrave MacMillan, 2013), p. 1–19; Juliane Hammer, *American Muslim Women, Religious Authority, and Activism* (Austin, TX: University of Texas Press, 2012).

33. Juliane Hammer, *American Muslim Women*, p. 140.

34. Frederick M. Denny, "Islam and Peacebuilding."

35. Ibid.

36. Geneive Abdo, *Mecca and the Main Street.*
37. Juliane Hammer, "Center Stage"; Asma Gull Hasan, *American Muslims*; Deepa Kumar, *Islamophobia and the Politics of Empire*; Nadirah Z. Sabir, "The Adventures of a Muslim Woman in Atlanta," in *Shattering the Stereotypes: Muslim Women Speak Out,* ed. Fawzia Afzal-Khan (Northampton, MA: Olive Branch Press, 2005), p. 39.
38. Nadirah Z. Sabir, "The Adventures of a Muslim Woman."
39. Ibid.
40. Ibid.
41. Carol L. Anway, *Daughters of Another Path*; Juliane Hammer, "Center Stage: Gendered Islamophobia and Muslim Women" in *Islamophobia in America: The Anatomy of Intolerance,* ed. Carl W. Ernst (New York, NY: Palgrave MacMillan, 2013), p. 107–144; Deepa Kumar, *Islamophobia and the Politics of Empire.*
42. Najwa Raouda, *The Feminine Voice of Islam.*
43. Yvonne Yazbeck Haddad, Jane I. Smith, and Kathleen M. Moore, *Muslim Women in North America.*
44. Narzanin Massoumi, "Beyond Personal Belief?"
45. Deepa Kumar, *Islamophobia and the Politics of Empire.*
46. Katherine Bullock, *Rethinking Muslim Women and the Veil: Challenging Historical and Modern Stereotypes* (London: International Institute of Islamic Thought, 2007); Stephen Sheehi, *Islamophobia: The Ideological Campaign Against Muslims* (Atlanta, GA: Clarity Press, 2011).
47. Yvonne Yazbeck Haddad, Jane I. Smith, and Kathleen M. Moore, *Muslim Women in North America.*
48. Tony Gaskew, "Confronting Political Islam"; Yvonne Yazbeck Haddad, Jane I. Smith, and Kathleen M. Moore, *Muslim Women in North America.*
49. Yvonne Yazbeck Haddad, Jane I. Smith, and Kathleen M. Moore, *Muslim Women in North America.*
50. Maria M. Ebrahimji, "In Search of Fatima and Taqwa," in *I Speak for Myself: American Women on Being Muslim,* ed. Maria M. Ebrahimji and Zahra T. Suratwala (Ashland, OR: White Cloud Press, 2011), p. 23–28; Yvonne Yazbeck Haddad, Jane I. Smith, and Kathleen M. Moore, *Muslim Women in North America.*
51. Aaron W. Hughes, *Muslim Identities: An Introduction to Islam* (New York: Columbia University Press, 2013).
52. Najwa Raouda, *The Feminine Voice of Islam.*
53. Aaron W. Hughes, *Muslim Identities*; Najwa Raouda, *The Feminine Voice of Islam.*
54. Katherine Bullock, *Rethinking Muslim Women*; Kirk Heriot, *Understanding Each Other*; Nousheen Yousuf-Sadiq, "Half and Half," in *I Speak for Myself:*

American Women on Being Muslim, ed. Maria M. Ebrahimji and Zahra T. Suratwala (Ashland, OR: White Cloud Press, 2011), p. 18–22.

55. Nousheen Yousuf-Sadiq, "Half and Half," p. 21.
56. Katherine Bullock, *Rethinking Muslim Women*; Yvonne Yazbeck Haddad, Jane I. Smith, and Kathleen M. Moore, *Muslim Women in North America*; Asma Gull Hasan, *American Muslims*; Juliane Hammer, "Center Stage"; Lori Peek, *Behind the Backlash.*
57. "Muslim Americans: Middle Class and Mostly Mainstream," *Pew Research Center.*
58. Lori Peek, *Behind the Backlash.*
59. Katherine Bullock, *Rethinking Muslim Women*; Haifaa Jawad, "Female Conversion to Islam, the Sufi Paradigm," in *Women Embracing Islam: Gender and Conversion in the West,* ed. Karin van Nieuwkerk (Austin, TX: University of Texas Press, 2006), p. 153–171.
60. Haifaa Jawad, "Female Conversion to Islam," p. 155.
61. Yvonne Yazbeck Haddad, Jane I. Smith, and Kathleen M. Moore, *Muslim Women in North America.*
62. Geneive Abdo, *Mecca and the Main Street*; Yvonne Yazbeck Haddad, Jane I. Smith, and Kathleen M. Moore, *Muslim Women in North America*; Lori Peek, *Behind the Backlash.*
63. Saleemah Abdul-Ghafur, Introduction to *Living Islam Outloud*; Katherine Bullock, *Rethinking Muslim Women.*
64. Maria M. Ebrahimji and Zahra T. Suratwala, Introduction to *I Speak for Myself: American Women on Being Muslim,* ed. Maria M. Ebrahimji and Zahra T. Suratwala (Ashland, OR: White Cloud Press, 2011), p. XV–XVI.
65. Juliane Hammer, "Center Stage," p. 116.
66. Deepa Kumar, *Islamophobia and the Politics of Empire,* p. 45.
67. Carl W. Ernst, Introduction to *Islamophobia in America,* p. 12.
68. Katherine Bullock, *Rethinking Muslim Women,* p. 225.
69. William R. Breakey, "Psychiatry, Spirituality and Religion," in *Religion in Politics and Society,* ed. Michael Kelly and Lynn M. Messina (New York: H. W. Wilson, 2002), p. 18–27.
70. Gordon W. Allport, *The Individual and His Religion* (London: Constable and Company, Ltd., 1950) p. 26.
71. Ibid.
72. Ibid., p. 11
73. Ibid.
74. Willy Jansen, "Two Contested Concepts."
75. Karin van Nieuwkerk, Introduction to *Women Embracing Islam.*
76. Rebekah Lee, "Conversion and its Consequences: Africans and Islam in Cape Town," in *Can Faith Make Peace? Holy Wars and the Resolution of*

Religious Conflicts, ed. Philip Broadhead and Damien Keown (New York, NY: I. B. Tauris and Co. Ltd., 2007), p. 124–133.

77. Karin van Nieuwkerk, Introduction to *Women Embracing Islam,* p. 11.
78. Karin van Nieuwkerk, "Gender, Conversion, and Islam: A Comparison of Online and Offline Conversion Narratives," in *Women Embracing Islam: Gender and Conversion in the West,* ed. Karin van Nieuwkerk (Austin, TX: University of Texas Press, 2006), p. 95–119.
79. Abdul Haqq Baker, *Extremists in Our Midst* (London: Palgrave Macmillan, 2011).
80. Karin van Nieuwkerk, Introduction to *Women Embracing Islam.*
81. Geneive Abdo, *Mecca and the Main Street.*
82. Debra L. Dirks, "Introduction: America and Islam"; Yvonne Yazbeck Haddad, Jane I. Smith, and Kathleen M. Moore, *Muslim Women in North America.*
83. Stefano Allievi, "The Shifting Significance."
84. Carol L. Anway, *Daughters of Another Path.*
85. Abdul Haqq Baker, *Extremists in Our Midst.*
86. Debra L. Dirks, "Introduction: America and Islam."
87. Yvonne Yazbeck Haddad, Jane I. Smith, and Kathleen M. Moore, *Muslim Women in North America.*
88. Ibid.
89. Yvonne Yazbeck Haddad, "The Quest for Peace in Submission: Reflections on the Journey of American Women Converts to Islam," in *Women Embracing Islam: Gender and Conversion in the West,* ed. Karin van Nieuwkerk (Austin, TX: University of Texas Press, 2006), p. 19–47.
90. Karin van Nieuwkerk, Introduction to *Women Embracing Islam,* p. 11.
91. Yvonne Yazbeck Haddad, Jane I. Smith, and Kathleen M. Moore, *Muslim Women in North America.*
92. Abdul Haqq Baker, *Extremists in Our Midst.*
93. Ibid.
94. Ibid.
95. Ibid.
96. Ibid.
97. Anne Sofie Roald, "The Shaping of a Scandinavian 'Islam': Converts and Gender Equal Opportunity," in *Women Embracing Islam: Gender and Conversion in the West,* ed. Karin van Nieuwkerk (Austin, TX: University of Texas Press, 2006), p. 48–70.
98. Ibid.
99. Ibid.
100. Abdul Haqq Baker, *Extremists in Our Midst.*
101. Monika Wohlrab-Sahr, "Symbolizing Distance."

102. Asma Gull Hasan, *Why I am a Muslim*; Kirk Heriot, *Understanding Each Other*.
103. Asma Gull Hasan, *Why I am a Muslim*.
104. Carol L. Anway, *Daughters of Another Path*; Asma Gull Hasan, *Why I am a Muslim*; Kirk Heriot, *Understanding Each Other*;, Rebekah Lee "Conversion and its Consequences."
105. Asma Gull Hasan, *Why I am a Muslim*; Kirk Heriot, *Understanding Each Other*.
106. Carol L. Anway, *Daughters of Another Path*, p. 86–87.
107. Geneive Abdo, *Mecca and the Main Street*; Carol L. Anway, *Daughters of Another Path*; Debra L. Dirks, "Introduction: America and Islam."
108. Karin van Nieuwkerk, Introduction to *Women Embracing Islam*.
109. Geneive Abdo, *Mecca and the Main Street*.
110. Katherine Bullock, *Rethinking Muslim Women*, p. xxiv.
111. Roy F. Baumeister, *Evil: Inside Human Violence and Cruelty* (New York: Holt Paperbacks, 1999).
112. Ibid.
113. Willy Jansen, "Two Contested Concepts," p. X.
114. Debra L. Dirks, "Introduction: America and Islam."
115. Rebekah Lee, "Conversion and its Consequences."
116. Yvonne Yazbeck Haddad, "The Quest for Peace in Submission."
117. Carol L. Anway, *Daughters of Another Path*.
118. Yvonne Yazbeck Haddad, Jane I. Smith, and Kathleen M. Moore, *Muslim Women in North America*.
119. Esra Özyürek, "German Converts to Islam and their Ambivalent Reactions with Immigrant Muslims," in *Islamophobia/Islamophilia: Beyond the Politics of Enemy and Friend*, ed. Andrew Shryock (Bloomington, IN: Indiana University Press, 2010), p. 172–192.
120. Ibid., p. 173–174.
121. Yvonne Yazbeck Haddad, Jane I. Smith, and Kathleen M. Moore, *Muslim Women in North America*.
122. Karin van Nieuwkerk, "Gender, Conversion, and Islam," p. 106.
123. Geneive Abdo, *Mecca and the Main Street*.
124. Ibid.
125. Yvonne Yazbeck Haddad, "The Quest for Peace in Submission."
126. Geneive Abdo, *Mecca and the Main Street*.
127. Karin van Nieuwkerk, "Gender, Conversion, and Islam."
128. Haifaa Jawad, "Female Conversion to Islam."
129. Geneive Abdo, *Mecca and the Main Street*.
130. Carol L. Anway, *Daughters of Another Path*, p. 14.
131. Asma Gull Hasan, *Why I am a Muslim*.

132. Yvonne Yazbeck Haddad, "The Quest for Peace in Submission"; Anne Sofie Roald, "The Shaping of a Scandinavian 'Islam."

133. Yvonne Yazbeck Haddad, Jane I. Smith, and Kathleen M. Moore, *Muslim Women in North America*.

134. Asma T. Uddin, "Conquering Veils: Gender and Islams," in *I Speak for Myself: American Women on Being Muslim*, ed. Maria M. Ebrahimji and Zahra T. Suratwala (Ashland, OR: White Cloud Press, 2011), p. 39.

135. Yvonne Yazbeck Haddad, "The Quest for Peace in Submission."

136. Ibid.

137. Yvonne Yazbeck Haddad, Jane I. Smith, and Kathleen M. Moore, *Muslim Women in North America*.

138. Anne Sofie Roald, "The Shaping of a Scandinavian 'Islam."

139. Stefano Allievi, "The Shifting Significance."

140. Carol L. Anway, *Daughters of Another Path*; Yvonne Yazbeck Haddad, "The Quest for Peace in Submission."

141. William R. Breakey, "Psychiatry, Spirituality and Religion."

142. Yvonne Yazbeck Haddad, "The Quest for Peace in Submission," p. 42.

143. Karin van Nieuwkerk, "Gender, Conversion, and Islam."

144. Ibid.

145. Yvonne Yazbeck Haddad, "The Quest for Peace in Submission."

146. Carol L. Anway, *Daughters of Another Path*; Yvonne Yazbeck Haddad, "The Quest for Peace in Submission."

147. Yvonne Yazbeck Haddad, "The Quest for Peace in Submission," p. 43.

CHAPTER 3

Islamophobia and the Talking Heads

The term *Islamophobia* was first used in print materials in 1991 meaning a "hatred of Islam and resultant fear or dislike of Muslims" and was first introduced to the Oxford English Dictionary in 1997.[1] Though the second part of the term – *phobia* – is generally understood in medical and psychological parameters to mean a debilitating fear of something (usually irrationally driven), the term *Islamophobia* is understood as a socialized fear, dislike, and distrust resulting in a rejection of Islam and those who are perceived to be Muslim. Interestingly, although the term was only first coined in 1991, academics and scholars had been discussing the concept of Islamophobia for approximately 66 years.[2] History reveals that Islamophobia existed in the United States as early as the Hoover Administration where Islam was already suspicious because it was associated with the African-American protests against white supremacy.[3] This social activism and a refusal to accept racial inequalities and a racially driven class system is what drew many African-Americans into black Muslim organizations and sparked their conversions to Islam in the first place;[4] yet, their conversion to Islam sparked claims that they were somehow even less American.

According to Allen, within the context of Islamophobia, Islam has the following assumed and incorrect features:

> Islam is seen as monolithic and static, rather than diverse and dynamic. Islam is seen as other and separate, rather than similar and interdependent. Islam is seen as inferior, not different. Islam is seen as an enemy, not as a partner.

© The Author(s) 2017
A.M. Guimond, *Converting to Islam*,
DOI 10.1007/978-3-319-54250-8_3

> Muslims are seen as manipulative, and not sincere. Racial discrimination against Muslims is defended, rather than challenged. Muslims criticisms of the West are rejected, not considered. Anti-Muslim discourse is seen as natural, not problematic.[5]

Although September 11, 2001 was used as the starting point for intense Islamophobia in the United States for the purposes of this study, any discussion of Islamphobia and 9/11 would be incomplete without recognizing that the Federation for American Immigration Reform (FAIR) and the Islamic Human Rights Commission (IHRC) were actively working to have Islamophobia be recognized as a global phenomenon by the United Nations in the days leading up to 9/11.[6] According to Mourchid, "a few days prior to 9/11, in the World Conference Against Racism, the United Nations recognized Islamophobia as a 'discriminatory and exclusionary phenomenon, similar to antisemitism or anti-Roma.'"[7]

Although formally recognized by the United Nations, recognizing Islamophobia at the societal level remained difficult because of the subjective nature of the definition. With no strong conceptual meaning of the term, many people continue to use the term *Islamophobia* in differing ways, and this non-consensus can make it easier for those who engage in Islamophobic behaviors and practices to deny its very existence. According to Hammer,

> Islamophobia is not about innate or natural fear of Islam or Muslims. Rather, it is an ideological construct produced and reproduced at the nexus of a number of political and intellectual currents that need to be taken into consideration and assessed critically in each instance or event of Islamophobic discourse and practice.[8]

It is the fluidity of the term Islamophobia what makes it difficult even for scholars to apply it even in a scholarly way.[9]

Islamophobia holds racism and discrimination as its core but transmits the message (both overtly and covertly) that Muslims are all to be feared because they are violent and hostile, and all are potential terrorists.[10] Although few Americans seek out accurate information regarding what Islam is and is not, Islamophobia "results for most from distant social experiences that mainstream American culture has perpetuated in popular memory, which are in turn buttressed by similar understanding of current events."[11] It is this *us* vs. *them* dichotomy that reminds us that

Islamophobia is so closely related to racism, and that racism provides the fuel in Islamophobic ideology,[12] an ideology that has become completely acceptable and institutionalized in the United States. According to Lean:

> The spheres of Islamophobia and racism overlap greatly. In the last 60 years, in particular, racist language has shifted away from overtly biological prejudices to include a strong cultural component. While derogatory views of blacks, for example have come to occupy a taboo and even disdainful corner of public social discourse, prejudices against groups with differing belief systems, not necessarily genes – is acceptable.[13]

CONTEMPORARY ISLAMOPHOBIA

Islamophobia increases in the United States any time that the United States actively engages in political maneuvers involving countries where there is a Muslim majority. In recent American memory, on April 19, 1995, when the Alfred P. Murrah Federal Building in Oklahoma City, Oklahoma was bombed, Arabs and Muslims were immediately targeted as initial suspects.[14] At the time, the United States was involved in the Middle East and the Gulf War, and because many believed that this attack had been perpetuated by Muslim extremists, it left many Americans being confused to learn that the actual perpetrator was actually Timothy McVeigh, a white American from the South.[15] History also reveals a backlash toward Muslims during the Iranian Hostage Crisis (1971–1981), the World Trade Center bombing of 1993, the Gulf War, and the USS Cole bombing in 2000;[16] however, September 11, 2001 finds the most prominent position in the American collective consciousness because it had the highest level of destruction and was the most shocking.

Although Islamophobia is most often linked to the United States and European countries, it is currently a global phenomenon with evidence supporting that it happens anywhere where Muslims are in the large visible minority status.[17] Similar to the United States, in Europe, Islamophobia forces Muslims to assimilate and integrate into Western society, effectually forcing them to choose between "modern and European" or "backward and oriental."[18]

Regardless of where they are, in essence, Muslims are viewed as "safer" and "good," the more secular they are in their practices.[19] This forced polarization of good vs. evil is deeply rooted in Edward Said's Orientalist thought processes[20] and Samuel Huntington's "Clash of Civilizations."[21] Huntington's "Clash of Civilizations" was originally a theory without much support, but over time people started to believe that Islam and the West were deeply pitted against one another in terms of morals and values and were on a collision course where only one could survive.[22] According to Kincheloe and Steinberg, Huntington's ideology pushes the Islamophobic agenda through perpetuating the ideas that

> there is an inevitable clash of civilizations between Western Christian nations and the Eastern Islamic and Confucian societies is injected into the discourse of U.S. foreign policy. If the United States does not act accordingly, the ideology asserts, bloody Islam will continue its warring tradition against the West.[23]

Although there has been research regarding the prevalence of Islamophobia in the United States, much of this high-priced "research" has been funded by groups which have been classified by the Southern Poverty Law Center as Islamophobic hate groups.[24] The results of this research have frequently been either fabricated or entirely misinterpreted to further the Islamophobic agenda and the Islamophobia industry.[25] This compounds the problem that Islamophobes, and those employing Islamophobic practices, rarely see their behaviors as problematic.[26]

As previously mentioned, the attacks of September 11, 2001 were not what started Islamophobia in the United states but they sparked the underlying anti-Muslim sentiments, and 9/11 was viewed as a catalyst for allowing Islamophobia to become more socially acceptable.[27] Prior to September 11, 2001, there were few public opinion polls about the national attitudes about Muslims; however, one pre-1993 World Trade Center bombing poll found that 62% of Americans said they did not know enough about Islam to form an opinion about Muslims.[28] These numbers would change drastically over the next 23 years.

In the 1 year following September 11, 2001, dozens of books were written and marketed which discussed the "problem" of "unruly and awful" Muslims within the American population.[29] Many Americans post-9/11 believed that Muslims were so "other" that they did not have many of the same relationship issues, work and school issues, or economic hardships that non-Muslims had,[30] a belief that is paramount in the othering of specific groups.

The American public voiced (and still currently voices) concern about the allegiances of the Muslim American community. An April 2002 study found that 44% of surveyed Americans believed that Muslim Americans were not doing enough to assist authorities with finding terrorist cells in the United States, and only 24% said that Muslim Americans cooperated fully with government authorities.[31] The reality is that Muslim Americans make the largest contribution in terms of tips toward counterterrorist initiatives and have proven to be an invaluable asset toward self-policing.[32]

The reality is that despite educational campaigns geared toward combating Islamophobia,[33] public opinion has grown increasingly negative and hostile toward Muslims. In a 2006 Gallup Poll, 33% of respondents said Muslims should carry special identification to help protect the general public from terrorist threats,[34] and many Americans advocate the continued surveillance of mosques and Muslim communities.[35] Interestingly, the FBI still actively scrutinizes American mosques and the American Muslim communities; yet in over 33% of all terrorist attacks in the years since September 11, 2001 – that is, in 48 out of 121 terrorist attacks – the intended damage and destruction by the would-be terrorists was foiled by a Good Samaritan Muslim who tipped off the police.[36]

A 2009 Gallup survey found that 53% of surveyed participants reported that they viewed Islam poorly.[37] In 2010, 28% of voters thought that Muslims should not be allowed on the US Supreme Court, approximately 33% indicated that Muslims should be barred from running for president, and 25% thought that President Obama was secretly a Muslim in pursuit of destroying the United States.[38] In 2010, ABC news and The Washington Post indicated that anti-Muslim sentiment was at an all-time high point with 73% of Americans having an unfavorable view of Muslims.[39]

In 2011, there was another burst of national Islamophobia after Osama bin Laden was captured and killed. At the time, CNN reported that half of the American public would be uncomfortable with women wearing the *burqa*, having a mosque in their neighborhood, or men praying in the local airport.[40] In the same study, 41% of the surveyed population indicated that they would be uncomfortable with an openly Muslim teacher at their local elementary school.[41] In 2011, another survey found that one-third of all Republicans interviewed believed the rhetoric that President Obama was a closet Muslim.[42]

The "Obama as Muslim" rumors and rhetoric continued, and during a 2012 Newsweek poll, 52% of surveyed Republicans indicated that they believed that President Obama had ties with Muslim Extremists and that he was actively pushing the United States to enact Sharia Law. In the research leading up to the writing of this book, I became increasingly aware that while many Americans are vehemently opposed to Sharia Law, it was difficult to find anyone who could articulate what it actually was, or anyone who could explain how it was either similar or different from the legal system in place in the United States.

The beliefs about President Obama's allegiances to Muslim Extremism continued and came to a head again during the 2015–2016 United States presidential race with a multitude of allegations and accusations targeted toward President Obama. This was just the tip of the proverbial iceberg however because Islamophobic discourse dominated a large portion of the Republican platform, and conservative candidates used widespread fear to fuel their agendum. What to do about the *Muslim problem* became a full-fledged political platform for some, specifically in the aftermath of the mass shooting and attempted bombing in San Bernadino, California. This horrific event was used by the then presidential hopeful Donald Trump who publicly called for a "total and complete shutdown" of the United States to Muslims. It was unclear to many whether this was a ban only on immigration, or if he was also suggesting that American Muslims traveling abroad (including Muslims who are deployed members of the US Military) should be denied reentry to the United States. Anyone who was not quick to use words like *terrorism* and *Muslim Extremism* was accused of being anti-American. At the time, studies showed that 45% of respondents supported a ban on Muslims in the United States, and 3 months later, a survey by YouGov found that this support had increased to 51%.[43]

Sheehi posited "that this correlation [between Muslims and violence/terrorism] translates into racist actions and prejudice which facilitates the passage of distinct domestic policies aimed at Muslim and Arab Americans."[44] Programs such as the USA PATRIOT and the NSEERS – also known as the INS Special Registration Program – both of which were products of the War on Terror, have inherently Islamophobic practices involved in their implementation.[45] Further, these policies such as USA PATRIOT and NSEERS are not only seeded from Islamophobia, but they also contribute to the furtherance of Islamophobia in that they increase discrimination through frequent instances of unsupported raids on families and businesses and "voluntary" interviews.[46] According to Hammer, programs that limit the civil liberties of Muslim men in America also specifically impact the women of the community as well because they

> are wives, mothers, sisters and daughters of the Muslim men taken away and deported for minor immigration infractions, fired for being Muslim, put

under surveillance for attending a mosque, forced to endure special registration and random searches and subject to material support for terrorism trials.[47]

MUSLIM AMERICAN RESPONSES TO ISLAMOPHOBIA

Fear and hostility toward Muslims leads to discriminatory and exclusionary practices that limit Muslim and Arab American involvement in social and political processes.[48] The perpetuation of stereotypical ideation, presumed guilt, and an increased exposure to hate crimes is what follows.[49] American Muslims have recognized that they must continue to be seen and heard in order to offset the Islamophobic discourse, which includes becoming more active members of the social sphere and becoming stronger contributors in local and larger-scale political processes.[50] In an ethnographic study based out of the Orlando, Florida area, Gaskew found that Muslim Americans were actively engaging in a process of balancing ethnic and national affiliations within their American and Muslim statuses.[51] This work also included a deep desire to overcome "a perceived environment of discrimination, alienation, fear of law enforcement and a loss of respect, honor, and dignity as the result of the USA PATRIOT Act."[52]

Due to overtly Islamophobic policies such as USA PATRIOT, many legitimate international and domestic American Muslim organizations have been forced to cut their fund-raising efforts and have been forced to close due to the perceived ties to extremist groups like Al Q'aeda.[53] Since the terrorist attacks of September 11, 2001, much of the Muslim community's financial support has shifted away from charity and toward legal defense or social action to educate and protect the community.[54] Since September 11, 2001, the Council on American Islamic Relations (CAIR) has been increasingly working toward bridging the schism between Muslims and non-Muslims in the United States.[55] As Islamophobic rhetoric has increased, CAIR has frequently been more inclined to combat intolerance with threats of lawsuits and legal recourse, but this has done little to actually reduce tensions and has done nothing toward education against misconceptions.[56]

ISLAMOPHOBIA FOR PROFIT

Terrorism is a deep concern for the American collective consciousness, and for many Americans, it has been indelibly etched to the perception of Muslims.[57] This link was cemented early in the period between September

11 and present day. In the days immediately following the terrorist attacks of September 11, President George W. Bush spoke at an Islamic Center and proclaimed that American Muslims "make an incredibly valuable contribution to our country [and] need to be treated with respect.... the face of terror is not the true faith of Islam. That is not what Islam is about."[58] While this may seem like a positive endorsement to Muslims in America, the 2001 declaration that the United States was not at war with Islam was only one part of the story. From that point forward, G.W. Bush's policies outlined the underlying and polarizing assumption that Muslims can be either good or bad, and that until they are proven to be innocent, they should all be suspected.[59]

Other politicians have contributed to perpetuate negative public sentiments toward Islam through their actions in the public eye. In 2000, during the New York race for US Senate, Hillary Clinton (D) received $50,000 in campaign contributions, and Opponent Rick Lazio – backed by the New York State Republican Party – alleged that she accepted the campaign contributions because she was anti-Israel, pro-terrorist, and a terrorist sympathizer.[60] After this became an increasingly charged campaign issue, Clinton returned the funds to her supporters so that she could distance herself from even the perception that her allegiances were maligned;[61] however, the seeds of the allegation had already been planted in the minds of many Americans. In 2003, while dressed in his uniform, General William G. Boykin, Deputy Undersecretary of Defense of Intelligence, publicly addressed multiple Christian groups about the true evils in the world, and contrary to public proclamations to the contrary made by other representatives of the federal government, Islam was the true enemy to Christianity, the West, and the United States. Official apologies were never issued.[62]

This attitude of Islam as the enemy has been relayed throughout the Conservative Christian community by not only well-known Evangelical Christian spokespeople, including Franklin Graham, Pat Robertson, and Jerry Falwell[63] but also politicians and media pundits who make claims of what Islam is and is not, without even having the basic understandings of what the faith represents.[64]

Islamophobia serves as a powerful tool used to the benefit of global political agendum,[65] a process which has become an industry within itself. The idea that Islam is oppressive to women is one that has been perpetuated by, and capitalized upon, by multiple American administrations in order to bolster support for overseas military initiatives.[66] On the other end of the spectrum, as Islamophobia increases, so does anti-American sentiment on the global scale, and those who "opt for conflict would welcome the intensification of Islamophobia and anti-Americanism."[67] By accepting an Islamophobic vein to political discourse, it could then be said that the American public is therefore helping to fund big businesses that profit off of war efforts. Indeed, Islamophobia is so ingrained into the American political discourse that we could find this kind of othering in every political dialogue. As Sheehi posited:

> Every discussion in the U.S. civil society and media about war, Iraq, and Afghanistan manifests Islamophobia. Every discussion about the war on terror is structured by Islamophobia. Every discussion on "repairing relations with the Muslim World" is underwritten by Islamophobic mindsets. Every discussion of Palestine is infused with Islamophobic precepts. Every discussion of oil and energy sovereignty is bounded by a strategic and willful hate and fear of Muslims.[68]

ISLAMOPHOBIA AS AN ENGENDERED PROBLEM

Islamophobia is an engendered cultural phenomenon. According to Hammer, this engendered phenomenon can be clearly identified in the "representation of Muslim men as violent terrorists (both against 'us' and Muslim women) and the representation of Muslim women as oppressed and silenced (by Muslim men, Islam itself, and Muslim culture)."[69] Being an engendered phenomenon means that men and women also experience Islamophobia in different ways.[70] According to Hammer, within the Islamophobic ideology, Muslim women are seen

> as objects of hate and crimes of discrimination, Muslim women have Islamophobia mapped onto them directly and as representations of Muslims in Americans society; [and] as objects of anti-Islamic discourse Muslim women are represented as victims of their religion, culture and Muslim men, and thus in need of saving, liberation, and intervention.[71]

From there, Muslim women in American society realize that while common rhetoric dictates that they are in need of liberation from a supposedly oppressive and marginalizing religion, they are also being ostracized and oppressed by the very same people who are claiming they need to be liberated in the first place.[72] The icing on the proverbial cake is that when Muslims draw attention to the way that they are being vilified and victimized (by mainstream America), they are accused of overexaggerating and trying to suppress the first amendment rights of the freedom of speech for the perpetrators of malicious treatment.[73]

THE TALKING HEADS

The cultural misunderstandings of all things Islam are not said to be an intentional misunderstanding but, rather, they come about because mainstream Americans are ignorant of the fact that they do not know enough about Islam in the first place.[74] Negative attitudes toward Muslims appear to be rooted in current events and media reports that link Islam with violence.[75] By repeatedly linking Muslims to terrorists   even through negative links such as "we are at war with terror, not Islam," – we suggest and reinforce the stereotype that all terrorists come from the Muslim faith, which is used to establish Islamophobic practices and policy.[76] With repeated references to *moderate* Muslims, the media reinforces the *good* vs. *bad* polarization inherent within Islamophobia.[77]

Shaheen noted that "during times of conflict, especially, media systems function as common carriers of government policies."[78] In this sense, the media serves an integral role in the spiraling of negative representations, where the government influences policies, which influences the media, which influences stereotypes, which in turn then influences the government. Staub noted that devaluation "can be transmitted by a culture through written and pictorial material, through everyday conversations, and the examples of people's behavior, or through guidance and instruction by parents,"[79] but this cycle must begin somewhere, and the media can be seen as a major conduit for misperceptions and the dissemination of inaccurate representations. In the wake of the September 11 terrorist acts, the media – who are generally responsible for writing the official script for how history is remembered – allowed this role to be filled by Secretary of Defense, Donald Rumsfeld, who was able to script the official updates to fit the political aims of the time.[80]

The media contributes to the negative framing of Muslims by covering stories that reinforce the consumer's previously existing beliefs about Islam and Muslims.[81] The Media works toward reinforcing the stereotype of Muslim men as "violent and fanatical," while Muslim women are portrayed as "weak and oppressed,"[82] as well as mute, enslaved, humiliated, and eroticized or demonized.[83] Even seemingly innocuous statements (such as those of Barbara Bush 2 months after September 11, 2001 when she said that we need to "focus on the brutality against women and children by the Taliban") have served to link Arabs and Muslims to violence and human rights violations – cementing the link in the American collective conscience.[84] According to Hammer, it is this:

> Juxtaposition of the oppressed lives of women in Afghanistan and Iraq [amongst other repressive cultures], and the prevalence of practices such as "honor killings" and violence against women with the lives and struggles of American Muslim women, even when it changes the perceptions of the latter, [that] still serves political purposes outside their control and interests.[85]

The Media and Metonymy

According to Nacos and Torres-Reyna, "by framing the news along the lines of traditional attitudes and prejudices of society's predominant groups, the news media convey stereotypes that affect a broad range of public perceptions, among them, how people think about race, ethnicity, and religion."[86] This selective media representation has contributed toward the development of negative stereotypes, particularly regarding the Middle East. In the media, Arabs are always associated with Muslims when in reality, only 20% of the world's 1.3+ billion Muslims hail from Arab countries,[87] and 15 million Arabs are Christian.[88] This *Arab equals Muslim* misperception is unfair to non-Arab Muslims as well as to non-Muslim Arabs and continues the process of marginalization and misinformation.[89] The reproduction of stereotypes of Muslim women reinforces the cultural attitude that Muslim women are inferior to Muslim men[90] and closely resembles early Orientalist thought. In the media, Muslim women are rarely portrayed as having roles of leadership and likewise are rarely shown in occupations requiring higher education, such as doctors, lawyers, philanthropists, etc., though Muslim women all occupy these spaces within the American public sphere.[91]

When Muslims are involved with illegal activities or nefarious plots, the news outlets are quick to reference his or her religious affiliation, something which rarely happens with Christians and Jews.[92] According to Gottschalk and Greenberg, the silence maintained by the media regarding Muslims until they are perceived as a threat means that Muslims become visible as people only when they represent threats *as Muslims*, and thus, they only exist as Muslims. This reinforces the negative view of Muslims and enduringly excludes from the perceived American norm.[93]

This negative perception of *Muslims as threat* might be countered should Muslims develop a stronger media presence, but currently there is no singular unified voice defending against untruths or unfair reporting.[94]

The Media Perpetuating Islamophobia for Profit

The problems with unfair and counterfactual media representations are compounded because Muslims are rarely given the space to use main-stream media to condemn violent events.[95] This one-sided representation does little more than reinforce negative stereotypes. It can also be said that the media – who is desperately attempting to oversimplify complicated situations so that consumers at all education levels can understand it – ultimately refines situations down so much that it leads to the creation of a single negative caricature that represents all of Islam.[96]

According to Norris, Kern, and Just, "decisions and common practices in news gathering – determining what and how stories are covered – contribute to these [negative] frames [of Muslims]."[97] The way that news is relayed and disseminated has a long history of enhancing general us vs. them dichotomies. As explained by Green,

> our society's nervous systems – the media, word of mouth – are far more likely to broadcast messages about our own group's painful experiences than about the painful experiences of others. As a result, our moral biases may, in some cases, be built into the systems that we use to perceive events in the world.[98]

Consumers of media must recognize that the media is influenced by the interests of the audience, political influences, and their ability to keep people engaged, and thus selling more of the sponsor's products through advertisements. For this reason, the media will continue to produce stories that reflect current dominant discourse. Monahan claimed that profiting off of the fears that the general public had regarding Muslims in the immediate aftermath of events such as September 11, 2001 was lucrative, stating that "September 11 remains a vital political resource for those who are willing and able to use it."[99]

Those who recognize the media's role in reaffirming negative stereotypes of Muslims will fault far-right, politically conservative media, such as FOX News.[100] According to research conducted in September 2011, 60% of Republicans, who enjoy and consume FOX News programming, believe that Muslim Americans are working to establish Sharia Law in the United states, and the attitudes of Republicans who do not consume FOX News are more consistent with their more politically liberal counterparts.[101]

Islamophobia in Television and Film

When thinking about how the media plays into Islamophobic discourse, most would be likely to identify nightly news as a contributing factor; however, assaults by the media are not solely tied to the major news outlets.[102] Immediately after September 11, 2001, there were 50+ fictionalized television programs that actively engaged in demonizing and vilifying Arabs and Muslims.[103] Although fictionalized TV shows portray Imams as being radicalized toward terrorism, real Imams like Imam Mohamed Maqid of Virginia have been actively working in conjunction with the FBI to assist with counterterrorism efforts. These types of positive representations are seldom highlighted by the media.[104]

There is questioning as to whether the mainstream American public has become so desensitized to vulgar denigrations of Muslims and Arabs that we no longer have an awareness that we are being exposed to them.[105] Exposure to negative images about Muslims and Arabs begins at an early age, and seldom do consumers recognize this exposure. Finkelstein posited that

> we are in a society where most people are taught nothing about Islam while being bombarded by the media with sensationalized, negative images . . . in Disney's animated feature Aladdin, the protagonist characters have light skin and American accents, whereas the villains are dark-skinned and have middle Eastern accents.[106]

It should be noted that while there have been some positive representations of Muslims and Arabs in films, these representations are fewer and farther between than the negative ones, thus they are completely overshadowed.[107]

There is a profitability in the denigration of Muslims, and some producers in the industry have recognized that creating "bash the Arab" films can quickly line their pockets.[108] Comedian and ventriloquist John Dunham created a YouTube sketch called "Achmed the Dead Terrorist," which played upon the negative framing of Muslims in America, and in 2009, it was the fourth most watched YouTube video ever.[109]

Islamophobia in Print propaganda

Immediately following September 11, 2001, a British group was found passing leaflets in Britain that simply stated "I. S. L. A. M.: Intolerance, Slaughter, Looting, Arson, Molestation of Women,"[110] but not all anti-Muslim print propaganda is as overt as this. In the United States, training centers for the FBI in Quantico Virginia were responsible for the dissemination of Islamophobic propaganda during trainings, which included slide shows, videos, and an extensive library full of books written by well-known Islamophobes.[111] At the local and community levels, textbooks used in American grade schools have been shown to reproduce negative attitudes toward minorities and downplay the historical impact on events that demean minority groups (including Muslims).[112] At the college level, humanities and history texts in the United States frequently carry both covertly and overtly anti-Islamic and Islamophobic messages.[113] It should be noted that while the reality is that Muslims have made significant contributions in medicine, mathematics, surgery, optics and ophthalmology, psychology, sociology, and the hard sciences, their contributions to the history in these fields are frequently downplayed[114] which further serves to marginalize their societal contributions and reinforce the idea that Muslims are backward, ignorant, and undeveloped.

Islamophobic Media Pundits, Religious Leaders, and "Experts"

Immediately after September 11, 2001, as the nation was turning to the news and other forms of media to garner a better understanding of what happened, there were few "experts" to be found, leaving the voices presented through the media as being either entirely absent or incredibly slanted.[115] Other than a handful of legitimate experts and specialists, few in the media knew very much about Islam or their religious beliefs.[116] Self-proclaimed experts (with little evidence to support their so-called expertise) ultimately were left picking up on sound bites from representatives of the religious right – leaders like Jerry Falwell, Franklin Graham, and Pat Robertson – who called the Prophet Muhammad a "terrorist" and made claims that Muslims were evil incarnate.[117]

Robert Spencer, a well-known Islamophobe, published five anti-Muslim books in the years following September 11 and, in the 7 years after the launch of his Islamophobic website, was earning an annual salary of $140,000.00 off of the profiteering of Islamophobic sentiments through his instant bestsellers.[118] In October 2012, Spencer's website which had over 31,000 entries to it was boasting 30,000 hits per day.[119] It was clear that there was money to be made off of Islamophobia and the reproduction of fear, and the internet has made this dissemination and profiteering easier. The anonymity of the internet allows those who develop or consume hate-filled messages to do so without fear of being held accountable.

Carter recognized that "cyberspace, viewed as ownerless but ideologically Western and white, is ripe for shaping and sustaining the same underlying oppression as that which constituted America's pioneer days."[120] Further, elaborated Carter, although people view the internet and technology as being democratic and revolutionizing social perceptions,

> technologically facilitated spaces may well be the newest forms of white havens where turmoil can be left behind and, concurrently, where a dramatic effort to protect and project whiteness as a normative pervasive cultural practice can be enacted and recovered.[121] (p. 271–272)

Another infamous Islamophobe who has made a name for herself through her online presence is celebrity blogger Pamela Geller. Geller, who worked hand-in-hand with Robert Spencer to piggyback off of the irrational fear of Islam, is a frequent "expert" on Islam with media outlets such as FOX News on her resume, though her only credentials certifying her expertise regarding Islam are those which are self-proclaimed after speaking engagements with Spencer and her blogging activities. While Geller denies that she is anti-Muslim, she continues to publish her blog entries and actively vocalize her propaganda-fueled opinions of Islam, always peddling them as *Truth*.[122] Gellar has taken an active role in speaking out against the oppression of women in Islam and has made this a focus point for her Islamophobic rhetoric, although it has been argued that in general, Gellar is not active in women's rights issues in the United States.[123] This attention to women's rights only in the *other* groups, with a complete disregard for women's rights issues within the person's own culture, should be cause for concern as it raises important questions about motivation.

The Place for Cassandras

Another type of "expert" that has been making a mark on the media and drawing attention to the plight of Muslim women is the stories of the *Cassandras*. *Cassandras* are token Muslim women who are "the native informants and 'insiders' whose role it is to confirm Islamophobia's stereotypes."[124] *Cassandras* are legitimized as experts by virtue of being Muslim, hailing from a Muslim country where patriarchy defines the balance of power, suffering abuses for their status as women, and for the mere fact that they have a vagina. Their stories are readily consumed by Americans who seemingly crave horror stories of women who suffer in the name of Islam.[125] Their supporters claim that these women are only being critical of Islam; yet, this is far from the truth.[126]

Because their stories are presented as autobiographical narratives, they are free from the requirements of the academy, no longer required to cite references, are not required to have historical basis, and are free to present opinions and bias as factual.[127] Irshad Manji, Ayaan Hirsi Ali, Azar Nafisi, and Nonie Darwish are some examples of women who have been chosen to give the Muslim "insider voice." According to Sheehi, these women "have benefited from being photogenic brown Cassandras . . . act as prophetesses who warn of the dangers of Islam and Muslims at a time when white America is seeking out brown faces to project and confirm their racist beliefs."[128] Although neither Hirsi Ali nor Manji has any professional or academic qualifications to classify them as "experts" on either the cultures they hailed from nor Islam in general, they both have been successful at making professional names for themselves based on their "insider claims" of expertise, and both have profited financially from these professional names.[129] Hammer noted that these women have

> been co-opted into the machinery of Islamophobic discourse and at times it
> seems hard to know where to draw the lines between those willingly parti-
> cipating in the reproduction of such discourse, for monetary reward and/or

to advance their political and intellectual agendas, and scholars, activists, and journalists, "native" or not, who seem to feed into Islamophobic discourse by buying into its premises or by supplying the "machinery" with additional arguments and material.[130]

As consumers of these insider voices, it is important to ask what the motives are behind the dissemination of their stories. According to Sheehi, consumers must be aware that

> typical of all tokens: they are selected, adopted and promoted by the dominant group on the basis of their willingness to perform in accordance with the group's needs – in this case, two wars against Muslim-populated countries with a third war against Iran already mounted in congress.[131]

Finally, it is important to note that this insider perspective works toward the overall gendering process found within Islamophobia and has been politicized to garner a large-scale support for intervention within the Muslim world under the guise of liberating women from their oppression.

NOTES

1. Lori Peek, *Behind the Backlash*, p. 36.
2. Chris Allen, *Islamophobia* (Surrey, England: Ashgate Publishing Limited, 2010).
3. Edward E. Curtis, IV., "The Black Muslim Scare of the Twentieth Century: The History of State Islamophobia and its Post-9/11 Variations," in *Islamophobia in America: The Anatomy of Intolerance,* ed. Carl W. Ernst (New York, NY: Palgrave MacMillan, 2013), p. 75–106.
4. Stephen Sheehi, *Islamophobia: The Ideological Campaign.*
5. Chris Allen, *Islamophobia*, p. 72–73.
6. Ibid.
7. Younes Mourchid, "The Dialectics of Islamophobia and Homophobia in the Lives of Gay Muslims in the United States," in *Teaching Against Islamophobia*, ed. Joe L. Kincheloe, Shirley R. Steinberg, and Christopher D. Stonebanks (New York, NY: Peter Lang Publishing, 2010), p. 189.
8. Juliane Hammer, "Center Stage," p. 108.
9. Aaron W. Hughes, *Muslim Identities.*
10. Ibid.
11. Peter Gottschalk and Gabriel Greenberg, *Islamophobia: Making Muslims the Enemy* (Lanham, MD: Rowman and Littlefield Publishers, Inc., 2008), p. 5.

12. Andrew Shryock, "Introduction: Islam as an Object of Fear and Affection," in *Islamophobia/Islamophilia: Beyond the Politics of Enemy and Friend*, ed. Andrew Shryock (Bloomington, IN: Indiana University Press, 2010), p. 1–25.
13. Nathan Lean, *The Islamophobia Industry*, p. 96.
14. Brigitte L. Nacos and Oscar Torres-Reyna, "Framing Muslim-Americans."
15. Nathan Lean, *The Islamophobia Industry.*
16. Brigitte L. Nacos and Oscar Torres-Reyna, "Framing Muslim-Americans."
17. Andrew Shryock, "Introduction: Islam as an Object."
18. Aaron W. Hughes, *Muslim Identities.*
19. Peter Gottschalk and Gabriel Greenberg, *Islamophobia: Making Muslims the Enemy.*
20. Katherine Bullock, *Rethinking Muslim Women.*
21. Samuel P. Huntington, *The Clash of Civilization.*
22. Ibid.
23. Joe L. Kincheloe and Shirley R. Steinberg, "Why Teach Against Islamophobia?" p. 21.
24. Nathan Lean, *The Islamophobia Industry.*
25. Ibid.
26. Andrew Shryock, "Introduction: Islam as an Object."
27. Lorraine Sheridan, "Islamophobia Before and After September 11, 2001," in *Confronting Islamophobia in Educational Practice*, ed. Barry van Driel (Staffordshire, England: Trentham Books Limited, 2004), p. 163–176.
28. Kambiz GhaneaBassiri, "Islamophobia in American History: Religious Stereotyping and Out-grouping of Muslims in the United States," in *Islamophobia in America: The Anatomy of Intolerance*, ed. Carl W. Ernst (New York, NY: Palgrave MacMillan, 2013), p. 53–74.
29. Lori Peek, *Behind the Backlash.*
30. Claude Salhani, *Islam Without a Veil.*
31. Brigitte L. Nacos and Oscar Torres-Reyna, "Framing Muslim-Americans."
32. Edward E. Curtis, IV., "The Black Muslim Scare."
33. Peter Gottschalk and Gabriel Greenberg, *Islamophobia: Making Muslims the Enemy.*
34. Lori Peek, *Behind the Backlash.*
35. Nathan Lean, *The Islamophobia Industry.*
36. Ibid.
37. Lori Peek, *Behind the Backlash.*
38. Nathan Lean, *The Islamophobia Industry.*
39. Ibid.
40. Ibid.
41. Ibid.
42. Stephen Sheehi, *Islamophobia: The Ideological Campaign.*
43. Peter Moore, "Divide on Muslim Neighborhood Patrols."

44. Stephen Sheehi, *Islamophobia: The Ideological Campaign*, p. 145.
45. Carl W. Ernst, Introduction to *Islamophobia in America*; Tony Gaskew, "Confronting Political Islam"; Stephen Sheehi, *Islamophobia: The Ideological Campaign*.
46. Amber Hague, "Confronting the Menace."
47. Juliane Hammer, "Center Stage," p. 120.
48. Parvez Ahmed, "Prejudice is Real and Exacts a Heavy Toll," in *Islamphobia and Anti-Americanism: Causes and Remedies*, ed. Mohamed Nimer (Beltsville, MD: Amana Publications, 2007), p. 15–20.
49. Ibid.
50. Louay Safi, "Truth and Vanity Shape Anti-Americanism."
51. Tony Gaskew, "Confronting Political Islam."
52. Ibid., p. xiv.
53. Jamillah Karim, *American Muslim Women*.
54. Yvonne Yazbeck Haddad, Jane I. Smith, and Kathleen M. Moore, *Muslim Women in North America*.
55. Claude Salhani, "The Problem is Knee-jerk Reactions and Counter-Reactions," in *Islamophobia and Anti-Americanism: Causes and Remedies*, ed. Mohamed Nimer (Beltsville, MD: Amana Publications, 2007), p. 93–97.
56. Ibid.
57. Peter Gottschalk and Gabriel Greenberg, *Islamophobia: Making Muslims the Enemy. p. 42*.
58. Jack G. Shaheen, *Reel Bad Arabs: How Hollywood Vilifies a People* (New York: Olive Branch Press, 2003), p. 3.
59. Nathan Lean, *The Islamophobia Industry*; Jack G. Shaheen, *Guilty: Hollywood's Verdict on Arabs After 9/11* (Northampton, MA: Olive Branch Press, 2012).
60. Brigitte L. Nacos and Oscar Torres-Reyna, "Framing Muslim-Americans."
61. Ibid.
62. Peter Gottschalk and Gabriel Greenberg, *Islamophobia: Making Muslims the Enemy*.
63. Amber Hague, "Confronting the Menace."
64. Jack G. Shaheen, *Guilty*.
65. Deepa Kumar, *Islamophobia and the Politics of Empire*; Nathan Lean, *The Islamophobia Industry*; Stephen Sheehi, *Islamophobia: The Ideological Campaign*.
66. Yvonne Yazbeck Haddad, Jane I. Smith, and Kathleen M. Moore, *Muslim Women in North America*.
67. Mohamed Nimer, Introduction to *Islamophobia and Anti-Americanism: Causes and Remedies*, ed. Mohamed Nimer (Beltsville, MD: Amana Publications, 2007), p. 9.
68. Stephen Sheehi, *Islamophobia: The Ideological Campaign*, p. 31.

69. Juliane Hammer, "Center Stage," p. 109.
70. Carl W. Ernst, Introduction to *Islamophobia in America*.
71. Juliane Hammer, "Center Stage," p. 110.
72. Juliane Hammer, *American Muslim Women*.
73. Stephen Sheehi, *Islamophobia: The Ideological Campaign*.
74. Asma Gull Hasan, *American Muslims*.
75. Kambiz GhaneaBassiri, "Islamophobia in American History."
76. Aminah B. McCloud, "Conceptual Discourse: Living as a Muslim in a Pluralistic Society," in *Muslims' Place in the American Public Square: Hope, Fears and Aspirations*, ed. Zahid H. Bukhari, Sulayman S. Nyang, Mumtaz Ahmad, and John L. Esposito (Walnut Creek, CA: AltaMira Press, 2004), p. 73–83.
77. Yvonne Yazbeck Haddad, Jane I. Smith, and Kathleen M. Moore, *Muslim Women in North America*; Peter Morey and Amina Yaqin, *Framing Muslims*.
78. Jack G. Shaheen, *Guilty*, p. xxii.
79. Ervin Staub, "The Origins and Evolution of Hate, With Notes on Prevention," in *The Psychology of Hate*, ed. Robert J. Sternberg (Washington, DC: American Psychological Association, 2005), p. 53.
80. Sara J. Ahmad, *Evaluating the Framing of Islam and Muslims Pre- and Post-9/11: A Contextual Analysis of Articles Published by the New York Times* (Saarbrucken, Germany: VDM Verlag Dr. Muller, 2008).
81. Geneive Abdo, *Mecca and the Main Street*.
82. Lori Peek, *Behind the Backlash*, p. 52.
83. Jack G. Shaheen, *Reel Bad Arabs*.
84. Yvonne Yazbeck Haddad, Jane I. Smith, and Kathleen M. Moore, *Muslim Women in North America*.
85. Juliane Hammer, *American Muslim Women*, p. 169.
86. Brigitte L. Nacos and Oscar Torres-Reyna, "Framing Muslim-Americans," p. 136.
87. Jack G. Shaheen, *Guilty*.
88. Jack G. Shaheen, *Reel Bad Arabs*.
89. Brigitte L. Nacos and Oscar Torres-Reyna "Framing Muslim-Americans"; Jack G. Shaheen, *Guilty*.
90. Stefano Allievi, "The Shifting Significance."
91. Jack G. Shaheen, *Reel Bad Arabs*.
92. Asma Gull Hasan, *American Muslims*.
93. Peter Gottschalk and Gabriel Greenberg, *Islamophobia: Making Muslims the Enemy*, p. 42.
94. Aminah B. McCloud, "Conceptual Discourse."
95. Peter Gottschalk and Gabriel Greenberg, *Islamophobia: Making Muslims the Enemy*.
96. Asma Gull Hasan, *American Muslims*.

97. Pippa Norris, Montague Kern, and Marion Just, "Framing Terrorism," in *Framing Terrorism: The News Media, the Government and the Public,* ed. Pippa Norris, Montague Kern, and Marion Just (New York, NY: Routledge, 203), p. 4.
98. Joshua Greene, *Moral Tribes: Emotion, Reason, and the Gap between Us and Them* (New York, NY: Penguin, 2013), p. 97.
99. Brian A. Monahan, *The Shock of the News: Media Coverage and the Making of 9/11* (New York, NY: New York University Press, 2010), p. 171.
100. Nathan Lean, *The Islamophobia Industry.*
101. Ibid.
102. Jack G. Shaheen, *Guilty.*
103. Ibid.
104. Ibid.
105. Ibid.
106. Beth Finkelstein, "Practical Educational Programming that Confronts Islamophobia," in *Confronting Islamophobia in Educational Practice,* ed. Barry van Driel (Staffordshire, England: Trentham Books Limited, 2004), p. 81.
107. Jack G. Shaheen, *Reel Bad Arabs.*
108. Ibid., p. 31.
109. Stephen Sheehi, *Islamophobia: The Ideological Campaign.*
110. Chris Allen, *Islamophobia.*
111. Nathan Lean, *The Islamophobia Industry.*
112. Lorraine Sheridan, "Islamophobia Before and After."
113. Amber Hague, "Confronting the Menace."
114. Ibid.
115. Claude Salhani, *Islam Without a Veil.*
116. Claude Salhani, "The Problem is Knee-jerk Reactions."
117. Mohamed Nimer, Introduction to *Islamophobia and Anti-Americanism.*
118. Nathan Lean, *The Islamophobia Industry.*
119. Ibid.
120. Vicki K. Carter, "Computer-assisted Racism: Toward an Understanding of 'Cyberwhiteness,'" in *White Reign: Deploying Whiteness in America,* ed. Joe L. Kincheloe, Shirley R. Steinberg, Nelson M. Rodriguez, and Ronald E. Chennault (New York, NY: St. Martin's Press, 1998), p. 271.
121. Ibid., p. 271–272.
122. Nathan Lean, *The Islamophobia Industry.*
123. Juliane Hammer, "Center Stage," p. 126.
124. Stephen Sheehi, Islamophobia: The Ideological Campaign, p. 94.
125. Ibid.
126. Kashif N. Chaudhry, "Hirsi Ali: Telling a Critic From an Islamphobe," The Huffington Post, April 30, 2014, http://huff.to/2aJjUy3.

127. Kashif N. Chaudhry, "Telling a Critic From an Islamphobe"; Stephen Sheehi, *Islamophobia: The Ideological Campaign*.
128. Stephen Sheehi, *Islamophobia: The Ideological Campaign*, p. 96.
129. Kashif N. Chaudhry, "Telling a Critic From an Islamphobe"; Aayan Hirsi Ali, *Infidel* (New York, NY: Atria, 2008); Stephen Sheehi, *Islamophobia: The Ideological Campaign*.
130. Juliane Hammer, "Center Stage," p. 129–130.
131. Stephen Sheehi, *Islamophobia: The Ideological Campaign*, p. 98.

CHAPTER 4

Prejudice, Privilege, and Hate

Humans are pattern seekers, and categorizations help us to interpret information from large groups and create thematic clusters which help interpret our lives. By categorizations, they work toward assimilating large amounts of information as quickly as possible, helping us to identify objects as well as out positionality with those objects, from being rational to less rational.[1] Categorizations can vary from simple (such as what we see with infants as they begin to explore the world around them) to far more complex. Complex categorizations happen as the result of projecting the complexity of our individual or group experiences onto the thing (or group) being labeled.[2]

Prejudice

Gordon W. Allport defined prejudice in his book *The Nature of Prejudice* as an "aversive or hostile attitude toward a person who belongs to a group simply because he belongs to that group, and is therefore presumed to have the objectionable qualities ascribed to that group."[3] Those who maintain views that are prejudicial are resistant to changing those views, even when there is evidence provided which undermines their established thought process. It is never easy to determine how much information is required for a person to create a belief about others, but those with prejudicial views have a tendency to claim that they have enough information to have created and maintained those views over time.[4]

The natural human process of categorization can easily pave the way for prejudice, but we must be cautious to not call all over-categorizations

© The Author(s) 2017
A.M. Guimond, *Converting to Islam*,
DOI 10.1007/978-3-319-54250-8_4

prejudice.[5] It is only when a person's beliefs are left unchanged following exposure to categorically contradictory information that we can begin the process of identifying that prejudice exists.[6] Although most people frequently think of prejudice as a negative thought or feeling, the more recent literature seems to be moving away from such value-laden connotations, toward a more neutral description of this phenomenon using terms such as *bias* or *in group favoritism* instead of *prejudice.*[7]

People who hold prejudicial views find ways to justify these views over time[8] and frequently avoid circumstances or situations that will bring their prejudicial views into question.[9] It can be argued that the Muslim community (as well perceived members of the Muslim community) currently faces a number of the five categories of prejudice which are defined as (1) antilocution, (2) avoidance, (3) discrimination, (4) physical attack, and (5) extermination.[10]

Gaylin noted that prejudice works in a cyclical process where beliefs are reinforced through avoidance.[11] Thus, we are unlikely to be invested in the process of correcting prejudicial behaviors or practices. According to Allport, even joking about specific group membership can fall within the beginning stages of prejudice as "mild animosity often underlies antilocution of the joking or derisive kind. Some of it is so gentle that it merges into friendly humor ... but even when jokes seem friendly they can sometimes mask genuine hostility."[12]

Stereotyping

Prejudice is developed during the process of categorization where stereotypes are attributed to the out-group. The term *Stereotype,* which originally was a term that was used in printing and publication (referring to a block printing process where identical prints were repeated and the quality deteriorated with each pull), was first used by Walter Lippman in the early 1900s when wrote a seminal treatise for "public opinion" and used the term to explain the way that beliefs about the out-group were relayed overtime, deteriorating into caricatures.[13] This definition of stereotypes ultimately being caricatures holds fast in contemporary discussion of prejudice and stereotyping.

Humans categorize to make meaning, but humans also stereotype to alleviate some of the hardships of categorizing in order to make meaning.[14] Quickly being able to determine who is friend or foe, or who can be identified as in-group vs. out-group in a quick and efficient manner, is one of the important skills that helps protect groups of people and ensure their survival.[15] According to Greene,

> we intuitively divide the world into *us* vs. *them*, and favor *us* over *them*. We begin as infants, using linguistic clues which historically have been reliable markers of group membership. In the modern world, we discriminate based on race (among other things), but race is not a deep innate psychological category.[16]

In order for people to develop their group identity, there must always be the presence of an *other* who becomes the subject of exclusionary practices. According to Gaylin, "by setting an alien population outside the moral community, the leaders lay the groundwork for possible stigmatization and demonization of the other."[17] This stigmatization and demonization of *other* serves the purpose of lessening a person's internal struggles: rather than blaming themselves for their own personal failures, people can lay blame on others when situations or personal performance does not meet the desired standards.[18]

Vilification and negative stigmatization are not always present in inter-group relationships, but there is an increased likelihood of prejudice at the societal level when perceived stereotypes of the target group appear to be incongruous with societal norms and standards of behavior.[19] The idea of a racial hierarchy is key to understanding modern racism and prejudice, although today's prejudice appears to be less about biological superiority, as opposed to cultural or religious superiority,[20] and in some cases, political affiliation.

Members of the out-group are more predisposed to negative stereotypes and mistreatment because the tendency is for people to homogenize their own groups. People are more likely to attribute negative personality traits to people from the out-group who have wronged them, and more likely to dismiss negative behaviors of their fellow in-group members as being a behavioral anomaly.[21] Empathy is more likely to be bestowed to those of the in-group, and positive arousal is more frequently stimulated between fellow in-group members, as is prosocial behavior, and this reinforces the power differential of being a part of the in-group, leading to a situation where in-group exchanges are almost always preferred to exchanges with one's out-group.[22] Rewards and resources are more likely to be bestowed upon those who are part of the in-group as opposed to those who are in the out-group.[23]

Prejudice as a Social Construct

Although early scholars indicated that prejudices are rigid and those holding prejudices are inflexible in terms of changing those beliefs,[24] Eagly and Diekman suggested that prejudices are indeed quite flexible and subject to change based on developing social discourse and changes to social context.[25] Stereotyping can serve three major functions in the formation of prejudice: (1) social causal – they see the stereotyped group as causing the event – specifically related to the current cultural discourse; (2) social justificatory – the stereotyping is used to justify maltreatment of the other; and (3) social differentiation – differences between groups are highlighted in favor of one specific group or another.[26]

When stereotypes are developed as a result of beliefs that were developed during armed conflicts with nations that are associated with the stereotyped group, those stereotypes stand up over time and frequently go unchallenged.[27] Greene noted that when it comes to intergroup conflict, "it seems that knowing which side of a dispute you're on unconsciously changes your thinking about what's fair. It changes the way you process the information."[28]

People who hold prejudices toward one group are more likely to be prejudiced toward other groups,[29] yet we live in a state of denial. According to Ehrlich,

> the culture of denial has so permeated American society that it has deeply influenced the way many whites think about prejudice. Many white people deny that discrimination against minorities persists and thus conclude that any interventions designed to equalize opportunities are uncalled for.[30]

Social intolerance allows the dominant group to become resistant to allowing the *other*, the right to live their *otherness*, and thus supports policy that strips them of their rights toward respect and personal independence.[31] Further, it ignores charges that policies should be modified to help level the power structure and social hierarchy.[32] Although overt discrimination has reportedly been on the decline since the 1950s,[33] institutionalized prejudice and racism permeates every level of our modern culture,[34] and deniability of prejudices leads to its further institutionalization.

Prejudice and Children

Children are automatically bestowed the group memberships of their parents;[35] therefore, children have the potential to be just as impacted by situations of prejudice and racism as the generations before them. If their parents are part of the out-group, children are more likely to suffer the consequences through both indirect and direct marginalization.[36] According to the available research, although children between the ages of three and four are not even able to readily distinguish between groups, they are already learning the group prejudices of their in-group.[37] Racial cues have been shown to have developed as early as 4 years old, and evidence also suggests that at 4+ years of age, children who are in the in-group can identify their ethnic group members and display in-group and out-group biases.[38] It is believed that younger children are more likely to identify with gender than race, but research is limited.[39]

Children as young as 3 years old appeared to understand in-group/out-group relations within their community.[40] One version of the Implicit Association Test (IAT) which was designed for children found that as early as age 6, children are mimicking the biases of the adults in their in-group.[41] The mimicking of these biases can lead to schoolyard bullying, name-calling, exclusion, and taunting.[42] Even for those who are part of the marginalized group, while they may still be loyal to the group they identify with, society dictates that they use the majority group as a reference for which to model societal standards of acceptance.[43] It should be noted that approximately 15% of complaints regarding anti-Muslim incidents happen in the school system, and this is second only to workplace incidents of Islamophobic discriminatory practices.[44] One glaringly obvious way of combating this would be to educate about various religions in the public schools, and though this would be legal under federal regulations, many teachers and faculty avoid the subject for fear of administrative sanctions or parental anger.[45]

Prejudice and Religion

In the literature, racial and ethnic prejudice and discrimination are well studied, but there is little research available on religiously based prejudice and discrimination.[46] Studies on racial prejudice outnumber studies on religious prejudice 18 to 1.[47] It has however been noted that religion can be a major catalyst for prejudice. Allport found that racial prejudice is more often noted in people who have strong religious identities, and that "closer analysis indicates that the religious sentiment in these cases is blindly institutional, exclusionist, and related to self-centered values,"[48] but this should not be interpreted that religion is the root of all prejudices. Nor should it be interpreted that specific religious doctrines teach hatred and exclusion. Instead, it is important to note that religion serves as a unifying characteristic that people use when developing their group identity, thus the relationship is corollary.

It has also been said that there is a corollary relationship between those who blindly accept the religious teachings and political/social leanings of their parents are more likely to hold negative prejudicial beliefs.[49] This could be a reason that although many people identify sameness within their religious group, there are often conflicts within religious in-groups regarding racism and identity.[50]

For those who straddle multiple group identities, the perceived incompatibility of those identities can lead to an increased intergroup conflict as each group seeks to lay claim to the individual.[51] This perceived incompatibility can also lead to an increase in intrapersonal conflict. For women with *identity intersectionality* (where a person is straddling two or more group identities), no singular identifier creates the lens that their experiences are interpreted through, or their overall social mobility.[52] According to Karim, "when we acknowledge that multiple subject positions like ethnicity, race, class, gender, region, generation, and religious perspective together frame women's experiences, individual identity reveals itself as far too complex to be imagined or fixed in any one space."[53]

Responses to Prejudice

Early in prejudice studies, it was believed that those who are victimized by prejudicial practices and policies display an increase in vigilance and hypersensitivity over being subjected to negative stereotypes.[54] More current research has shown that the people suffering from prejudice and discriminatory actions are actually more likely to minimize, deny, or dismiss the presence of prejudice as a precursory factor.[55]

According to Major and Vick, those being prejudged are aware that others hold negative views of them and are concerned with being subjected to *stereotype threat* – a term which they have defined as a "psychological predicament that occurs when people are aware of the negative stereotypes that others hold of their social group and are anxious that they

may confirm them, either in their own or others eyes,"[56] or *attributional
ambiguity* – a term used to reference an "uncertainty about whether their
outcomes (both positive and negative) are due to their own merits or
shortcomings, or to prejudice and discrimination based on their social
identity."[57] Although being subjected to highly prejudiced people and
being in highly discriminatory settings can be quite traumatic on an
individual, Major and Vick found that women and ethnic minorities
appear to have difficulty in recalling specifics about times when they
were subjected to this maltreatment, even when they can clearly articulate
that such maltreatment is a violation of law.[58]

There are two general categories for reactions to discrimination stress:
approach and avoidance.[59] Coping strategies for dealing with being victimized due to prejudice appear to vary depending on the individual's own
personal history and the overarching social context that they are exposed
to.[60] Regardless of how the increase of stress is handled, if left unacknow-
ledged and untreated, the cost of discrimination stresses to those who
experience it has the potential to be disastrous. Muslim Americans who
experience discrimination, identity fracture, poor coping, and psychological stress are at higher risk for compromised physical and mental health.
One such consequence to mental health would be complete identity
fracture. And yet, many Muslim American women choose not to seek
mental health treatment because they worry that their identification as
Muslim might prejudice the health-care worker and interfere with
appropriate diagnosis and treatment.[61]

PRIVILEGE

The United States has a long history of valuing whiteness, and privileging
those who fall into this racial category, and in modern contexts, we see
evidence of racial privilege, gender privilege, heteronormative privilege,
cisnormative privilege, and religious privilege. In studies of privilege, the
majority of the information available pertains to racial privilege, more
specifically the privilege bestowed upon whites over blacks.[62] Although
the United States prides itself on having policy requiring the separation
of church and state, Christianity – more specifically Protestantism – is
the majority religion with many policies being built around it.[63] For
this reason, the United States uses the values of Protestantism as the
guide of modeling behavioral norms and also for defining who may be
its ideological and political enemies.[64]

Johnson noted that in terms of privilege, there is a distinction that must be articulated between the individual identity and the group identity, writing "individuals aren't what is actually privileged. Instead, privilege is defined in relation to a group or a social category. In other words, race privilege is more about *white* people than it is about white *people*."[65] Today, with the reshaping social context, Italians, Greeks, Jew, and the Irish have acculturated as such that they are considered white by most people, or they can easily pass for white – reaping the benefits of such group affiliation,[66] but it is important to remember that these groups were once not considered part of the white privileged majority.

This can illustrate how our position in the world, and race in general, are part of a much larger social construct, therefore whiteness is not as static as many would believe.[67] In the United States, whiteness was historically interpreted as having an absence of "one-drop" of blood from sub-Saharan African descent, but because of the constantly changing social context for who is part of an in-group, it has become increasingly difficult to identify exactly what white and whiteness are.[68]

In the literature, as well as in dominant discourse, it is clear that the term *race* only appears to be applied to those who are nonwhite.[69] This exclusion of whites in the discourse on race and multiculturalism reinforces the notion that whites are the norm and people from other races are a deviation from the norm.[70] Apple explained that "race as a category is usually applied to 'non-white' peoples. White people usually are not seen and named. They are centered as the human norm, 'others' are raced; 'we' are just people."[71]

The privileges that come from whiteness are the product of birth, and not merit, and few who benefit from said privileges are aware that their status of birth is the reason that they have the opportunities that they do. According to Rothenberg (2008),

> because of its invisibility, it has helped foster the illusion that those who succeed do so because of their superior intelligence, their hard work, or their determination, rather than, at least in part, their privilege. The power of whiteness is that it gives certain people an advantage without ever acknowledging that this is the case.[72]

Today, there are two classifications for those who benefit from white privilege: those who are from Caucasian descent, who have no mixed relations in their bloodlines, and those who are white amongst other characteristics and can easily blend into white society.[73] Modern reform and conservative Jews, Italians, Irish, and any mixed ethnic fair-skinned people in the American melting pot would classify into this second status.

Privilege: A Hierarchy

Inherent within the theory of white privilege are the ideas of Eurocentrism, androcentrism, patriarchy, and heterosexism. Within this discursive and derisive lens of privilege, anything that is not Caucasian, European, Protestant, and Male is excluded from the norm. This creates a privilege hierarchy. Denial of racial tensions and inequalities compounds the problem. Instead of recognizing that there is a systemic problem, people instead assume that those who are not on the benefiting end of privilege are being overly sensitive or are in other ways – other than related to their status as non-privileged – to blame.[74]

The evolution of white privilege was one where group identity was strengthened over time through deliberate and conscientious actions as early as the colonial period so that whites would remain in power within the developing nation.[75] It is through the intergenerational transmission of these stories, and through stereotypes which bestow negative attributes – such as laziness, poor planning, or a heightened spontaneity – power and political control was maintained.[76] Groups such as the Irish and Eastern European Jews were able to quickly assimilate and distance themselves from the traits that had been attributed to blacks, and through this process, they (though many people despised them) were able to overcome their less privileged status and pass for white-other.[77]

This struggle to maintain the status quo in terms of power would easily explain why whites still continue to benefit from privilege despite the fact that an African-American man has served as president. This might also explain why far right political candidates began circulating rumors that President Barack Obama was a secret Muslim in the first place, and why his birth certificate was the topic of much speculation.

HATE

Although hate has been well researched, there is no singular, cohesive, and commonly accepted definition of it.[78] According to Royzman et al., the overwhelming variances and contradictions found in the definitions "have to do with the weighting of feeling and (affect-free) judgment, with some authors emphasizing a negative feeling toward the object of hatred and others emphasizing a negative judgment about that object."[79] In Sternberg's *Duplex Theory of Hate*, hate has been identified as possessing the following attributes:

> Hate is very closely related psychologically to love.
> Hate is neither the opposite of love nor the absence of love.
> Hate, like love, has its origins in stories that characterize the target of the emotion.
> Hate, like love, can be characterized by a triangular structure generated by these stories.
> Hate is a major precursor of many terrorist acts, massacres, and genocides.[80]

Scholars agree that hate is made up of three components that have been sometimes called the *Triangular Theory of the Structure of Hate*. This triad of components includes (1) intimacy – or the negation of intimacy as seen through distancing; (2) passion – as seen in anger and fear; and (3) decision – otherwise known as the commitment to hate.[81]

These three components work together in various ways and are displayed as seven distinct types of hate. If one displays only a negation of intimacy, they display a cool hate; if the person displays only passion, they display hot hate; and if the person displays only a commitment to hate through acts like devaluation, they display a cold hate.[82] Similarly, a person is displaying boiling hate when they present with a negation of intimacy and passion; a person is displaying simmering hate when they present with a negation of intimacy and a commitment to hate; and the same person would present with seething hate if they present with a combination of passion and commitment. Burning hate would be the most dangerous form of Sternberg's types of hatred in that it presents with all three components of the triangular structure of hate and leads to a desire for total annihilation.[83]

As people traverse through difficult stages of life or experience various hardships, they become frustrated by their inability to fulfill their basic human needs, and thus the foundations of hatred are laid.[84] It is far easier on the ego and psyche for an individual to project their failures on someone other than themselves and even better to project those failures on someone outside of their in-group.[85] This desire to project failures outward instead of internalizing them causes people to scapegoat the other, and to develop ideologies where the other is cause for their hardship, therefore the cause of evil.[86] The objects of hatred are then viewed as being immoral, dangerous, or evil – by their mere existence, not necessarily through their works or deeds.[87]

Because the person then sees themselves as the victim and the object of their hatred as the perpetrator – or the evil enemy – the person finds a way to absolve themselves of any adverse actions that come to the object of their hatred.[88] It then becomes easier for the hater to internalize assaults (including verbal, physical, emotional, sexual, and the threat – these types of assaults) as retaliatory, rather than offensive.[89]

True hatred – as opposed to the feelings that are frequently uttered by children when faced with new vegetables or unpleasant situations – is an emotion that can follow a person throughout their lifetime "allowing them to feel delight in observing or inflict suffering on the hated one. It is always obsessive and almost always irrational."[90] These sustained emotions can be heightened in the ongoing presence of ideological differences, such as those between religious groups and within specific religious denominations, even if the groups have come to agreement to live in harmony.[91]

Although most religious people claim that their religions do not advocate for hatred, there is an ideological system in place within religion which sets the stage for hatred to grow out of religious affiliation.[92] Because religious people believe that they are on God's side and they believe in God's teachings, they believe that they are on the side of right, and those who oppose them are on the side of evil. To even dialogue with people who are perceived as evil diminishes the religiously righteous person's own sense of goodness because those who are "in bed" with evil are considered tarnished as well. Thus, the religious person must see those who do not share the same affiliation as evil in order to protect their own self-conceptualization of goodness.[93]

As a culture, once the collective conscience deems that it is acceptable to hate an out-group – in this case, the evil religious other – the more socially acceptable it is to hate, and the more ingrained that hatred becomes.[94] Although hatred often sprouts from seeds of prejudice and heightens after exposure to perceived confirmations of those prejudices, one should be cautious to remember that not everyone who holds prejudges will find their emotions elevated to the level of hatred.[95]

Social Acceptability of Hate

Like prejudice and privilege, hate is also socially constructed and social conflict plays an important role in the development of hatred.[96] Hatred is frequently developed over time and it can come about if there is a minor harm between groups that has no intervention.[97] Once a person harms someone as the product of hatred, they are primed to harm the members of the same hated group in the future, which can create the cyclical cycle that is oft times found within the hate phenomena.[98] Once a culture deems it morally acceptable to hate a group, propagandists use this hatred, appealing to the cultural fear to create overarching generalizations.[99] These generalizations transfer the negatively charged attitudes toward the targets of hatred, and this can lead to an oversimplification of the larger social problem that allows for hatred as more and more people join the cause and bandwagoning happens.[100] Political and other high-profile leaders frequently lead the charge against this "outed" group, and once this happens, it can be difficult to reverse.[101]

Hate and Bias Crimes

Originally, the term *hate crime* was developed for political and legislative purposes so that serious criminal acts (including murder, rape, assault, arson, some acts of intimidation, kidnapping, and manslaughter) that were aimed at a victim – because of their status as out-group members – could carry statutorily serious consequences.[102] In the understanding of hate crimes, *hate* is defined as "roughly that which motivates a deliberate act of physical violence or intimidation against a member of a minority group by him or her being a member of that group,"[103] but this definition itself is problematic because it lays the focus of the offending act on the victim and who or what the victim is – rather than laying the focus and responsibility squarely with the offenders.[104] Because the term *hate* in *hate crime* is so problematic, many scholars on issues of hate are now preferring the terms of *bias crimes* or *bias incidents*.[105]

At the national level, FBI hate crimes statistics only track those criminal activities which are punishable under federal law – which excludes any activities which are punishable at the state level only. The rates and types of incidents in the United States can be difficult to track. Hate crimes statistics only include acts which are reported to the authorities, acts which have been reported to the state and local authorities as hate crimes, and then are relayed to the FBI, and the most heinous of crimes.[106] These statistics are problematic as has been estimated only 25% of all ethno-violent incidents were reported to authorities in the first place.[107] Hate crimes statistics would not include behaviors which are noncriminal such as simple housing discrimination or workplace discrimination, but some scholars indicate that these are also acts of ethno-violence (though not recognized as such through legal channels).[108] Indeed, group defamation – or indirect verbal aggression – should be included in the discussions of hate and bias as it is believed to be nearly as traumatic for victims as a physical assault does pose a reasonable threat to the person's safety or security.[109]

During an escalating conflict, as tensions become heightened and spiral toward violence, "hate shifts from a means to achieve political ends to being an end in itself that consumes lives, businesses, communities, and social institutions."[110] As hatred grows and takes on a less rational and more paranoid appearance, those who hate begin to feel more and more justified in using violence to achieve their end goals.[111] Those who hate believe that they have been wronged at the hands of the objects of their hatred, and they take the offensive, adopting an attitude of *get them before they get us.*[112] Because much religious hatred evolves from the devaluation of the beliefs of one religious group over another, during hate crimes against religious group, the perpetrators adopt the belief that they are acting out the moral right, and therefore their acts of violence are not wrong and they cannot be punished.[113] This was explained by Baumeister and Butz who said,

> If God and goodness are on our side, then those who oppose us must have embraced the cause of evil, and therefore it is appropriate (perhaps even obligatory) to hate them.[114]

It is not unusual to see bias crimes occurring at the hands of groups of people. Groups of offenders frequently seen as co-perpetrating bias crimes because "people in crowds, each believing that he or she cannot be individually identified in the midst of so many others, can depart from socially approved standards of conduct."[115] It isn't necessarily that the culture encourages violence, but rather violence is more likely to be encouraged when the social structure indicates that violence will not be punishable and people are not taught nonviolence.[116] It is through this safety in groups, a lack of individual accountability, and a culture that doesn't teach nonviolence that mob mentality develops in situations of hate and bias crimes, and people become victims of wilding style violence.

Hate and Bias Crimes Against Muslim Americans

Hate crimes against Muslim Americans are on the rise, and in 2009, this group was experiencing more discrimination in the Unites States than any other religious group.[117] Reported crimes against Muslims and those perceived to be Muslim (Arabs, Middle Easterners, South Asians, and Sikhs) have included vandalism and firebombings (homes, businesses, and mosques), physical altercations (including, but not limited to hand-to-hand beatings, stabbings, and shootings), and verbal assaults. Muslim women have reported being spat upon, shoved, beaten, discriminated against in the workplace and in the educational system, and had their scarves forcibly removed.[118] Children frequently witness their parents being victimized and are also bullied and harassed in the schoolyard.[119] Muslim women who used to have people stare or ask questions based on curiosity prior to 9/11 were suddenly being approached with outright hostility instead.[120]

In September 2004, Andrea Armstrong, a Muslim co-ed at the University of South Florida, was forced off of the basketball team because she was wearing hijab while playing.[121] Armstrong petitioned the NCAA to be allowed to wear her religious clothing in practice and games but later quit the team. Armstrong's friends later revealed that Armstrong had actually quit the team because she had been receiving hate emails regarding her petition. On August 23, 2002, a 37-year-old Florida doctor was arrested in a thwarted mosque bombing. In a search of the man's home, authorities found a list of 50 mosques, improvised explosive devices, a gas bomb with timer, grenades, and upward of 40 other weapons.[122] In 2003, a 13-year-old boy was arrested in New York for making Islamophobic slurs toward a Muslims girl at school and then punching her in the face.[123] In 2012, a teacher in a Louisiana school forcibly removed a Muslim student's hijab after making derogatory remarks regarding Islam.[124] In 2001, two board members of the Jewish defense league were arrested for conspiracy to bomb a local mosque, the Muslim Public Affairs Council offices, and the office of Congressman Darrel Isa.[125] The listing of specific incidents could continue.

The point is that, for the most part, Arab and Muslim bashing has become an acceptable practice in American culture, whereas if this treatment was against any other religious or ethnic group, there would be less social acceptance, and possibly even massive public outcry. Tracking of hate crimes against Muslim Americans has only happened since 1995, and in the pre-9/11 years, they were even more significantly underreported than they were in the aftermath of 9/11. In general, there was very little focus on Muslim Americans pre-9/11. So, that makes tracking the longevity of this phenomena difficult.[126]

In 2001, the FBI received 481 reports of anti-Islamic hate crimes, almost all of which happened between September and December 2001, most of which were reported in the 9 weeks' post-9/11.[127] This number rose from a total of 28 crimes in the previous year.[128] The US Commission on Civil Rights had anticipated backlash against the Muslim community in the wake of 9/11 and went live with a hate crimes hotline on September 13, 2001. At the height of the backlash against Muslim Americans, this hotline reported an astonishing 70 calls per hour.[129] In the 9 months immediately after 9/11, CAIR indicated that there were over 1,715 incidents of hate crimes, discrimination, and profiling, including 303 reports of actual violence.[130] In the 1 year after September 11, 2001, the American-Arab Anti-Discrimination Committee and CAIR officially documented over 200 reports of violence, threats, and harassment against Arab American and Muslim American students.[131]

In the 1 year post-9/11, the Equal Employment Opportunity Commission (EEOC) investigated a total of 654 cases of discrimination in the workplace that were related to post-9/11 backlash and 706 cases of religious bias.[132] In these cases, approximately 75% of the claimants had been unlawfully terminated. By May of 2004, anti-Muslim incidents increased in the United States by an additional 70%, with 1,019 reports of violence or verbal abuse.[133] The rate of attacks on mosques has not declined since President Barack Obama was inaugurated.[134]

Generally bias crimes have been significantly underreported by the media. One study in Maryland found that only 1 in 82 incidents of bias crimes was reported in the press.[135] Similarly, in Chicago, the Chicago Commission on Human Relations found that "only 9 percent of the [total] bias crimes reported to the commission were mentioned in the press."[136] According to Ehrlich, "to gain coverage, they have to be 'worthy victims'.... victims are 'worthy' only if their victimization can be used by the gatekeepers of news to fit their agenda."[137] This *worthiness* is something that is denied because of dominant Islamophobic discourse. Although the media has covered some of the more serious instances of hate crimes against the Muslim and Arab communities, this caused an increase of fear in the Muslim community.[138]

Coping Strategies for Victims of Hate and Bias Crimes

Responses and coping strategies for the victims of bias crimes can range from revisiting the incident, anger, fear, social isolation or withdrawal, fantasizing about exacting revenge, disenfranchisement, and more.[139] Disenfranchisement may lead Muslims to seek acceptance through strengthening ties within their own faith communities – building relationships off of distrust of the West – or it may lead to them leaving the United States for other communities around the world, causing an American brain drain.[140] According to Ehrlich,

> trauma can be understood only from the standpoint of the victim. It is the victim's personality and past experiences, the immediate situation in which the incident occurs, and the victim's perception of the incident that determine the level of trauma. The same incident that debilitates one person may be of relatively little consequence for another.[141]

Although coping strategies vary greatly, many Muslim Americans appear to cope with their victimization with increasing self-denial. Many are believed to minimize empirical evidence that the cultural climate is becoming increasingly hostile.[142]

While there has been minimal research into how American Muslims and Arab immigrants have coped with an increasingly negatively charged social climate toward Muslims, in the years since September 11, 2001, there has also been a noticeable absence of the voices of women. The women who are frequently used as evidence of needing emancipation from a supposedly misogynistic religion are being left out of dialogue concerning their own outcomes, and without focusing on this population, we are left with only a partial understanding of the story. For this reason, this research is designed to fill in the gaps within the literature, bring voice to women who have so frequently overlooked within scholarship, and who want to share what their shared lived experiences are of being a white female American who has converted to Islam since September 11, 2001.

Notes

1. Gordon W. Allport, *The Nature of Prejudice*.
2. Peter Batelaan, "Intercultural Education in Europe: A Recent History of Dealing with Diversity and Learning to Live Together," in *Confronting*

Islamophobia in Educational Practice, ed. Barry van Driel (Staffordshire, England: Trentham Books Limited, 2004), p. 57–58.

3. Gordon W. Allport, *The Nature of Prejudice* (Cambridge, MA: Addison-Wesley Publishing Co., 1954), p. 7.
4. Ibid.
5. Ibid.
6. Ibid.
7. Martha Augoustinos and Katherine J. Reynolds, "Prejudice, Racism and Social Psychology," in *Understanding Prejudice, Racism and Social Conflict,* ed. Martha Augousinos and Katherine J. Reynolds (London: SAGE Publications Ltd., 2001), p. 1–23.
8. Gordon W. Allport, *The Nature of Prejudice.*
9. Carol S. Dweck and Joyce Ehrlinger, "Implicit Theories and Conflict Resolution," in *The Handbook of Conflict Resolution: Theory and Practice (2nd ed.),* ed. Morton Deutsch, Peter T. Coleman, and Eric C. Marcus (San Francisco, CA: Jossey-Bass, 2006), p. 317–330.
10. Gordon W. Allport, *The Nature of Prejudice;* J'lein Liese, "The Subtleties of Prejudice: How Schools Unwittingly Facilitate Islamophobia and How to Remedy this," in *Confronting Islamophobia in Educational Practice,* ed. Barry van Driel (Staffordshire, England: Trentham Books Limited, 2004), p. 63–76.
11. Willard Gaylin, *Hatred: The Psychological Descent into Violence* (New York: Public Affairs, 2003).
12. Gordon W. Allport, *The Nature of Prejudice,* p. 50.
13. Peter Gottschalk and Gabriel Greenberg, *Islamophobia: Making Muslims the Enemy.*
14. Gordon W. Allport, *The Nature of Prejudice;* Nelson M. Rodriguez, "Emptying the Content of Whiteness: Toward an Understanding of Relation Between Whiteness and Pedagogy," in *White Reign: Deploying Whiteness in America,* ed. Joe L. Kincheloe, Shirley R. Steinberg, Nelson M. Rodriguez, and Ronald E. Chennault (New York, NY: St. Martin's Press, 1998), p. 31–62.
15. Joshua Greene, *Moral Tribes.*
16. Ibid., p. 54.
17. Willard Gaylin, *Hatred,* p. 163.
18. J'lein Liese, "The Subtleties of Prejudice."
19. Alice H. Eagly and Amanda B. Diekman, "What is the Problem? Prejudice as an Attitude-in-context," in *On the Nature of Prejudice: Fifty Years After Allport,* ed. John F. Dovidio, Peter Glick, and Laurie A. Rudman (Malden, MA: Blackwell Publishing, 2005), p. 19–35.
20. Martha Augoustinos and Katherine J. Reynolds, "Prejudice, Racism and Social Psychology."

21. Samuel L. Gaertner and John F. Dovidio, "Categorization, Recategorization, and Intergroup Bias," in *On the Nature of Prejudice: Fifty Years After Allport,* ed. John F. Dovidio, Peter Glick, and Laurie A. Rudman (Malden, MA: Blackwell Publishing, 2005), p. 71–88; Penelope J. Oakes and S. Alexander Haslam, "Categorization on Trial for Inciting Intergroup Hatred," in *Understanding Prejudice, Racism and Social Conflict,* ed. Martha Augousinos and Katherine J. Reynolds (London: SAGE Publications Ltd., 2001), p. 179–194.

22. Samuel L. Gaertner and John F. Dovidio, "Categorization, Recategorization, and Intergroup Bias"; Penelope J. Oakes and S. Alexander Haslam, "Categorization on Trial."

23. Gordon W. Allport, *The Nature of Prejudice*; John F. Dovidio, Samuel L. Gaertner, and Adam R. Pearson, "On the Nature of Prejudice: The Psychological Foundations of Hate," in *The Psychology of Hate,* ed. Robert J. Sternberg (Washington, DC: American Psychological Association, 2005), p. 211–234; Joshua Greene, *Moral Tribes.*

24. Gordon W. Allport, *The Nature of Prejudice.*

25. Alice H. Eagly and Amanda B. Diekman, "What is the Problem?"

26. Peter Morey and Amina Yaqin, *Framing Muslims.*

27. Jack G. Shaheen, *Guilty.*

28. Joshua Greene, *Moral Tribes.* p. 85.

29. Howard J. Ehrlich, *Hate Crimes and Ethnoviolence: The History, Current Affairs, and Future of Discrimination in America* (Boulder: Westview Press, 2009).

30. Ibid., p. 10.

31. Willard Gaylin, *Hatred.*

32. Howard J. Ehrlich, *Hate Crimes and Ethnoviolence.*

33. Leonard Berkowitz, "On Hate and its Determinants: Some Affective and Cognitive Influences," in *The Psychology of Hate,* ed. Robert J. Sternberg (Washington, DC: American Psychological Association, 2005), p. 155–184; John F. Dovidio, Samuel L. Gaertner, and Adam R. Pearson, "On the Nature of Prejudice."

34. Martha Augoustinos and Katherine J. Reynolds, "Prejudice, Racism and Social Psychology"; Beth Finkelstein, "Practical Educational Programming."

35. Gordon W. Allport, *The Nature of Prejudice.*

36. Gordon W. Allport, *The Nature of Prejudice*; Juliane Hammer, "Center Stage."

37. Howard J. Ehrlich, *Hate Crimes and Ethnoviolence.*

38. Drew Nesdale, "The Development of Prejudice in Children," in *Understanding Prejudice, Racism and Social Conflict,* ed. Martha Augousinos and Katherine J. Reynolds (London: SAGE Publications Ltd., 2001), p. 52–72.

39. Ibid.
40. Ibid.
41. Joshua Greene, *Moral Tribes*, p. 52.
42. Joe L. Kincheloe, Shirley R. Steinberg, and Christopher D. Stonebanks, "Re-educating Against Miseducation," in *Teaching Against Islamophobia*, ed. Joe L. Kincheloe, Shirley R. Steinberg, and Christopher D. Stonebanks (New York, NY: Peter Lang Publishing, 2010), p. ix–xii.
43. Gordon W. Allport, *The Nature of Prejudice*.
44. Beth Finkelstein, "Practical Educational Programming."
45. Ibid.
46. Lorraine Sheridan, "Islamophobia Before and After."
47. Ibid.
48. Gordon W. Allport, *The Individual and His Religion*, p. 66.
49. Ibid., p. 66.
50. Ibid.
51. Samuel L. Gaertner and John F. Dovidio, "Categorization, Recategorization, and Intergroup Bias."
52. Jamillah Karim, *American Muslim Women*.
53. Jamillah Karim, *American Muslim Women*, p. 91.
54. Gordon W. Allport, *The Nature of Prejudice*.
55. Brenda Major and S. Brooke Vick, "The Psychological Impact of Prejudice," in *On the Nature of Prejudice: Fifty Years After Allport*, ed. John F. Dovidio, Peter Glick, and Laurie A. Rudman (Malden, MA: Blackwell Publishing, 2005), p. 193–154.
56. Ibid., p. 142.
57. Ibid., p. 144.
58. Ibid.
59. Adriana Faur, "A Qualtitative Analysis of Cultural Discrimination Stress," (doctoral dissertation, The University of Toledo, 2008).
60. Gordon W. Allport, *The Nature of Prejudice*; Brenda Major and S. Brooke Vick, "The Psychological Impact of Prejudice."
61. Yvonne Yazbeck Haddad, Jane I. Smith, and Kathleen M. Moore, *Muslim Women in North America*.
62. Michael W. Apple, Forward to *White Reign: Deploying Whiteness in America,* ed. Joe L. Kincheloe, Shirley R. Steinberg, Nelson M. Rodriguez, and Ronald E. Chennault (New York, NY: St. Martin's Press, 1998); Paula S. Rothenberg, Introduction to *White Privilege: Essential Readings on the Other Side of Racism*, ed. Paula S. Rothenberg (New York: Worth Publishers, 2008), p. 1–5.
63. Kambiz GhaneaBassiri, "Islamophobia in American History."
64. Ibid.

65. Allan G. Johnson, "Privilege as Paradox," in *White Privilege: Essential Readings on the Other Side of Racism,* ed. Paula S. Rothenberg (New York: Worth Publishers, 2008), p. 17.
66. Paula S. Rothenberg, Introduction to *White Privilege.*
67. Joe L. Kincheloe and Shirley R. Steinberg, "Addressing the Crisis of Whiteness: Reconfiguring White Identity in a Pedagogy of Whiteness," in *White Reign: Deploying Whiteness in America,* ed. Joe L. Kincheloe, Shirley R. Steinberg, Nelson M. Rodriguez, and Ronald E. Chennault (New York, NY: St. Martin's Press, 1998), p. 3–30; Nelson M. Rodriguez, "Emptying the Content of Whiteness"; Paula S. Rothenberg, Introduction to *White Privilege.*
68. Joe L. Kincheloe and Shirley R. Steinberg, "Addressing the Crisis of Whiteness"; Nelson M. Rodriguez, "Emptying the Content of Whiteness"; Philip C. Wander, Judith N. Martin, and Thomas N. Nakayama, "The Roots of Racial Classification," in *White Privilege: Essential Readings on the Other Side of Racism,* ed. Paula S. Rothenberg (New York: Worth Publishers, 2008), p. 29–34.
69. Michael W. Apple, Forward to *White Reign*; Richard Dyer, "The Matter of Whiteness," in *White Privilege: Essential Readings on the Other Side of Racism,* ed. Paula S. Rothenberg (New York: Worth Publishers, 2008), p. 9–14.
70. Richard Dyer, "The Matter of Whiteness."
71. Michael W. Apple, Forward to *White Reign*, p. x.
72. Paula S. Rothenberg, Introduction to *White Privilege,* p. 3.
73. Clinton B. Allison, "Okie Narratives: Agency and Whiteness," in *White Reign: Deploying Whiteness in America,* ed. Joe L. Kincheloe, Shirley R. Steinberg, Nelson M. Rodriguez, and Ronald E. Chennault (New York, NY: St. Martin's Press, 1998), p. 229–224.
74. Linda Faye Williams, "The Construction of Race: American Social Policy at the Dawn of the New Century," in *White Privilege: Essential Readings on the Other Side of Racism,* ed. Paula S. Rothenberg (New York: Worth Publishers, 2008), p. 91–95.
75. George Lipsitz, "The Possessive Investment in Whiteness," in *White Privilege: Essential Readings on the Other Side of Racism,* ed. Paula S. Rothenberg (New York: Worth Publishers, 2008), p. 67–90.
76. Ibid.
77. Philip C. Wander, Judith N. Martin, and Thomas N. Nakayama, "The Roots of Racial Classification."
78. Edward Royzman, Clark McCauley, and Paul Rozin, "From Plato to Putnam: Four Ways to Think About Hate," in *The Psychology of Hate,* ed.

Robert J. Sternberg (Washington, DC: American Psychological Association, 2005), p. 3–36.

79. Edward Royzman, Clark McCauley, and Paul Rozin, "From Plato to Putnam," p. 4.
80. Robert J. Sternberg, "Understanding and Combating Hate," in *The Psychology of Hate,* ed. Robert J. Sternberg (Washington, DC: American Psychological Association, 2005), p. 38.
81. Edward Royzman, Clark McCauley, and Paul Rozin, "From Plato to Putnam"; Robert J. Sternberg, "Understanding and Combating Hate"; Robert J. Sternberg and Karin Sternberg, *The Nature of Hate* (Cambridge, NY: Cambridge University Press, 2008).
82. Edward Royzman, Clark McCauley, and Paul Rozin, "From Plato to Putnam"; Robert J. Sternberg and Karin Sternberg, *The Nature of Hate.*
83. Robert J. Sternberg and Karin Sternberg, *The Nature of Hate.*
84. Willard Gaylin, *Hatred*; Robert J. Sternberg and Karin Sternberg, *The Nature of Hate.*
85. Willard Gaylin, *Hatred.*
86. Robert J. Sternberg and Karin Sternberg, *The Nature of Hate.*
87. Ervin Staub, "The Origins and Evolution of Hate."
88. Willard Gaylin, *Hatred.*
89. Ibid.
90. Ibid., p. 34.
91. Ibid.
92. Willard Gaylin, *Hatred*; Joshua Greene, *Moral Tribes.*
93. Roy F. Baumeister, *Evil.*
94. Ibid.
95. Willard Gaylin, *Hatred.*
96. Robert J. Sternberg and Karin Sternberg, *The Nature of Hate.*
97. Ervin Staub, "The Origins and Evolution of Hate."
98. Ibid.
99. Robert J. Sternberg and Karin Sternberg, *The Nature of Hate.*
100. Ibid.
101. Ervin Staub, "The Origins and Evolution of Hate."
102. Howard J. Ehrlich, *Hate Crimes and Ethnoviolence.*
103. Edward Royzman, Clark McCauley, and Paul Rozin, "From Plato to Putnam," p. 9.
104. Howard J. Ehrlich, *Hate Crimes and Ethnoviolence.*
105. Ibid.
106. Lori Peek, *Behind the Backlash.*
107. Ibid.

108. Ibid., p. 34.
109. Ibid.
110. Susan Opotow, "Hate, Conflict and Moral Exclusion," in *The Psychology of Hate,* ed. Robert J. Sternberg (Washington, DC: American Psychological Association, 2005), p. 126.
111. Leonard Berkowitz, "On Hate and its Determinants."
112. Ibid.
113. Roy F. Baumeister and David A. Butz, "Roots of Hate, Violence, and Evil," in *The Psychology of Hate,* ed. Robert J. Sternberg (Washington, DC: American Psychological Association, 2005), p. 87–102.
114. Ibid. p. 97.
115. Leonard Berkowitz, "On Hate and its Determinants," p. 172.
116. Roy F. Baumeister, *Evil.*
117. Nathan Lean, *The Islamophobia Industry.*
118. Yvonne Yazbeck Haddad, Jane I. Smith, and Kathleen M. Moore, *Muslim Women in North America.*
119. Ibid.
120. Lori Peek, *Behind the Backlash.*
121. Yvonne Yazbeck Haddad, Jane I. Smith, and Kathleen M. Moore, *Muslim Women in North America.*
122. Mohamed Nimer, "Muslims in the American Body Politic," in *Muslims' Place in the American Public Square: Hope, Fears, and Aspirations,* ed. Zahid H. Bukhari, Sulayman S. Nyang, Mumtaz Ahman, and John L. Esposito (Walnut Creek, CA: AltaMira Press, 2004), p. 145–164.
123. Shaila K. Dewan, "Muslim Girl Punched in Face: Boy is Arrested," *New York Times,* September 17, 2003, http://nyti.ms/2aoM95G.
124. Council on American-Islamic Relations (CAIR), "Louisiana Teacher Removed After Hijab Incident," *CAIR-Council on American Islamic Relations,* July 13, 2012, http://bit.ly/2aD1VGN.
125. Mohamed Nimer, "Muslims in the American Body Politic."
126. Lori Peek, *Behind the Backlash.*
127. Ibid.
128. Geneive Abdo, *Mecca and the Main Street.*
129. Lori Peek, *Behind the Backlash.*
130. Geneive Abdo, *Mecca and the Main Street.*
131. Lori Peek, *Behind the Backlash.*
132. Ibid.
133. Beth Finkelstein, "Practical Educational Programming."
134. Stephen Sheehi, *Islamophobia: The Ideological Campaign.*
135. Howard J. Ehrlich, *Hate Crimes and Ethnoviolence.*

136. Ibid., p. 48.
137. Ibid., p. 45.
138. Lori Peek, *Behind the Backlash.*
139. Howard J. Ehrlich, *Hate Crimes and Ethnoviolence.*
140. Amber Hague, "Confronting the Menace."
141. Howard J. Ehrlich, *Hate Crimes and Ethnoviolence,* p. 148.
142. Geneive Abdo, *Mecca and the Main Street.*

CHAPTER 5

Methodological Considerations

This study used a qualitative transcendental phenomenological approach to shed insight on what it means to be a Caucasian female American who has converted to Islam in post-9/11 America. This methodological decision was supported by the fact that data on shared lived experiences are not easily measured through quantitative means and are frequently contingent on contextual markers and societal norms of the generation. Because I approach social science research from a subjective ontology where there may be no solitary "absolute" truth, and an epistemology that rejects empiricism in favor of becoming as "close as possible to the participants being studied,"[1] a qualitative phenomenological method was most appropriate.

In transcendental phenomenology, there is a clear division between the phenomena that is experienced (the *noemata*) and the way that it is experienced (the *noesis*).[2] For this reason, the researcher must work toward transcending their own ego by being aware of their own intention (their own consciousness) and separating their personal experiences from the phenomena as much as possible.[3] According to Moustakas, this type of research is known as "'transcendental' because it adheres to what can be discovered through reflection on subjective acts and their objective correlates."[4] This process is heavily methods driven and relies on *epoche* as the researcher sets aside their own experiences and biases so that the information garnered is analyzed with a perspective that is not overshadowed by the life experiences of the researcher themselves.[5]

© The Author(s) 2017
A.M. Guimond, *Converting to Islam*,
DOI 10.1007/978-3-319-54250-8_5

Epistemologically, I accept the notion that there is a connection between the lived experiences and how they are interpreted by the individual; however, I also strongly subscribe to Moustakas's notion of transcendental phenomenology that "each experience is considered in its singularity, in and for itself."[6] Further, I am also a firm believer that it is important to understand my own experiences and to be aware of them so that I can separate my beliefs from the social phenomenon that is being studied.

It should also be noted that I subscribe to a research epistemology which is deeply rooted in the feminist perspective. I believe strongly that social science research is an opportunity to not only generate knowledge but to also help empower and uplift people who have been marginalized.[7] I strongly believe in the teachings of Gillies and Alldred, who argued that the voices of female – and feminist – scientists can "help eliminate distortion, ignorance and prejudice, and thereby reform the otherwise inadequate practices of positivist research."[8] I also agree with Gillies and Alldred who argued that without feminist research, "women's subjectivities come to be defined through masculinist knowledge structures,"[9] and believe that it is my ethical responsibility as a female social scientist to ensure that these knowledge structures are changed to create space at the proverbial table for contributions *by* women to the discourse *regarding* women and women-related issues.

BRACKETING

I recognize that through the collection and analysis of data, I play a role in the production and reproduction of the narratives.[10] A researcher can use a stringent bracketing process to help allay any biases that may be present by the researcher projecting their own preconceived notions of the phenomenon onto the participants.[11] I recognized early in this research that bracketing my own experience was necessary to help limit projection of my own thoughts and feelings onto the experiences of those participating in the study.

The bracketing process during the conceptualization and execution of this research was an ongoing and dynamic process. Initially, I outlined and reflected on my experiences after having completed a 28-day personal project where I wore hijab to determine if I would be treated any differently based on my appearance as a Muslim. This project, the responses to the project, and my subsequent personal awareness were used as the starting point of the bracketing process. From there, I considered and outlined my experiences with religion and conversion, with religious identity, with seeking a religious community, and with my own feelings as I witnessed a more recent American terrorism event (the Boston Marathon bombing). A more complete explanation of my bracketing statements can be found in Chapter 1 under the "Why me?" section.

SAMPLE

In keeping with the traditions of phenomenological research, I initially aimed to identify 8–12 participants[12] through a snowballing technique by asking personal contacts for introductions to potential participants; however, this proved slightly problematic. Although common understanding of phenomenology dictates that those who participate in research are considered "coresearchers" and tend to be addressed as such, based on the fact that the women in this study referred to themselves as "participants" throughout the data collection process, they will be referenced throughout this manuscript as "participants."

In my early contacts with potential participants, I was told on multiple occasions that there would be some hesitancy by members of the female Muslim Convert community due to fears of being marginalized. I recognized that these hesitancies may have been grounded in a combination of experiences (including personal, anecdotal, and hyperbolic experiences), and I respected their hesitancy to participate. I was also told that there is great concern in the Muslim population with having their voices recorded, and there was great fear that recordings would be modified or spliced together (should they wind up in the wrong hands).[13] Although my initial requests for participation fell short, ultimately I did find that I could use social media to reach out to Muslim American organizations and specifically groups of female converts to Islam. After much explanation and rapport building, I was able to ask them to post calls for participation in this project. This resulted in the identification of nine participants to be interviewed via telephone or Skype. Thus, the purposive sample was met.

It should be noted that although nine participants were interviewed, there was a technical issue with one of the participants where the interview was repeatedly interrupted by loss of internet connection, the interview was never completed, and subsequent contact attempts to finish the interview with the participant received no response. This interview was not transcribed and was not included in the dataset. Thus, the final sample size was eight.

All participants met the criteria of inclusion in this phenomenological study in that they were all Caucasian females over the age of 18 who had converted to Islam since September 11, 2001 and who were over the age of 18 at the time of their conversion. For the purposes of this study, the term Caucasian was defined if the participant met two criteria: did they perceive themselves as Caucasian, and would a reasonable person look at them and also perceive them to be Caucasian? Participants varied based on age, ranging from 26 to 59 years old, and were chosen to geographically represent three categories of residential community: urban, suburban, and rural living. Five participants were from urban communities, two were from suburban communities, and one was from a rural community. In trying to garner the most geographically diverse population, I ensured that no state was represented more than once. I was unable to identify participants from the Pacific Northwest, The West Coast, the American Southwest, Alaska, or the Hawaiian Islands.

The participants each also had different marital statuses which ranged from never married, married, widowed, subsequent marriages, divorced, and estranged. As a way to help maintain the confidentiality for their families and any minor children, I did not specifically ask questions about their children, nor did I track this information. During the interview process, each participant was advised that they would receive a pseudonym in the final analysis and was asked whether they would prefer a traditionally American name or a Qur'anically based pseudonym. Requests for specific pseudonyms were honored where applicable. A table of demographic information is presented in Table 5.1.

DATA COLLECTION

During my initial contact with each participant, I described and explained the purpose of this study and solicited participation from them. Once they showed interest in participation, I emailed them copies of the consent paperwork to review and indicated that if they had questions or concerns about the process, than I would address those issues prior to obtaining their signatures. After I addressed questions and concerns, I asked each participant to return the consent forms to me via either email or United States Postal Service (USPS) and waited for their return. Once returned, I scheduled either telephonic

Table 5.1 Demographics of participants

Name/ Pseudonym	Age	Religion prior to conversion	Geographic location	Marital history
Reilly	37	Catholic	Urban PA	Married after conversion
Nawal	59	Catholic	Urban MN	Widowed prior to conversion, not remarried
Emily	44	Christian (Lutheran, Mormon, Presbyterian)	Suburban NH	Divorced prior to conversion, married Muslim living overseas after conversion
Sumaya	34	Southern Baptist	Urban IL	Married to immigrant Muslim after conversion, divorced
Amy Marie	45	Catholic	Suburban OH	Married immigrant Muslim after conversion, estranged
Lynn	39	Catholic	Rural ME	Divorced prior to conversion, married Muslim living overseas after conversion
Jessica	33	Catholic	Urban LA	Married after conversion to Caucasian convert
Jena	26	Catholic	Urban NJ	Married after conversion to American/Arab Muslim

or Skype-based interviews with each participant at a time which would be most respectful of their schedules.

Upon making contact with the individuals via phone or Skype, I verbally reviewed the purpose of the study and answered any questions that they had regarding procedure or protocol. I reminded them that their participation was voluntary and this ensured that the participants did not feel coerced into participation. I did not pressure the participants to reveal any information that they were uncomfortable with. At the culmination of each interview, I asked if the participants had stated anything that they wished that I would withhold from the final analysis. Some of the participants who had mentioned spouses or children by name asked to have this information redacted, and the ages of children to be shielded in the research manuscript. One participant also asked that her location be shielded from the research manuscript as well.

The interviews were conducted over a 37-day period between the dates of June 4, 2014 and July 10, 2014. The latter half of the interview period coincided with the Muslim holy month of Ramadan. In the same way that Pollio et al. suggested that a person's present can affect the way they interpret their past;[14] it is possible that the coinciding of Ramadan with a number of the interviews caused the participants to interpret and describe their experiences with this phenomenon in a different way than they would while not observing this holy time.

Data was collected through the application of phenomenological interviews which included nine open-ended questions. These questions had been developed based on Moustakas's model where questions are utilized to elicit descriptive and explanatory responses about the phenomena itself, as well as uncover how each participant experienced – and subsequently processed – the phenomena.[15] The main questions asked during the interview were a variation of Creswell's primary questions of: "What have you experienced in terms of the phenomenon? [And] What contexts or situations have typically influenced or affected your experiences of the phenomenon?"[16] The interview questions were aimed at developing a better understanding of the research questions which were:

- RQ_1: What is the shared lived experience of Caucasian female American converts to Islam in post-9/11 America?
- RQ_2: What impact does the increasingly hostile social climate toward Muslim Americans have on these spiritual, social, physical, and mental integration of the participants?
- RQ_3: How is conflict experienced between Caucasian female American converts to Islam and their non-Muslim counterparts?
- RQ_4: How is conflict experienced within the selves of Caucasian female American converts to Islam in post-9/11 America?

Interview questions were designed to assist the researcher in fleshing out a more representative textural description during data analysis. During the narrative interviews, the questions focused on describing the experiences of what it means to be in this population and explaining how Islamophobia may affect the participant's spiritual, social, physical, and mental well-being.

I began each interview by asking a few questions to establish basic rapport. For example, I began the interviews by asking for the participant to state their age and date of birth. I then asked each participant what type of religious upbringing they had. This question generally allowed the participant to become comfortable talking about their faith. I followed that question up with "What did religion look like growing up?" Asking this question began to identify the data which was relevant to this phenomenon. I then moved on to ask questions which were geared toward getting a better understanding of how they experienced the phenomenon being explored. These questions included "Can you tell me a little about the experiences that led to your conversion to Islam?" and "Can you tell me about the experience that you had when you told your non-Muslim friends and family about your conversion? How did they react and what did that mean to you?" Follow-up questions were aimed to unpack the experiences that discrimination and Islamophobia have on the participant and how these experiences are processed. Follow-up questions included highlighting whether their relationships changed or stayed the same after their conversion, what types of struggles that they had since their conversion, whether they chose to wear hijab and what that was like, and whether they had experienced an impact on their mental health.

Toward the end of each interview, I reminded the participant that they would be assigned a pseudonym to protect their anonymity and suggested that they could choose whether it be Qur'anically based or a more traditional American name. Although this was not initially planned as an interview question to elicit data, I found it to be quite revealing about the way each participant viewed and subsequently identified themselves. This question allowed them to choose (and have control over) how they would prefer to be identified in the research manuscript for a study designed in part to look at the mutual exclusivity of Muslims and Americans that is inherent in Islamophobic discourse, but it also revealed information as to how they felt about this mutual exclusivity.

I finished the interview by asking whether there was anything else that they wished that I had asked about or that they would like to share. The majority of the participants used this opportunity to reflect on things that they had already shared, but in a couple of cases, this provided me with new information. With one participant, we were going over the next steps after the recording was stopped, and she asked me to turn the recording back on because our conversation was progressing back into something else that she had wanted to discuss. In this case, I turned the recorder back on, and I allowed her to speak freely.

While some pioneers in social science research suggest that the researcher be rigid and stick to the specific previously designed questions during each phenomenological narrative interview,[17] due to my feminist epistemology, I chose instead to refrain from too much rigidity during the interview protocol. For me, it was important to allow my participants the opportunity to have their voices be heard and I felt that a rigidity in the questions would ultimately derail the organic nature of storytelling within the context of narrative dialogue. For this reason, I asked follow-up questions quite informally and in keeping with my conflict resolution background, I employed reflective listening skills to ensure clarity. At times, the participants addressed planned follow-up questions on their own without prompting, and in this case, I allowed them to direct the dialogue in any way that they deemed fit. Using this skill, I was able to build rapport, encourage each participant to continue sharing their respective story, and convey to them that I believed that their story had value.

I also understood that appropriate responses to stories which are amusing or sad essentially work toward building rapport and thus help elicit more textually rich data;[18] thus, I worked toward keeping my responses from sounding too stoic. Furthermore, coming from a conflict analysis and resolution perspective, I recognized that throughout the interviews, I needed to remain aware that nonverbal communication patterns can oft times highlight discrepancies between what is felt and what is said, or they can be used to confirm and validate the utterances of the participant.[19]

In order to remain as close to the data as possible, I personally transcribed the interviews, verified them for errors, and forwarded a copy of the transcripts to the participant to review, clarify, or elaborate if they desired.

ETHICAL CONSIDERATIONS

It should be noted that because the participants for this research were all within a marginalized community in the United States, there were a number of specific ethical considerations (beyond consent) to address. First and foremost, I recognize that when approaching research from a feminist perspective, the researcher must first seek to ensure that the benefits of the research will outweigh the risks to those involved.[20] Through my feminist lens, I recognize that the current research in the field that neglects to include female Muslims does little more than allow for the "active reproduction of dominant cultural accounts of individual subjectivity."[21] This exclusion of female Muslims from research does little more than allow for perpetual marginalization and othering, and ultimately, I believed that the contributions of this proposed research helped fill a void in the existing literature while causing minimal risk to those involved.

I also had to recognize that social science research has the potential for interfering with the lives of the participants, and an imbalance of power between researcher and participant can increase the likelihood for mental health issues to arise for the participant, including anxiety, self-esteem damage, guilt, shame, and an increase in stress.[22] I helped to create empowered participants and protect their autonomy by ensuring that each participant agreed to take part in the research on a completely voluntary and coercion-free basis, and I was certain to check with each participant at the end of the interview process that they were not in any imminent psychological discomfort. Further, I had researched religiously based counseling providers in each participant's respective location and had references and recommendations on hand should they need to speak with someone in a therapeutic capacity. Although some of the participants revisited some painful experiences in order to share their stories, none of them indicated that they needed these recommendations.

Because the participants in this research were chosen from both personal contacts and through a quasi-snowballing referral technique, I had to constantly evaluate the process to ensure that the line between access and consent was not muddied. I remained aware that the constant negotiation and mapping of ethical issues were paramount, and my reflexivity was one of the most important assets that I had.[23] For this reason, I was certain to treat consent as an active process, rather than a single moment in time. Further, this active process of consent helped to build and strengthen rapport and helped foster the understanding that this research would not be used to victimize or marginalize. Building strong rapport also helped to alleviate the issues that Muslims currently are facing with trusting non-Muslims in terms of consent, paperwork, signing documents, etc.

DATA ANALYSIS

After transcription and verification of the interviews with the participants, I reviewed each transcript individually and with equal weight following the methodology presented by Moustakas.[24] Then, by hand, I highlighted the key phrases of each statement which related to this phenomenon. Along the margins, I wrote formulated meanings of each key phrase which revealed the horizons of the experiences (and ultimately how those experiences are processed by the participant). One cannot possibly exhaust all possible meanings during the process of horizonalization and new information can help to contribute to the generation of new knowledge,[25] thus the horizonalization process for this study continued until formulated meanings were exhausted within context of place, time, and information provided. Analysis became cyclical and dynamic in nature. In this stage, I also employed an in vivo coding method, using the participant's own words as much as possible to assist with the next stage of the phenomenological reduction model.

Using the in vivo coding method, the invariant meanings (also known as the horizons) were clustered together into thematic groups.[26] I created a new Word document for each individual participant and categorized each formulated meaning into thematic cluster. I overlapped the thematic clusters of each participant to develop the thematic clustering for the entire data sample.

These thematic clusters were then used to develop the textural descriptions of what participants experienced. According to Moustakas, the development of the structural description includes "thinking and judging, imagining and recollecting, in order to arrive at core structural meanings."[27] For the purposes of this study, I viewed each interview protocol individually and wrote textual and structural descriptions for each participant regarding what it means to experience being a Caucasian female American convert to Islam in post-September 11 America.

In the final step of data analysis, the textural description and structural descriptions were further refined to reveal the development and articulation of the overarching essence, or *essential, invariant structure*, of the phenomena that was researched.[28] In this stage of analysis, I used the textual and structural descriptions of each participant and viewed them in totality alongside the thematic clusters of formulated meanings to explore the commonalities and differences between the various participants in the study.

CREDIBILITY AND VALIDITY

It is important to be mindful that within phenomenology, the emphasis is less on replicability than it would be in quantitative research. Instead, the researcher determines whether the study met criteria for validity. For this reason, this criteria was met by asking whether it was confirmable with the research participants, and whether it was reliable and credible in that the data backed up the findings.[29]

To ensure that the research findings were congruent with the statements of the participants, I employed a vigorous process of member checking. To ensure that I was hearing both what was and was not being said, during the interview process, I asked participants to clarify statements that might have ambiguous meanings. After transcription of the interviews, I forwarded copies of the interview protocol to each participant and asked them to review and clarify anything that they believed might be ambiguous as well. During the various stages of the phenomenological reduction process, I forwarded each participant their textural and structural descriptions and asked for their input to ensure that I was not misinterpreting their experiences with the phenomenon in question. In the final stages of analysis, I spoke with the participants to ensure that they were confident that their voices had been heard and that I had accurately represented the essence of what it means to have experienced being a Caucasian female American convert to Islam in post-9/11 America. To that end, I was confident that the study was credible.

In terms of reliability and credibility, I employed a rigorous audit trail throughout the analysis process. This audit trail began with my personal bracketing statement, continued to include the protocol transcripts, the transcripts coded for formulated meanings which included the horizonalization, the documents containing both individual and group thematic clustering of horizons, the textual and structural descriptions for each participant, and my personal memos during the process. According to Pollio et al., "the criterion of validity becomes whether a reader adopting the worldview articulated by the researcher would be able to see textual evidence supporting the interpretation, and whether the goal of providing first-person understanding was attained."[30] By submitting the audit trail and subsequent manuscript to members of my research committee to determine whether they would come to the same conclusions, it became clear that I had reached Pollio et al.'s criteria of validity. The following chapter outlines the research findings.

NOTES

1. John W. Creswell, *Qualitative Inquiry and Research Design: Choosing Among Five Approaches* (Thousand Oaks, CA: SAGE, 2007), p. 18.
2. Clark Moustakas, *Phenomenological Research Methods*.
3. Ibid.
4. Ibid., p 45.
5. Ibid.
6. Ibid.
7. Rosalind Edwards and Melanie Mauthner, "Ethics and Feminist Research: Theory and Practice," in *Ethics in Qualitative Research*, ed. Melanie

Mauthner, Maxine Birch, Julie Jessop, and Tina Miller (London: SAGE Publications, 2002), p. 14–31.

8. Val Gillies and Pam Alldred, "The Ethics of Intention," p. 34.
9. Ibid., p. 34.
10. Maxine Birch and Tina Miller, "Encouraging Participation: Ethics and Responsibilities" in *Ethics in Qualitative Research,* ed. Melanie Mauthner, Maxine Birch, Julie Jessop, and Tina Miller (London: SAGE Publications, 2002), p. 91–106.
11. Howard R. Pollio, Tracy B. Henley, and Craig J. Thompson, *The Phenomenology of Everyday Life* (Cambridge: Cambridge University Press, 1997).
12. John W. Creswell, Qualitative Inquiry and Research Design.
13. This may sound hyperbolic to some, but this is a very real fear for some participants, and this fear may not entirely be ungrounded. At the time of the study, the news was abuzz with a story about the recent subpoena issued by the police in Northern Ireland. The police had subpoenaed Boston College in federal court for the confidential recordings taken during The Belfast Project. The subsequent release of these confidential recordings led to the arrest and brief detention of Sinn Fein President Gerry Adams for his role in a 40+-year-old murder.
14. Howard R. Pollio, Tracy B. Henley, and Craig J. Thompson, *The Phenomenology of Everyday Life.*
15. Clark Moustakas, *Phenomenological Research Methods.*
16. John W. Creswell, *Qualitative Inquiry and Research Design,* p. 67.
17. Ibid.
18. Howard R. Pollio, Tracy B. Henley, and Craig J. Thompson, *The Phenomenology of Everyday Life.*
19. Neil H. Katz, Marcia Kopplman Sweedler, and John W. Lawyer, *Communication and Conflict Resolution Skills (2nd ed.)* (Dubuque, IA: Kendall Hunt Publishing Company, 2010).
20. Pam Alldred and Val Gillies, "Eliciting Research Accounts: Re/producing Modern Subjects?" in *Ethics in Qualitative Research,* ed. Melanie Mauthner, Maxine Birch, Julie Jessop, and Tina Miller (London: SAGE Publications, 2002), p. 53–69; Jean Duncombe and Julie Jessop, "'Doing Rapport' and the Ethics of 'Faking Friendship,'" in *Ethics in Qualitative Research,* ed. Melanie Mauthner, Maxine Birch, Julie Jessop, and Tina Miller (London: SAGE Publications, 2002), p. 91–106; Val Gillies and Pam Alldred "The Ethics of Intention: Research as a Political Tool," in *Ethics in Qualitative Research,* ed. Melanie Mauthner, Maxine Birch, Julie Jessop, and Tina Miller (London: SAGE Publications, 2002), p. 32–52; Tina Miller and Linda Bell, "Consenting to What? Issues of Access, Gate-keeping, and 'Informed Consent,'" in *Ethics in Qualitative Research,* ed. Melanie

Mauthner, Maxine Birch, Julie Jessop, and Tina Miller (London: SAGE Publications, 2002), p. 53–69.

21. Pam Alldred and Val Gillies "Eliciting Research Accounts," p. 162.

22. Elizabeth Murphy and Robert Dingwall, "The Ethics of Ethnography," in *Handbook of Ethnography,* ed. Paul Atkinson, Amanda Coffey, Sara Delamont, John Lofland, and Lyn Lofland (London: SAGE Publications, 2001), p. 339–51; Ken Plummer, "The Call of Life Stories in Ethnographic Research," in *Handbook of Ethnography,* ed. Paul Atkinson, Amanda Coffey, Sara Delamont, John Lofland, and Lyn Lofland (London: SAGE Publications, 2001), p. 395–406.

23. Maxine Birch and Tina Miller, "Encouraging Participation."

24. Clark Moustakas, *Phenomenological Research Methods.*

25. Ibid.

26. Ibid.

27. Ibid., p. 79.

28. John W. Creswell, *Qualitative Inquiry and Research Design.*

29. Ibid.

30. Howard R. Pollio, Tracy B. Henley, and Craig J. Thompson, *The Phenomenology of Everyday Life.*

CHAPTER 6

Findings

This phenomenological study presents the shared lived experiences of Caucasian female converts to Islam in post-9/11 America. All participants met the criteria of inclusion in this study in that they were all Caucasian females over the age of 18 who had converted to Islam since September 11, 2001 and who were over the age of 18 at the time of their conversion. The participants varied in age from 26 to 59 years old and geographically represented three categories of residential community: urban, suburban, and rural living. Five participants were from urban communities, two were from suburban communities, and one was from a rural community. Within the sample, no state was represented more than once. The participants each had different marital statuses which ranged from never married, married, widowed, subsequent marriages, divorced, and estranged. Some of the participants had children, but this was not formally tracked as a way to help maintain the confidentiality of their families. The participants described varying level of religious practice prior to their conversion, and they came from varying Christ-based religious upbringings. Six of the participants identified Catholicism as the religion of their upbringing, while one referenced Southern Baptist, and another referenced a childhood that included a variety of Christian dogmas including Lutheran, Mormon, and Presbyterian. All participants either chose a pseudonym for themselves or had one assigned to them. This chapter presents the key findings obtained through analysis of eight in-depth interviews.

© The Author(s) 2017
A.M. Guimond, *Converting to Islam*,
DOI 10.1007/978-3-319-54250-8_6

The results of this study inform the understanding of what it means to be a Caucasian female American convert to Islam in post-9/11 America. The overarching essence of these phenomena is the renegotiation of status, and this was experienced and discussed by the participants in five distinct ways: (1) the role of personal choice, (2) identity, (3) experiences with marginalization and victimization, (4) serving as ambassadors of Islam, and (5) the impacts of marginalization. The overarching themes and patterns of this phenomenon will be presented in this chapter, including subthemes wherever appropriate. Although in phenomenology, the goal is to highlight the shared lived experiences of the group experiencing the phenomenon in question, in this chapter, quotations are included wherever applicable in order to illustrate how this phenomenon is experienced. These quotations should be interpreted as the embodiment of the overall experience rather than as indicative of personal individual experiences. For a more complete textural description of the experiences of each individual, please see Appendix B.

Figure 6.1 represents the key themes that emerged through data analysis. It does not include subthemes, but they will be included in the discussion of each theme.

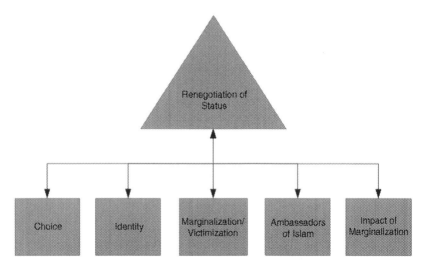

Fig. 6.1 Thematic structure for the experience of being a Caucasian female American convert to Islam

THEME 1: CHOICE

In the first theme, participants spoke about the many choices that they faced throughout the conversion experience. This theme shed light into better understanding the research question of what is the shared lived experience of Caucasian female American converts to Islam in post-9/11 America, as well as began to highlight possible understanding in terms of the research question regarding how conflict is experienced within the selves of this population. The theme of choice was separated into two interrelated subthemes (see Fig. 6.2) of both the personal choice to convert, and the personal choice surrounding the choice of covering (adopting hijab and other modest forms of dress). Personal choice appeared to be a recurring theme for all of the participants, and this is particularly important considering how the recurring dominant discourse regarding Muslim women is that they are being oppressed and blindly follow the demands of their male counterparts.

Subtheme 1: Choice in Converting

All of the participants in this study reported that their conversion was a nonlinear process that they were actively engaged in. The majority of the participants reported that they were seekers of a religious understanding from an early age and this sparked an active inquiry into religion as an adult, as described in this statement:

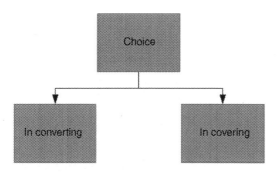

Fig. 6.2   Subthemes under choice

> I was always a seeker … I searched, I think I read about just about every type of religion, including maybe non-religion if you want to include it or call it, like you know Atheism. Some people think that's a religion, some people don't. But I searched. I searched just about everything. (Reilly, age 37)

Similarly, another woman added:

> I would go along with friends from school, um whatever religion. I know I went to Baptist church, went to the Nazarene church, and other churches. So I – I always wanted to have you know, God in my life. So after the divorce, and not being able to go to the Catholic Church, I just started searching, I guess. (Amy Marie, age 45)

Inquiry into Islam took different forms for each participant, but the majority of the women in this study discussed the inquiry process as including reading, watching videos, discussions with people online, in-person networking, visits to mosques, and self-directed study of theology. As one participant explained, she

> Looked around for a Qur'an and I couldn't find one at the bookstore. I didn't think to look online, so I went on Skype and I found Saudi Arabia, and I found a friend there. And I asked him please send me books from you know, and of the Qur'an, and about Islam. (Sumaya, age 34)

The depth of the research that informed the personal decision to convert was similarly reflected upon by another participant who reported:

> I was rooming – roommates with a friend of mine from high school in the dorm, and she and I kind of – we had these really deep philosophical existential conversations that would last hours and hours. You know, normal kids would be out in the clubs. We did that too, but she and I would spend most of our time in the library researching this stuff. (Jessica, age 33)

All of the participants spoke about unpacking culture from religion, a process which also included unpacking their own internalized Islamophobia. As explained by one participant:

> I was really, I was kind of weary of the people because all I know was what I saw on TV, and all the bad negative images, and it was, I was scared of them. (Sumaya, age 34)

Another participant directly named this weariness as Islamophobia stating, "of course I had all that Islamophobia that I hadn't – that I had to get rid of so to speak, or to put in order" (Nawal, age 59). And as another woman reflected on her conversion experience, she noted that unpacking culture and religion can be a difficult process. She stated:

> It took me a long time to really recognize in myself that I wanted – to admit to myself that I believed in Islam. Because even before 9/11, this was well before 9/11 (from '98 on), to grapple with the stereotypes culture taught me, and it was hard to disentangle the two. OK, and once I did, it was just a completely different experience. And I don't have to be Arab. There's nothing to do with Arabs, and so on and so forth. So it was a process, it took from 98, well into November 2001 [which] was when I converted, when I took the faith. And it um, it was a wild ride. (Jessica, age 33)

Resonation of the teachings of Islam was a recurring theme amongst the participants in this study. As one woman explained, "kind of clicked for me" and it "kind of made sense, kinda the principles I agreed with" (Reilly, age 37). Not only was there a deep resonation with the teachings of Islam, but the participants all spoke of how the faith appealed to their greater logic. As one participant explained:

> And when I realized that, I still get goosebumps. When I realized that, only God of Creations could have dictated that – that, being the timing of the five daily prayers – that was the straw that broke the camel's back – as my reading had explained the truth in the Islamic claim that the Christian Bible was not in its original form and not reliable as the infallible word of God. And no one in the desert could have realized that something like 1400 years ago. So right then and there, I realized that Islam was the truth and it frightened me. Because I thought, well what do I do now? (Nawal, age 59)

Another participant added:

> There reached a point where I had to say, you know what? There's no way that people 1400 years ago could have known this. You know, certain things, you can't argue with that. I mean, at the time, they were arguing about whether the world was flat or not. And Mohammed in fact, not only did he say it was round, but that it was egg shaped. It wasn't perfectly round, and we just found this out with science when we got the satellites. You know, within the last hundred years, we have the formation of embryonics,

it's in the Qur'an...and I'm like wait a minute. It was only in the last 50 years that we came up with this. How can he have said that – that you know, a baby is formed first by two droplets...you know, that the male sperm is what determines gender. That you know, you can't even know how babies are formed, let alone what kind of gender. You know, so again, a lot of good things that were coming up and I – I had to accept the fact. OK, this is that guy, I just felt this was the world of God. (Lynn, age 39)

All of the participants in this study spoke about the role of personal choice in the conversion process, but regardless of the paths that their inquiry into Islam took, they each owned the conversion process and were clear to convey ownership of the personal choice to convert. The following statement exemplifies the personal experiences with choice that all of the women shared:

I can honestly say that I accepted Islam on my own. Not because someone told me something and I believe it. I did the research myself. What hurts me even more is from my family, they believe it's because of him, and that I've been brainwashed. Everyone knew me as a hard-headed stubborn independent person, and then as soon as I converted, "oh, she must have been brainwashed by some guy." What an insult to me. I mean, come on, give me a break. You really think that low of me that I can't make up my own mind? (Lynn, age 39)

All of the women in this study indicated that the decision to convert was entirely on their own, and that they entered the conversion process after doing a significant amount of research. The overwhelming majority of the women in this study reported that Islam was congruent with the beliefs that they had already established in terms of gender equality and humanitarian works. All of the women claimed feeling as if Islam resonated with them at their core. For the women in this study, choice in the decision to convert was a recurrent theme.

Subtheme 2: Choice in Covering

All of the women in this study spoke about the personal choice and introspection that went into deciding whether to adopt hijab or not. Six of the participants actively wore hijab in public all the time, one of the participants was in the transition toward wearing hijab full time, and one of the participants had chosen to stop wearing hijab after she began experiencing health impacts due to the stress surrounding her conversion. The amount of introspection into the choice to wear hijab varied based on their own respective journeys through the conversion process. As one participant explained, the choice to cover immediately set her apart from the mainstream American community, and this was something that she found herself considering:

> I took it for granted. That my life as a white American Christian woman, I took for granted. Because when I converted, all of a sudden, I felt every single eye on me every time that I walked out of my home...cuz I started wearing hijab. It was my own decision. (Emily, age 44)

Another participant found that her decision to wear hijab was significantly impeded by her husband, who did not want her to show outward identifiers of faith so that she could blend in better with the dominant culture. She explained:

> I told my fiancé then (husband now) – I said I want to go get hijab, I don't know where to get them, you know? I just – take me to the store. I tried it for months, he didn't bring me. And finally I had to say "you can't stop me from wearing them. It's my right as a Muslim woman, this is literally going against Allah to not bring me." And he said I had to understand that he's from [a] post 9/11 world – two weeks afterward, he remembers a guy coming up to the car when he was with his mom, and hitting on the window and telling her to go back to her home country. And I didn't understand the impact that it was gonna have, so I thought I was really like mentally prepared. (Jena, age 26)

All of the participants, whether they currently choose to wear hijab or not, shared that the wearing of hijab doesn't change who they are in their hearts. As one participant reflected:

> It's just that I am an American. And I happen to be Muslim, you know? It's – because I wear something on my head, does that make me any different than if I wear a baseball cap? Or I dyed my hair purple? Or a mohawk? Or pierced my nose? Or you know, anything that American women do, you know? Just because we're not...whatever, doesn't mean that they're hated and different than who they are. I am who I am. You know? I'm still me. (Lynn, age 39)

For all of the women in this study, the decision on whether to adopt the hijab or not was one that required great introspection. This introspection led to a choice which was not free from personal turmoil. The amount of introspection into the choice to wear hijab or not varied based on their own respective journeys through the conversion process; yet, each participant was adamant that she maintained ownership of all aspects of this decision and the decision-making process which led to their adopting hijab or not.

THEME 2: IDENTITY

All of the participants in this study spoke about the theme of identity. This theme incorporated various aspects of their identity (and the shift of identity) – including their beliefs, their social practices, and how they saw themselves overall. Not only does this theme go toward answering the research question of what is the shared lived experience of Caucasian female American converts to Islam in post-9/11 America, but this theme also appeared to answer the question regarding how conflict is experienced within the selves of Caucasian female American converts to Islam in post-9/11 America. Further, it goes toward informing what impact the increasingly hostile social climate toward Muslim Americans has on the spiritual, social, physical, and mental integration of the participants. As one participant explained, post-conversion identity integration was not as difficult as some would expect because she felt that she had always been deeply rooted as an American in her identity. She explained:

> That's all that I've ever known my entire life, is that I'm an American. But an American is my history. . . . I don't know how to explain it. It's like yeah, my American part of me is who I am, who my past generations have been. They've been here, they came here years and years – like hundreds of years ago, and I can't deny my past. (Emily, age 44)

Another participant echoed these thoughts, reporting:

> I haven't dropped my culture. I'm just following a religion that's different from some of my culture. But um, I would say American . . . because I still identify myself [that way]. (Reilly, age 37)

Other participants felt as if they were having people assign identities to them, identities which were perceived to be congruent within dominant

Islamophobic discourse, yet had no basis in either the participants' belief systems or their philosophy on life. As one participant intimated:

> I guess my biggest problem was – I was always one of those staunch feminist types, you know? So many people have this impression now that I was wearing this because I had a Muslim husband, you know? And I was being oppressed, and wearing this is – how much I have changed to allow that to happen to myself. And for me, it was like a big problem. People thought I wasn't who I was anymore. That I was just a silent partner. And even, I have found acquaintances from high school, and I see them out and about town, and they won't approach me anymore. (Jena, age 26)

Some of the participants found that the process of integrating practices of their new religion with their previous social practices was difficult. This caused them to enter into a long process of integrating their new practices with old, causing introspection over how they identified themselves in general. One exemplary statement is as follows:

> [I had to] figure out: OK, now who is actually Emily? Emily the Muslim, who am I? And that's what I've been working on, trying to figure out where's the middle ground between this extreme Muslims that all that, to Emily who is all that? And I'm trying to figure out who I am in the middle. (Emily, age 44)

For all of the participants in this study, identity and the renegotiation of identity was a significant theme. As the women in this study adopted new faith practices after their respective conversions, they had to integrate and juxtapose these new faith practices and beliefs with their previously established identities. For some, this was a relatively smooth process, and for others, this process was drawn out and difficult. Regardless of how they experienced this process of integrating the various aspects of their identities, each participant in this study clearly articulated how they viewed and identified themselves in terms of religion, nationality, race, and gender. Each was clear that these are not mutually exclusive categorizations.

THEME 3: MARGINALIZATION/VICTIMIZATION

Theme 3 encompassed experiences with marginalization and victimization. This theme serves to inform the research question of how conflict is experienced between Caucasian female American converts to Islam and

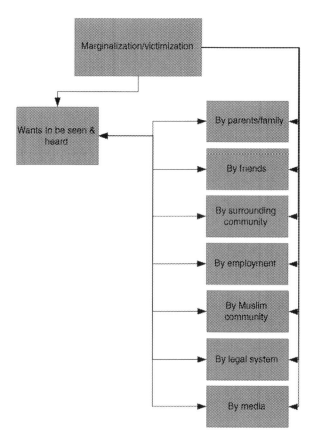

Fig. 6.3 Subthemes under marginalization/victimization

those around them, but it also serves to inform what impact that the increasingly hostile social climate toward Muslim Americans has on the spiritual, social, physical, and mental integration of the participants.

The thematic umbrella of marginalization and victimization consists of two distinct interlocking components (see Fig. 6.3). In the first component, all participants in this study expressed a strong desire to be seen and heard. In the second component, all of the participants touched upon ways that they have been victimized and marginalized. Though each of the participants experienced various forms of marginalization and victimization from various sources, in all cases, the women in this study made statements to the effect that the process of marginalization and the inability to have space to be seen and heard within society are deeply intertwined.

Subtheme 1: Wanting to be Seen and Heard

All of the participants in this study reflected on the desire to have a platform to be seen or heard. As one participant explained after realizing that she could not find representations of herself anywhere within either the American community as a Muslim, or the Muslim community as a Caucasian American, she felt that she was being marginalized. She wanted the ability to be seen as representative of both. As she explained, she was

> Not represented anywhere, on any level…you don't ever see, even on the WhyIslam.org where they show this whole video thing, they don't even show a white woman in a hijab. At least they show a white man…but they didn't actually show it as a white woman in hijab. Well where am I in that picture? (Emily, age 44)

One woman explained that there is too much assumption and conjecture about Muslim women; yet, there still is no opportunity to find out from the source what the needs and issues are for this population. She explained:

> America is so focused on the scarf and it's like oh, for God's sake. Why not be concerned about what I believe and why? You know? Why don't you think about God? Why don't you go find out what it is I believe, instead of being angry or being whatever it is you're thinking because somebody else told you? It's like, I was in their shoes you know? 6 years ago, I was just like them. (Nawal, age 59)

Another participant indicated that by fighting for the space to enter the discourse on the significant issues pertaining to Muslim Americans as Caucasian converts to Islam, this can help change the perception of Islam. As she reported:

> This is the thing people, we can be American and Muslim. But I don't know if that micro-situation that I'm in right now…[as] an indication that things are getting better. I'm not sure. I think they will get better whether or not people convert, just because we're fighting for our space to say what we need to say. And I'm hoping people listen. I don't know. (Jessica, age 33)

Multiple participants indicated that they were participating in this study
for the opportunity to hopefully achieve some validation and understanding about their experiences with being a Caucasian female American
convert to Islam in a post-9/11 American culture. One exemplary statement is as follows:

> I was hoping that if they read it in print – like a newspaper (just cuz it's in
> print doesn't mean it's true), but I'm hoping that they can just see it. Not
> just my words, but if they can see it, it will help. That's what, one of the
> things that I'm hoping from this [study]. They can read it, maybe it will
> spark an interest, start making them see. Send a copy of it to my parents. I'm
> hoping your [research manuscript] can get through [to them]. Maybe not
> my own words, but yours. (Lynn, age 39)

Three participants indicated that there was cause for concern that they
were victimized through both the Muslim community and through the
legal system and were frustrated that they had not been given the opportunity to speak for themselves. All of the participants in this study spoke
about the importance of being able to be seen and heard as Muslim
women. All of the participants recognized that by not being given the
opportunity to speak for themselves in relationship to the issues that
directly affect them as Caucasian Muslim women, they are inevitably cast
into the role of victim. Each participant recognized that by using their
voices and being more visible in the public sphere, they would be able to
develop a much stronger sense of personal autonomy in terms of their
psychosocial outcomes.

Subtheme 2: Marginalization

A recurring theme amongst all of the participants was marginalization
and/or victimization. For some, this marginalization came from family
and friends, and for others, this marginalization came from the greater
community that they were situated in. Some of the participants spoke
about how they were treated by the Muslim community or how they
were treated by law enforcement and the criminal justice system. All
participants reported a belief that the media plays an active role in the
marginalization of Muslim Americans. No two participants experienced
marginalization in the same way, and their experiences ranged from being
treated as an "outcast," to being assaulted, and to more serious

aggressions (one participant reported that her community experienced a serious hate crime which was highlighted by the media at a national level). All of these subthemes are interrelated and inform one another, and both inform wanting to be seen and heard, as well as are informed by wanting to be seen and heard.

Subtheme 2a: By Parents and Family
Six of the eight participants in this study reported that they were marginalized by their parents and family, while another reported that she was not forthcoming about her conversion experience with her family because she was fearful of the ramifications. As she explained:

> I was overseas for a little while, and when I was in Jordan – and if you didn't put some type of scarf on your head, whether it's wrapped tight or casually, you were judged. You know, just like you know Muslims are judged here, without a scarf in Islamic countries, you are looked at . . . I just casually had it on my head, and it was cold so I had a scarf on. Anyway, my mom saw that picture and she said "Oh My GOD!! You are wearing a scarf!" And she just came unglued. And I thought, well I'm not saying – I wasn't even a Muslim yet, and it's like "well I'm not saying nothing." (Nawal, age 59)

For some of the participants who reported marginalization by their family, this marginalization was experienced in the form of family using their change of religion as a point to be brought up during unrelated arguments. One participant intimated how her family used her change of religion to force her into a role of pious submission during disagreements:

> There's been arguments between me and my mother that have nothing to do with religion? But the religion will always be brought into it . . . when the arguments would come up. "well I thought you were a Muslim and Muslims don't act like that," you know, this and that, and trying to put me down, and you know – stuff like that. I'm like, you know, I retaliate in words, but basically tell her "so what? I'm allowed to get angry." I mean, like I said, I'm not a saint just because I'm a Muslim. (Reilly, age 37)

The experiences of marginalization by parents and family also came in the form of shunning. As one woman reported:

> You know, we would call and say "hey, you want to get together?" And "OK, I'll come," but the treatment was like Jessica is not here, she's an

alien . . . so that was hard to deal with. Um just proving to them that I'm still myself. That I haven't become the death by some alien lifeform, that was difficult. (Jessica, age 33)

Another participant explained that she similarly did not receive the validation that she deserved and was treated as if she had died. She stated:

At one point, I did go to my mother and sat her down, and told her that this is – *I've become a Muslim, do you have any questions?* But by then, the gossip and the assumption and the speculation had already gone so far into her own mind that she was so upset with me that she couldn't talk to me. And in fact, she still is the same way today. I tried to talk to her about it, she starts crying *I don't want to talk about it*. It doesn't get talked about, and she – she says that her daughter died. You know, I'm right here. (Lynn, age 39)

In some cases, the treatment from family took on a more threatening role, as one woman reported:

My parents told me if I do my thing in their house, meaning praying, that they're gonna call the police. And that, they also said to me that I wasn't welcome in their house anymore. (Sumaya, age 34)

Two of the participants were greatly saddened that their children were brought into the patterns of victimization through custody battles. After her children were placed into the custody of her non-Muslim American husband, one participant clearly outlined how Islamophobia plays a role in her current relationship with her children. As she explained:

Now he has fed them so much Islamophobic stuff. You know anti-Islam, anti-Muslim hate stuff that you know – my oldest daughter stopped talking to me. My younger daughter, she's just trying to avoid me so it is hurtful. My youngest daughter, we chat through a game. You know, we can text each other, send messages through this game, talk to each other here and there. You know, I'll Skype when I can, if I see she's online, I'll call. But usually she's only – see, he's always there. When he's not there, they'll talk to me no problem. When he's there – my oldest daughter, she tends to seek his approval or show off, do crazy things. Like take a piece of bacon and then eat it in front of me and say "oh this is so good." (Lynn, age 39)

The majority of the participants in this study spoke about having been marginalized or victimized by their parents or family. While this marginalization and victimization varied from participant to participant, it is important to note that marginalization from family ranged from antilocution to overt discrimination.

Subtheme 2b: By Friends

Six of the women in this study spoke about how their relationships with friends had changed since their conversion. Some of the women spoke about how they can relate this directly to their changes of social practices and no longer consuming alcohol. For these women, their change of relationships was a renegotiation process, which sometimes meant resetting boundaries, no longer participating in certain social practices like visiting nightclubs or chatting with various friends online the way they had previously. Others found that social media exacerbated the problem of marginalization and hate speech, stating things such as "online it is a whole different world, and I can get attacked left and right" (Emily, age 44). Emily went on further to exemplify the experiences with social media by stating:

> When I actually converted, or reverted, I actually would post random things, and I had a lot of people actually say a lot of mean things. Making comments to me about Islam, or random things. And I have a person who I used to go to church with, and I've actually seen in a news-feed where he had actually wrote to "kill all the Muslims," blah blah blah. And so I actually went and it was very opening, because he, you know, he came back and was like "well I was just stating something about something that was going on in another country." And I was like "OK." But I said, "do you know specifically about what's going on in another country? Or are you hearing about it from a news media source that you have no clue about?" It's like, cuz they'll tell you anything that they want to. And so, we ended up talking about it.... (Emily, age 44)

Some of the participants reported that they experienced a complete isolation from friends. The following is an embodiment of the experience that these participants underwent:

> Everybody had a negative reaction, for the most part. My friends stopped talking to me, and my family, they started harassing me. And they would

make negative comments about Islam and the Muslims. And directly toward me. (Sumaya, age 34)

Other participants felt that they needed to continue attending social events to try to retain and renegotiate social connectivity. These women recognized that although they were still invited, there was a significant change to the dynamic. One woman explained that at social gatherings where she was the only one abstaining from alcohol, she felt that people began to show their true colors:

> And they tell me "then why don't you just take off the hijab, wouldn't that just make things easier if we didn't all have to have this?" And I told them "I don't know why I have to do it, it's not gonna change who I am, it's not going to change my heart as a person," you know? I don't expect them to take off a cross, I never have and I never would. I never went to a young Jewish man and been like "take off that yarmulke," you know like that's – I don't know. And I don't think those same people that tell me I should take this off would have the nerve to go up to a Jewish man and say "why are you wearing this, and this is what's separating us," you know? Or to a Jewish woman and say it, it's just really [an] open secret that we're allowed to pick on certain people. (Jena, age 26)

For the majority of the participants in this study, the conversion to Islam had a negative impact on their relationships with friends. For some, this impact was caused by a change of social behaviors as they adopted new religious practices, but for others, this negative impact was the result of the conversion itself. While the marginalization and victimization varied from participant to participant in regards to their respective relationships with family and friends, it is important to note that this marginalization and victimization spanned the range from antilocution to overt discrimination.

Subtheme 2c: By the Surrounding Community
All of the participants in this study reported that they were aware of, and impacted by, the increasingly Islamophobic sentiments, and the increasingly hostile social climate. For one participant, although she had not experienced hostility toward her in her community, she was aware that she had misjudged how openly she would be accepted. But for the overwhelming majority of the participants, there were poor outcomes in the

surrounding community. As one woman who hadn't experienced Islamophobia-based violence explained:

> Everyone has been, if anything it has been – it's a really weird dynamic. I mean, when I have hijab, it's like so odd. More people open doors for me, and more people go out of their way to like, let me go by. But I don't know if it's because they're being like – but I know it's like, it's almost like "here let me actually let you go through first." Like they are being so extra kind ... which is totally opposite of how I feel internally.... I would walk out of my home, I always felt that I was being stared at. And I remember the first time I was driving with the hijab and I had another car driving by me, and she was pointing at me. Like there's two women in the car and she was pointing at me, and was laughing at me.... You know, just like random things. And um, so like, I can't blend in because when I converted, all of a sudden, I felt every single eye on me every time that I wanted out of my home.... And Muslim women, when they wear hijab, [people] see that. Just like they see the color of your skin. And all of a sudden, I'm an outcast. (Emily, age 44)

Other participants explained that in public, they experienced an openly hostile attitude expressed by those they came into contact with. As one woman explained:

> So I've gotten, like I said, the stares, remarks, rude comments, laughing. You know, things like that. And I'll just say something sarcastic right back ... I was in CVS – no Rite Aid – and I was in back of a white guy who was maybe in his thirties. And he turned around and he said "we don't wear towels in America" in front of my children. (Reilly, age 37)

Two of the participants reported that they had suffered minor physical assaults while wearing hijab in public. One participant had an egg thrown at her outside of her new home, and another had a man attempt to rip her hijab off of her while she was riding the bus. One of the participants mentioned that she had more serious concerns for her physical safety, explaining:

> People would come up to me and scream at me, and just the vilest things. Walking down the street, people would roll down their window and "F this" and blah, blah, blah. The [Islamic Center of Savannah] was shot at and burned down during the time that I lived there. So it was – I felt betrayed. I might cry. I've never cried about this before. (Jessica, age 33)

Another participant explained that her marginalization by the surrounding community was also found in her interactions with medical and mental health counselors. Instead of having her overall mental health diagnosed, she felt that she actually was having her hijab diagnosed. As she intimated:

> When I would go to the doctor and when I would wear hijab, because I tried to get counseling because I felt like I needed counseling because I was getting angry. And I, I know I just needed to talk about it, and I thought I could go to the doctors to talk about it and they would right away ask me why I would wear the hijab, like changed my religion. They would diagnose me changing my identity, and you know act like there's something wrong. Like you can't change your religion without it being something wrong. (Sumaya, age 34)

Although many of the women talked about their own experiences of marginalization and victimization in the general community, a couple of the women reported that they were comforted by being stood up for when others were openly being rude or mocking them. As one woman intimated:

> It just happened so many times to me that people make snide comments and strangers behind me will tell them to shut up. I don't tell people to shut up, you know? So many people have defended me, I think that's finding the unity in Islam – that's not in Islam so much – but in finding the greater community around me in Americans. So I'm fortunate. This really is very good, very great. (Jena, age 26)

All of the participants in this study were acutely aware that their conversion to Islam set them up for marginalization and victimization from the surrounding community, particularly as Islamophobic sentiment increases and becomes more socially acceptable. The majority of the women in this study reported that they had experienced marginalization and victimization by the surrounding community, and while this was experienced differently from person to person, it is important to note that this marginalization and victimization spanned the range from antilocution to physical attack.

Subtheme 2d: By Employment
Although multiple participants discussed their fears about marginalization and victimization at the hands of their employer or their coworkers,

many of the women who discussed the role of marginalization in employment indicated that they felt that they had misjudged the acceptance and tolerance that they received. Alternately, one woman explained that the experiences she had in the workplace as a recent convert to Islam fell within the scope of the overarching sense of anti-Muslim sentiment that is occurring in the surrounding community. In her own words:

> I did get harassed at work, at more than one job. Because I am white, and I'm a convert to Islam. I would wear hijab and I would have people make direct comments to me, or they would go behind me and harass me, like cause problems for me at work, trying to sabotage my performance or make me look bad. I had people play jokes on me. (Sumaya, age 34)

The subtheme of victimization and marginalization by employment was not a theme which the participants spoke about in great depth. For the most part, when participants discussed the issue of how their conversion was received by their employers and colleagues, this discussion was cursory and revealed that they were surprised to have misjudged the responses they received. Because the fears regarding telling employers/colleagues was a recurrent theme for many of the participants, and the actual instances of feeling persecuted for the decision to convert to Islam as experienced and relayed by one participant, it is included in this research manuscript to help develop a well-rounded conceptualization of the varying ways in which the participants experienced victimization and marginalization.

Subtheme 2e: By the Muslim Community

Five of the participants in this study spoke about the Muslim community and their relationship with it. One of these participants spoke about how she was openly accepted into her local Muslim community and wanted to clarify that she did not experience any type of marginalization. Another one of the participants explained that she is mostly exposed to Muslim international students through the local college, and that they treat her as if she is a novelty. She stated:

> I don't want to say they're fascinated, but they're like "wow, we heard that there's American reverts, and now we know one" ... and "you make me love my faith more." (Nawal, age 59)

Four of the participants spoke specifically about the cliquishness of the Muslim community. As one woman reported:

> I'll stand out because I'm an American.... You know, during Ramadan everybody brings all their meals for – to celebrate *Iftar*, and I'm like, I'm – this will be my second full year at Ramadan – and I'm sitting here going "OK, well you're gonna be bringing Bosnian food, you're gonna bring all this, and do I bring like macaroni and cheese?" (Emily, age 44)

Another woman echoed these sentiments and focused on her exclusion stating:

> There are the converts from America, white people, mostly women. Then there's the women who are from Iraq or wherever the Muslim countries, and the feeling is like, they're judgmental. They're – They're better than you. And so it's not very welcoming. It's not like I can go to the mosque, at least the ones in my area. I can't go there and find a sister who will you know, take me under her wing and be my buddy, and help me with everything that I want to learn and know. (Amy Marie, age 45)

Similarly, another woman indicated that being subjected to the cliquishness of the Muslim community only exacerbated her overall feelings of marginalization. In her own words:

> I have to honestly say, more of the feedback that I get that is hurtful is from other Muslimahs, like other – especially Arab Muslimahs. Like they look at me almost in that cultural phenomenon of African American women that look at black men and white women, there's a stigma against it. I find it's also very alive and well in the Arab American community. Like "what she's doing marrying an Arab boy?" You know "wearing hijab?"...It's hard because you feel this distance all of a sudden from your own culture because you're publicly displaying something that isn't – and the culture that you thought was going to be that community that brings you – for the most part saying "oh no, that was nice of you to try, but this is *our* thing."...Do I think there's a place for me in the Palestinian American community as a Muslim here? I don't know that there is much of a place for me. I don't think that I'm ever gonna really be part of their community. I think I'm always gonna be married to a part of their community and be on the outside of that circle. (Jena, age 26)

Two participants in this study indicated that the cliquishness of their respective Muslim communities was even more alarming as they had been exploited by people within them, and they couldn't find support to help stop the exploitative behavior. One exemplary statement is as follows:

> So being a white convert and being a white Muslim convert, I'm being alienated. Or I feel like I'm being alienated from the Muslim community here. Cuz I'm white and a convert, and it gives people most people [the impression] that I work for the government. Which is not true.... I have been exploited. I feel like I have had people try to take advantage of me. It's like the [immigrant Muslim] lady who I came here [to help], her intent and purpose for me being here was for me to take over her organization, that's what she told me. And also to try to get me to marry somebody for a green-card. And um, her intention was to put me in trouble. To get me in trouble so she could cover [her illegal activity]. Or help her friend or whatever. And from my point of view she's, I feel like she's trying to sell me. (Sumaya, age 34)

Victimization, marginalization, and exploitation by the Muslim community were recurring themes for the majority of the participants in this study. This victimization, marginalization, and exploitation was cause for great concern for the participants in this study, as they felt that this only compounded and exacerbated the hostility that they face within the general public. For the women who experienced victimization and marginalization from the Muslim community, this victimization and marginalization had been unanticipated prior to their conversions, and they felt that it had exacerbated their issues of feeling isolated. It is important to note that this victimization and marginalization by the Muslim community spanned the range from antilocution to overt discrimination.

Subtheme 2f: By the Legal System
Although only three participants openly discussed how they had been marginalized in the legal system, this subtheme still requires acknowledgment as one of the ways in which the participants felt victimized or marginalized. Two of these women lost their children during custody battles that were partially fueled by their conversions to Islam. As one woman stated:

> My parents said that I needed supervised visits, ah the court appointed an attorney to my parents and the attorney was asking me if I believed Islam, if I believed in the Qur'an, if I believed in my husband having four wives, if I'm gonna force my kids to wear hijab. And also, they asked me if I support

Israel. And I was like "I don't know what the hell this has to do with me being a mom." (Sumaya, age 34)

The other woman likewise shared her situation of discrimination in the courts:

There was discrimination. Because I never even had a speeding ticket. I've never broken the law. I went to – in college, my major was [pertaining to law] . . . I have no record. I've never done anything wrong. And you know, I went to trial – it was supposed to just be my ex in front of the judge – and tell my story, and my ex showed up with an attorney. Which I found out, he of course got a credit card and went into debt to pay for – which in Islam you know [is not encouraged]. I paid off all my debt. I couldn't afford to buy it, but after the first day of trial, my mother realized uh oh, and offered to cut me a check and retain an attorney for me. Because I was completely unprepared. I went with my story and my speech . . . all of the anti-Islamic stuff my ex was posting on Facebook, all of the hate phone calls and voice-mails he would leave me, um there's this song about open season on Muslims, he would call my home and play it on my answering machine, so when I came home – all this stuff, I could not submit as evidence. (Lynn, age 39)

One woman reported that her husband had actively been involved with the FBI regarding his own nefarious behaviors and was actively exploiting her. She reported that the FBI was actively watching her movements, and that further, instead of being able to find help from law enforcement and protection against her husband's exploitation and abuse, she was instead marginalized and treated as collateral damage. In her own words:

They made a deal with him that he would search for terrorists online, do fake things in chat-rooms and stuff like that to try and find terrorist cells. And instead of doing the right thing – which is what every other American would have happen to them – he [should] have gone to prison and he would have been kicked out of the country. (Amy Marie, age 45)

Although only three participants openly discussed how they had been marginalized in the legal system, this subtheme still requires acknowledgment as one of the ways that the participants reported being victimized and marginalized. For the women who experienced victimization and marginalization from the legal system, this victimization and marginalization had been unanticipated and led to significant levels of stress.

Victimization and marginalization by the US legal system spanned the range from antilocution to covert discrimination.

Subtheme 2g: By the Media
All of the participants in this study spoke about the role of the media in perpetuating the marginalization of Muslims in America. As one participant explained:

> Here in America we have got the rapists, the murderers, the attacks and stuff like that. But when do we in America attach a religion to these criminals? We don't. We don't say the Baptist rapist, the Christian murderer, or whatever it is, you know? But it's very convenient to attach to these criminals the – the Muslim faith. (Amy Marie, age 45)

Another participant further reflected:

> The Christian drunk driver killed a family of four, they don't put Christian in there. But if it's a Muslim man, regardless of you know, it would be in the news. When most everyone is Christian, and you look at the police blotter in the newspaper, almost all of them are Christian, but they don't make the headlines, you know, sell papers. So I mean, even molesting priests don't even make the news anymore. It's all kept hush, hush. So it, again, yeah it's the media. (Lynn, age 39)

The participants in this study also indicated that although the media actively reproduces misrepresentations of Muslims in general, they also marginalize the American Muslim population; by stifling the voices of Muslim Americans, the media does not allow for the active reproduction of positive voices. The embodiment of this idea was shared by one participant as follows:

> Two percent of the Muslim population are creating such problems for the world. For Americans and American Muslims. They have terrorized us as well. And the media just ignoring, Ignoring the Sheiks and Imams – the people who say this isn't right, this isn't Islam. Just ignoring that and coming to say "where are the voices? Where are the Muslims?" saying that. We're here. We're trying. You won't let us. I felt betrayed in that I thought that I had freedom of religion, but I did not. (Jessica, age 33)

All of the participants expressed deep frustration over the way that they were represented and depicted in various forms of media. All of the participants felt that the media functioned in a way which perpetuated myths about Muslims and left little room for the introduction of more accurate representations to reshape the discourse.

THEME 4: AMBASSADORS OF ISLAM

The fourth theme to emerge was that of Ambassadors to Islam, in which all of the participants spoke about the various ways that they had served as representatives of Islam or educators about Islam. This theme serves to inform the research question of what impact does the increasingly hostile social climate toward Muslim Americans have on the spiritual, social, physical, and mental integration of the participants. It also serves to inform the research question of how conflict is experienced (and mitigated) between Caucasian female American converts to Islam and those around them. As one participant explained:

> I'm just smiling and trying to like, make people feel at ease. Just going into public and having to be Islam's representative, having to be the person that – kind of like the ambassador to, feelings of good will…I am an American. I never had to give that up to be a Muslim, and I never did give that up. I love my country, I love – I love the American people because there are so many good, even though I have seen a lot of bad. I know that there is good, you know? And I can't blame people who have been convinced to hate me, because they don't know. You know? And I am not a threat to you. I'm not. There's no reason to be frightened of me. (Jessica, age 33)

Some of the participants indicated that they frequently found that they were having to correct false assumptions about Islam. One exemplary statement regarding this correction of misconceptions and assumptions is as follows:

> They were like "oh my God, what did you do?" Like, "why did you do it?" "How can you cover?" They weren't vicious about it, they just had a lot of questions. So I had to explain myself over and over to everybody. And most of them said "oh my God, I couldn't do that, that's hard." And a lot of people would say "did you do it for a guy?" I get that all the time. "Did you do it for a man? Did you do it for a man?" Oh my God, how many times do I [hear]

that. "Do you cover because your husband makes you? Does your husband
beat you?" Oh my God, it's almost laughable at times. (Reilly, age 37)

Other participants explained that clarifying the separation between religion and culture helps to build and strengthen relationships. Further
educating the family on what Islam is and is not, and the process they
took during the conversion process was helpful to navigate the process of
renegotiating their relationships. As one participant reflected:

Just recently [I] went down to Florida, and actually went to see [my
brother], and he accepted me one hundred percent, and he was fine. Of
course he was asking me all kinds of questions. And my other brother who is
totally Christian, he's OK with me the way that I am, he doesn't have any
problem with me. My mom is one hundred percent [supportive]. She
doesn't know anything about it and she just wants to learn and understand.
(Emily, age 44)

All of the participants in this study reported feeling as if they were serving
as ambassadors of Islam since their respective conversions. For some of the
participants, this meant that they felt as if they were being perceived by
others as the token representative of Islam and therefore they needed to
behave accordingly. For others, this role of ambassador to Islam meant
that they were functioning in a role of Islamic educator to those around
them. For all of the participants in this study, serving as ambassadors to
Islam meant clarifying misconceptions and confronting stereotypes and
misunderstanding.

THEME 5: IMPACT OF MARGINALIZATION

In the final theme, all of participants discussed the impact that marginalization had on them. This final theme serves to inform all of the
research questions of this study, but most specifically how conflict is
experienced between Caucasian female American converts to Islam and
those around them, and how conflict is experienced within the selves
of Caucasian female American converts to Islam in post-9/11 America.
The theme of impact of marginalization can be broken into two
subthemes of emotional responses and coping strategies (see
Fig. 6.4). These subthemes are interconnected and work to inform
one another.

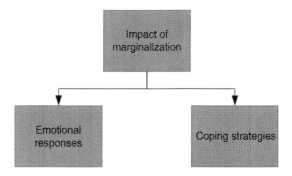

Fig. 6.4 Subthemes under impact of marginalization

Subtheme 1: Emotional Responses

All of the participants spoke about their emotional responses to the marginalization that they received due to their conversion to Islam. Emotional responses included loneliness and isolation. As one participant explained "It's got to do with all of your social connections. I was very much alone. But that's OK, because it allowed me to read and to really know what I believe and why" (Nawal, age 59). Another participant reflected on this isolation and loneliness stating "it's like, the most lonely existence ever. The only thing is, if I had to change anything over again, I would never change. It's just because the reward is so much bigger than everything here" (Emily, age 44).

Other participants experienced confusion, frustration, disappointment in those around them, and sadness. Speaking on the sadness, one participant explained:

> I had a man on the bus try to rip off my hijab. And I cried for weeks after it, you know? I just want to – I never thought it would happen, it makes me so much sadder at times, but you know? But, we say we pray for those people for peace, so they don't have to hurt anyone else. Because I have my peace. It's sad. (Jena, age 26)

Some of the participants indicated that due to levels of stress at various stages of the conversion process, they began to experience physical manifestations of that stress on their bodies. As one participant intimated, "I was under so much stress that I ended up losing my hair and all that kind of stuff" (Emily, age 44). Another participant reflected similarly:

I was very healthy before and all of a sudden, my health started deteriorating and I'm somebody who seems to cope with stress, but it was coming out in my health. And my last doctor said the reason why I'm having all these problems is because of the stress. (Sumaya, age 34)

All of the participants spoke about their emotional responses surrounding the turmoil that was created in their lives as they renegotiated their statuses. All participants reported feeling varying levels of sadness, frustration, isolation, disappointment, confusion, and stress. All participants also reported that although they experienced these negative feelings, they believed that the greater rewards of the afterlife made these negative emotions worthwhile in the end.

Subtheme 2: Coping Strategies

All of the participants spoke about their coping mechanisms for dealing with the sadness, frustration, isolation, disappointment, confusion, and stress. While some participants used an active approach of tackling perceived injustices head on, some of the participants chose to avoid situations that might increase these emotional responses. Some chose to seek out guidance and support from others who may have had the same experiences, others chose to avoid thinking about the negativity that they have encountered since their conversion altogether.

Although they handled their emotional responses differently, all of the women in this study indicated that they took great solace and found comfort in their faith and found that they were comforted through God. As one participant reflected:

I feel that this is definitely a touch from God, you know. I feel like it makes me a stronger person. It makes me realize that the only thing that's there for you is God. Because the way I make it through life is through Him. (Sumaya, age 34)

Similarly, another participant added:

If it wasn't for my faith, I would be, I think, suffering from severe depression. Absolutely. I am 100% sure of it. The only thing that seems to keep me together is my faith. Because I've seen people lose it for less. No, and who could have done this? I've gone from full-time mother 13 years, I can't imagine any woman having their children taken away like that wouldn't be devastated. And yeah it hurts, yeah I was upset, but I knew that it would get better at some point. Trust that God loves us, he doesn't allow bad things to happen to us without a purpose. I know that something in the end, waiting...he should be waiting for us. It should be great. (Lynn, age 39)

A third participant, who indicated that she struggled with depression and anxiety earlier in life, expanded on these thoughts, intimating:

[People] either become more withdrawn or they learn how to deal. And I think my faith has been a tool. And being a Muslim, a visible Muslim has helped me.... I think that this about me has been such a positive [thing]. Through understanding my faith and understanding the peace that comes with, how do you say it? Doing what I feel I was created to do – worship God and everything else comes through that – the spiritual aspect...the day to day aspect of being forced to do the scary things. And I think that's kind of been a really good exposure therapy for me. I've felt that I've been backed into a corner and being there with my faith, and understanding that lashing out is not gonna get me through, but having to figure out a way to be – to come out of that corner in a good and positive way. I think that has been positive – and you know your mental disorders will never go away. But I think my coping mechanisms that I've come across in the past 12 and a half years really [have] been profoundly helpful to me. (Jessica, age 33)

All of the participants in this study discussed their coping strategies for dealing with the negative emotional responses to the victimization and marginalization that they received due to their conversion to Islam. For all of the participants, while the coping strategies varied, the personal comfort that they garnered from God and their faith was palpable. In the end, all of the participants intimated that they were so soothed by the teachings of their faith that if they could travel back to the time immediately prior to their conversions to Islam with the information that they now know about the obstacles they had faced in the wake of their respective conversions, they would not have done anything differently.

The findings presented in this chapter speak to the general thematic issues that Caucasian female American converts to Islam in post-9/11 America have experienced. The essence of these phenomena is the renegotiation of status, and this essence was discussed by the participants in five distinct ways: (1) the role of personal choice, (2) identity, (3) experiences with marginalization and victimization, (4) serving as ambassadors of Islam, and (5) the impacts of marginalization. In the next chapter, the discussion of these findings will be presented and framed through the theoretical frameworks of prejudice, privilege, and hate. Using these theories, readers can better understand what it is like for these women as they navigate the change of religion which forced them to confront their status shift from majority to minority. From there, the limitations and implications of this study will be discussed.

CHAPTER 7

Discussion, Limitations, and Implications

The previous chapter presented the findings of this study regarding the shared lived experience of being a Caucasian female convert to Islam in post-9/11 America. This study revealed a variety of themes including the role of personal choice, identity, experiences with marginalization and victimization, serving as ambassadors of Islam, and the impacts of marginalization. Subthemes under the larger theme of marginalization and victimization included marginalization by parents/family, by friends, by employment, by surrounding community, by the legal system, and by the media. These subthemes exist because they represent the various conflict types and levels that were experienced by the participants.

The discussion presented in this chapter is framed through the theoretical frameworks of prejudice, privilege, and hate. Using these theoretical lenses, readers can better understand what it is like for these women to confront their status shift from majority to minority. The overarching essence of these phenomena of what it means to be a Caucasian female American convert to Islam in post-9/11 America is the renegotiation of status, and the various ways that this essence was relayed through phenomenological interviews will be discussed in depth following the same pattern of presentation as the previous chapter.

© The Author(s) 2017
A.M. Guimond, *Converting to Islam*,
DOI 10.1007/978-3-319-54250-8_7

THE ROLE OF PERSONAL CHOICE

All of the women in this study perceived a shift in their social position as they converted to Islam, indicative of the shift from being part of the social majority to now being a member of the social minority. At the same time, they also discussed the importance of personal choice in both the decision to convert and the decision to adopt hijab (which they understood would turn them into visible minorities).

In Converting

The women who participated in this study all expressed a passion for Islam and a deep resonation of Islamic teachings. Further, they all actively expressed that their personal choice to convert was informed through a process of inquiry in which they engaged in in-depth research regarding the teaching of Islam and a personal introspection of their own beliefs which is aligned with van Nieukerk's studies in The Netherlands.[1] All of the women shared the experience of finding that Islam greatly appealed to their intellect.

The shared experience of choice, as explained by the participants in this study, falls squarely within the discourse on religious conversion and also helps to better understand how religious conversion to Islam can be represented within the discourse on religious conversion. As Jansen explained, conversion as experienced can take on "a wide variety of forms and meanings, which can only be understood in the specific contexts and specific power relations of the individuals and groups involved."[2]

The emphasis on choice in conversion, as expressed by the participants in this study, supports Haddad's research that found that for many converts to Islam, conversion itself was not the initial purpose of investigating Islam,[3] and the research of Haddad et al. found that desire to marry a partner from the Muslim faith was also not a motivating factor into the inquiry and investigation of Islam.[4]

To varying degrees, all of the participants in this study referenced the process of unpacking culture from religion as they navigated their decision to convert. This appears to reflect research by Roald who found that many converts are faced with discerning which practices are those that are cultural and those which are religiously based.[5] Further, these participants in this study recognize that although the religious text remains the same, there are various different cultural practices that inform the way that Islam is to be practiced and interpreted, a finding that is consistent with the research developed by Kumar.[6]

In Covering

All of the women in this study spoke about choice while discussing their respective thought processes that went into deciding whether to adopt hijab. The concept of covering and the deep introspection surrounding the choice to cover that was illuminated through this study reflects the findings of Bullock who studied the role of the hijab in Canada and found that those who choose to cover are aware of the cultural implications and ramifications related to choosing an outward identifier of their Muslim faith.[7]

Though the stereotype is that Muslim women observe the hijab because they are being forced to by the men in their lives, all of the women who spoke about hijab indicated that their adoption of hijab had nothing to do with the men in their lives and was entirely a decision that they made on their own, a finding supported by Bullock[8] and Peek.[9] Further, the findings in this study relating to the role of personal choice in covering reflected the findings of Hughes[10] and Raouda,[11] who found that many Muslim women who choose to cover indicated that it is less about what they believe that Muslim women *should* do, and more about how they express themselves as Muslim women, and how they present their identity.

Identity

All of the participants in this study spoke about the theme of identity, although they each spoke about it in varying ways. This theme included the various ways that they changed and renegotiated their beliefs, changed their social practices, and how they saw themselves overall. Some of the participants found that the process of integrating practices of their new religion with their previous social practices was difficult. This caused them to enter into a long process of integrating their new practices with old, causing introspection over how they identified themselves in general.

A recurring subtheme in this study was that participants felt as if they were having people assign identities to them, identities which were perceived as being congruent within dominant Islamophobic discourse, yet had no basis in either the participants' belief systems or their philosophy on life. This mirrors the findings presented by Beiten and Allen who studied Arab American couples in the wake of September 11, 2001 and found that the couples felt "pressured to decide whether they are Arabs or Americans, with little room in between, resulting in feelings of frustration, confusion and anger."[12] Participants in this study reported that the American public was trying to highlight the mutual exclusivity of being Muslim and America, forcing a label on them. There was a rejection of the idea that they must choose between being American and Muslim, and the women were adamant that they did not have to choose from the two because they were still American while being Muslim.

Some of the participants discussed the perceived mutual exclusivity of being a feminist and a Muslim. They explained that prior to their conversion to Islam they were strong supporters of feminist issues. They wanted to be clear that there was no incongruence between being feminist and being Muslim. This concept corresponds with statements made in Ebrahimji's research that found that woman can straddle multiple group identities harmoniously, and that American Muslim women want to acknowledge that there isn't a mutual exclusivity toward being a Muslim and an American,[13] and that they the two are not at odds with one another or at odds with feminist thought process.

Finally, many of the participants in this study reported that they were aware of their new precarious social position as they experienced the shift from membership in the social majority to membership in the social minority. This supports Bullock's assertion that she herself had to navigate prejudice, racism, and discrimination as her privilege was stripped from her after conversion.[14]

Experiences with Marginalization and Victimization

All of the participants in this study reported that they had a twofold experience with being marginalized and victimized. All of the participants spoke about their strong desire to be seen and heard, and each had experienced marginalization and victimization from various sources (and to varying degrees). In all cases, the women in this study made statements to the effect that the process of marginalization and the inability to represent themselves and their own experiences within the general society are deeply interlaced.

Wanting to be Seen and Heard

All of the participants in this study felt that they were unrepresented or underrepresented in the issues that specifically pertain to them as Muslims and as Caucasian female American converts to Islam. Instead, the participants felt that they were either being completely ignored in the discourse, or that people were making gross overgeneralizations about who they are and what their unique needs are. This reflects the findings of Hammer who noted that women in Islam are "not spoken to, but rather spoken about, a common feature of much of the Islamophobic discourse as we have seen it reincarnate in various forms over the last decade."[15] In this study, the participants wanted the opportunity to speak for themselves, which Kumar,[16] Bullock,[17] and Sheehi[18] all indicated would be paramount in reshaping the orientalist-based unsubstantiated claims about how women were being tyrannized at the hands of their male counterparts, as well as help to combat the socially accepted treatment of Muslims that is rooted in a feigned objectivity toward Islam which is deeply rooted in xenophobia. The findings in this study regarding the participants' desire to be seen and heard are also reflective of Haddad et al.'s finding that Muslims (regardless of their nationality or immigrant status) are being excluded from discussions relating to their community, and the expressed concerns that Muslim voices are excluded from task forces that are specifically designed to address violence against women.[19]

At a personal level, the women in this study wanted the opportunity to be seen as more than just their headscarves and were frustrated that they were seemingly excluded from even the debates over whether headscarves should be permitted or not. This closely mirrors the research presented by Abdul-Ghafur,[20] Bullock,[21] and Yousuf-Sadiq.[22] Finally, at the societal level, the women in this study expressed great frustration over a lack of representation and not having the space to be seen or heard, which was also noted by Ebrahimji and Suratwala.[23]

Marginalization and Victimization as Experienced

All of the participants in this study reported experiencing covert and overt marginalization and victimization from various sources. These experiences of marginalization fall within Allport's continuum for prejudice which states that there are five levels of prejudice: (1) antilocution, (2) avoidance,

(3) discrimination, (4) physical attack, and (5) extermination.[24] The participants in this study experienced the first four of these levels but none stated feeling as if they were personally being actively pursued for extermination. It is important to note that during the writing of this manuscript, just over 2 years after the interview portion of this research concluded, I made contact with some of the participants in this study. These participants indicated that they feared for their safety during the 2015–2016 Republican Primary and as the then Republican presidential hopeful Donald Trump's political campaign gathered support through an increase of Islamophobic rhetoric. Despite the fact that Mr. Trump officially stated in March 2016 that he was not in favor of internment camps for Muslims in the United States, the participants that I spoke with during the Summer of 2016 remained fearful that we were moving toward policy that would isolate Muslim Americans and bring the United States one step closer to a society that would allow for extermination. In the weeks after the 2016 election, President-elect Donald Trump and his advisors once again appeared to be doubling down on their ideas of registries for Muslims in the United States, but only time will tell what will happen next.

The participant's experiences with marginalization and victimization reflect the findings of Eletreby who studied the phenomenology of being a black male who converted to Islam.[25] Eletreby found that participants, "experienced, indirectly, religiously driven racism. As white, male allies, they witnessed xenophobia directed at friends, spouses, and family members, they are able to hear anti-Muslim sentiment from coworkers unaware of their religious identities."[26] These were the same anti-Muslim sentiments that participants in this study expressed.

The findings in this study regarding how the participants experienced marginalization and victimization also directly reflect van Nieuwkerk's Dutch study which found that "female conversion to Islam summons up particularly fierce battles because gender issues have been pivotal in the construction of otherness between 'Islam' and the 'West'. Female converts are thus regularly treated with hostility."[27] In a similar study in Germany, Özyürek also found that white converts to Islam experienced othering and exclusion from relationships that had existed prior to their conversions.[28]

Some of the participants in this study noted that the choice of adopting the hijab and thus adopting the visible identifiers of minority status as a Muslim caused an increase of friction in their encounters with others. This finding is reflective of the findings of Bullock[29] and Jawad.[30]

It should be noted that half of the participants in this study spoke about the cliquishness of their local Muslim community and discussed how they felt that this exclusion further compounded their feelings of being marginalized. These women struggled to figure out their social placement within both the mainstream American community and their local Muslim community. The statements made to this extent directly reflect the findings of Karim who found that converts are left feeling as if they no longer fit in amongst their old or their new communities and are left straddling the two.[31]

SERVING AS AMBASSADORS OF ISLAM

In one way or another, all of the women in this study expressed that they were serving as ambassadors of Islam. For some of the participants, this ambassadorship was evident in their strong desire to help educate others on what Islam is and is not. The findings of this study are congruent with Abdo's findings that women within the Muslim community – whether they are converts or born-Muslims – are diligently working to highlight the differences between the Qur'anic doctrine that emphasizes equality and patriarchal cultural practices,[32] thus working to undo generations of androcentrist attitudes.

Other participants found that they served as ambassadors to Islam through their defending of their decision to convert and having to explain their conversion to those around them. These findings are aligned with the findings of van Nieuwkerk's Dutch study, where it was found that recent Caucasian female converts to Islam frequently act as both defenders of their choice to convert, but also as defenders of their newly established Muslim identity.[33]

Other participants in this study reported that they served as an ambassador to Islam every time they left the house because they were perceived to be representations of the greater community of Muslim women, which appears to be congruent with Major and Vick's assertion that those in minority status are concerned by *stereotype threat* – a term developed to discuss the "psychological predicament that occurs when people are aware of the negative stereotypes that others hold of their social group and are anxious that they may confirm them, either in their own or others eyes."[34]

The Impact of Marginalization

In the final theme, all participants discussed the impact that marginalization had on them. This theme is broken into two subthemes of emotional responses and coping strategies. These subthemes are interconnected and work to inform one another.

Emotional Responses

All of the participants in this study discussed their emotional responses to the marginalization that they received due to their Conversion to Islam. These emotional responses included sadness, frustration, confusion, stress, disappointment in others, anxiety, loneliness, and isolation. Some of the participants intimated that their emotional responses to their conversion experiences were so severe that they began to experience physical manifestations of that stress on their bodies. As Abdo indicated, these factors can contribute to social conflict as experienced through the conversion process.[35] Further, these findings regarding emotional responses are congruent with Anway's study which found that "disillusionment, confusion, unanswered questions – these describe the early religious experience of many women."[36]

Coping Strategies

All of the participants in this study spoke about their coping mechanisms for dealing with the sadness, frustration, confusion, disappointment in others, stress, anxiety, loneliness, and isolation that have come about since they entered into the conversion process. While some participants used an active approach of tackling perceived injustices head on, some of the participants chose to avoid situations that might increase these emotional responses. Some participants chose to seek out guidance and support from others who may have had the same experiences, while other participants chose to altogether avoid thinking about the negativity that they have encountered since their conversion.

This is reflective of Allport's assertion that coping strategies for dealing with the emotional responses to prejudice appear to vary depending on the individual's own personal history and the overarching social context that they are exposed to.[37] Further, the findings of this study reflect the coping strategies that were found to be utilized in Faur's study of families are marginalized and victimized due to their religious identity of Paganism.[38] Faur found that participants in her study had four ways that they approached being marginalized: "(1) fighting back, (2) reasons for fighting back, (3) not accepting blame, and (4) stand up for own culture/be 'oppositional;'" and there were five ways that participants avoided situations: "(1) general avoidance of thoughts, (2) ignore people who discriminate, (3) avoiding actions which might precipitate prejudice, (4) rejecting American identity, and (5) avoiding people who discriminate."[39] All of these fight or flight approaches were mentioned by the participants in this study.

Although each of the participants in this study had a different way of handling their emotional responses and approached situations which they were being marginalized or victimized, all of the women in this study indicated that they took great solace and found comfort in their faith. They each indicated that they were deeply comforted through God and the teachings of Islam. Despite marginalization and victimization, and despite poor emotional responses (due to sadness, frustration, confusion, stress, disappointment in others, anxiety, loneliness, and isolation), the findings of this study indicate that the participants had overall positive experiences with the conversion process and post-conversion life and believe that any negative emotional responses helped to build their respective characters and faiths.

A ROAD MAP TO UNDERSTANDING THE CONFLICT

The conflicts experienced by the Caucasian female American who has converted to Islam in post-9/11 America are of grave importance, and understanding the way that these conflicts manifest and the roles that they serve is paramount. For the purpose of this discussion, it is important to remember that conflict has been defined by Wilmot and Hocker, external conflict is defined as being an "expressed struggle between at least two interdependent parties who perceive incompatible goals, scarce resources, and interference from others in achieving their goals."[40] Similarly, internal conflict would be the personal struggle between two seemingly incongruent interdependent feelings or thoughts. Although people experience internal and external conflicts differently, conflict is an inevitable part of the human existence which can help change our trajectory.

Conflict falls into one of two categories: expressive or instrumental.[41] Expressive conflicts are those which generally manifest from a desire to express and discharge frustrations, tensions, and negative emotions; while instrumental conflicts manifest for the purpose of creating a means to the ends (or in the pursuit of alternative outcomes).[42] This study found that the conflicts as experienced by Caucasian female Americans who have converted to Islam since September 11, 2001 are both expressive and instrumental, varying based on the source and directionality of the conflict behaviors. When analyzed through a holistic lens including the larger societal structure and the positionality of the self, we can develop a pictorial representation of this conflict including both the expressive and instrumental (see Fig. 7.1).

The map of conflict as experienced by Caucasian female American converts to Islam in post-9/11 America (Fig. 7.1) illustrates how an individual (notated as *self*) is surrounded by circles representing each type of influence that they come into contact with as they navigate through their daily lives (parents/family, friends, employment, surrounding community, the legal system, and the media). At this level, the conflicts that the Caucasian female American convert to Islam faces are expressive in nature. The individual experiences marginalization and victimization due to increased tensions and frustrations on the part of the general public regarding the tragedy of September 11, 2001, the Boston Marathon Bombing, and other similar atrocities that people claiming an affiliation to Islam have committed. These tensions and frustrations are stoked in part by much larger Institutional machine, which has been labeled "structural system." Within the individual, as conflict increases with each of the individual's societal influences, conflict within the self-increases. This increased internal conflict triggers reactionary emotional responses and an implementation of coping strategies.

At the outermost level of this diagram of the conflicts as experienced by the women in this study, we have the structural system. The structural system includes the national policies and procedures which have been set up in order to marginalize Muslim and Arab Americans, including programs such as USA PATRIOT and NSEERS. At this level, the conflicts are instrumental in nature in that they serve to help further both domestic and international political initiatives. The arrows from the outer circle representing the structural system are representative of the pressure that comes from the top-down and helps to influence the feelings and stoke the embers of underlying tension and hostilities toward the Muslim American population.

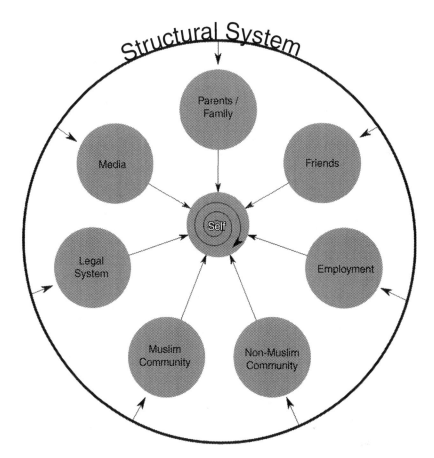

Fig. 7.1 Map of conflict as experienced by Caucasian female American converts to Islam in post-9/11 America

LIMITATIONS

It is important to remember that this study was not without limitations. One of the most oft cited limitations in phenomenological research has to do with the biases that the researcher brings to the study. While I acknowledged my previous experiences with this specific phenomenon in as concise and transparent way as possible, I also recognize that despite the bracketing process, there is always a possibility – however minor – that my own beliefs and personal history could have influenced my analysis of the data. To reduce these limitations, I employed a vigorous series of member and peer-checking opportunities. Reception of early analysis of the data by both the participants in the study and peers in the field of social sciences has confirmed that this limitation has been accounted for.

A limitation presented itself quite early during the research design, while defining the terms white and Caucasian. I am acutely aware that the term white or Caucasian is a somewhat socially constructed identifier. Defining these terms was more difficult than one might imagine, but ultimately I relied on whether a person looking at them would reasonably believe that could be categorized as white or Caucasian, and I simultaneously ensured the participants self-identified themselves as white or Caucasian for the purposes of their inclusion in the study. I did not make any efforts to verify their affiliation with this group, and at the end of the day, I believe that this limitation was managed fairly thoroughly.

Another limitation of this study was related to the sample itself. The sample in this study consisted of eight participants, and although the participants provided enough information to achieve data saturation and help us better understand their experiences with this phenomenon, we must remain cognizant that the findings of this study cannot be applied to the entire population of Caucasian female American converts to Islam. It should also be noted that all of the participants in this study reported coming from variances of a Christ-based dogma, with six of the participants identifying with a rearing that was aligned with Catholicism. The research design did not call for the participants to come from specific religious upbringings, and this proclivity toward Catholicism was an unpredicted phenomenon, but it is worth noting in the limitations of this study. It is possible that the experiences of participants hailing from non-Christ-based religious upbringings might have been relayed in a different manner. Further, participant's actual experiences with the conversion process might as well as the interpretation and internalization of said conversion process might have been different had they hailed from a wider scope of religious foundation (e.g., Buddhism, Hinduism, Judaism, Atheism, etc.).

It should also be noted that within the sample population, only one participant was under the age of 30 years, and no participant was under the age of 26 years at the time of this study. While participation criteria allowed any Caucasian American woman over the age of 18 who had experienced this phenomenon to participate, interestingly, nobody under the age of 26 years even responded to my requests for participation. While unintended, this proved quite valuable in terms of my own conceptualization and analysis of the presented data. It is a distinct possibility that having a higher mean and median age as beneficial because it focused on developmentally mature reasoning. Current literature on mental maturity suggests that the full development of the prefrontal cortex does not happen until the age of 24 or 25; thus, the cognitive maturity may not be evident.[43] Because it has been suggested that those who have fully developed brain connections are less likely to be swayed by emotions, those over the age of maturity in the prefrontal cortex may are said to be less impulsive in their decision-making processes and more likely to follow through with their long-term commitments (i.e., the commitment to follow another religious path and engage in the arduous conversion process). While this research was designed to include the experiences of Caucasian female American converts to Islam at any age, ultimately I recognize that it was the *mature* conversion experiences and processes that this research was aimed to illuminate.

In addition, I also had to recognize that while I elicited participation from many people within the target demographic, I received a number of declinations to participate stating that they were afraid that I would marginalize them, or that their recordings would be given to the government or otherwise used for unintended reasons. For this reason, the sample population consisted only of women who believed that the value of having the opportunity to have their voices be heard outweighed their fears that this study would be used as a tool for marginalizing and victimizing them further. How different might the stories be had they come from a demographic that was not already feeling as if they were being targeted for hatred and discriminatory practices?

All of the limitations pertaining to the sample population could be explored in future research. These other areas of research might include studies of the conversion experiences of Caucasian American women who came from non-Christ-based religious upbringings, the study of the conversion experiences of non-Caucasian American women, and even the conversion experiences of Caucasian American males. To tackle the fear of marginalization that was evidenced by the poor response levels to request for participation, alternate data collection methods could be used which might inform a quantitative analysis of the prevalence of the five thematic findings of this study. Alternately, future grounded theory studies could be aimed at understanding how relationships are affected for Caucasian female Americans who have converted since September 11. Further study might also focus on the efficacy of intervention strategies for women dealing with the ramifications of Islamophobia. Finally, with the constantly changing social climate and the increase of Islamophobia, it is possible that longitudinal studies might be of great benefit. These possible areas for future research are greatly needed to inform the development of supportive programming to assist with their various levels of emotional responses experienced by these women.

IMPLICATIONS AND CONCLUSION

This study has contributed significantly to the current literature where there is a threefold deficit. At present, female Muslims are significantly underrepresented in the literature, conversion to Islam since September 11, 2001 has been grossly understudied, and studies of the nonimmigrant American Muslim experience are quite notably lacking. If research is reflective of the interests of the general population, it should set off alarm bells in the academy that media pundits (and other talking heads) devote such a large amount of time speaking about the Muslim community without having adequate social science research to support the claims that they make. The absence of the Muslim voice sends the unspoken message that this community is not worthy of research and perpetuates the prevailing negatively charged dominant discourse. Despite the limitations of this study, and a need for further in-depth research, there are several implications for this study that may prove useful to both the academy and policy makers. This research manuscript concludes with a general summarization of the key implications of this research.

It is important to recognize that the women in this study experienced victimization and marginalization at varying levels, and they clearly articulated a desire for increased recognition and protection. As Islamophobia increases and remains unchecked, the more socially acceptable it becomes – thus increasing the likelihood that we will see a greater amount of incidents which fall on Allport's scale of prejudice,[44] including an increase in assaults toward these women. These women are a cog in the wheel of ongoing dehumanization, othering, and demonization of Muslims in America and it would not be irresponsible to suggest that if left unchecked, extermination could be an outcome. As policy makers, we cannot turn a blind eye to the marginalization of Caucasian female American converts to Islam, and we certainly cannot allow them to become casualties of the politics that Islamophobia fuels and is fueled by.

The Caucasian female American converts in this study found themselves caught straddling identities with one foot planted in a culture that rejects them, and for many, the other foot planted in a receiving culture that is less than welcoming to them. The women in this demographic have differing needs than other minority groups, and because they constantly have to face and deal with misconceptions regarding both their faith as Muslims and their national identity as Americans, they find themselves on the margins of society. The reality is that globally, conversion to Islam is happening at an astonishing rate, and this means that the face of Islam is changing as well. At the national level, conversion to Islam is increasing in the Caucasian demographic, and we can anticipate in the years to come that more women will find themselves facing the themes that this study presented. For this reason, there is a social urgency in further research on their experiences which can be used to help develop strategies for how to support them and their unique needs.

Finally, the findings of this study imply that the cultural acceptance of the absence of voices representing the Caucasian female American Convert to Islam helps to perpetuate the marginalization of this demographic. By not providing the opportunity for these women to be heard, they are excluded from the opportunity to help reshape the discourse that specifically pertains to them. The women in this study desired the opportunity to speak for themselves and actively engage in creating an alternate discourse, and this study offered them the platform (albeit a small platform) to help others better understand their experiences. During the member-checking stage of analysis, I was told by nearly all of the participants that they were grateful that I chose them to participate, and they were thankful that there are people who are assisting them to create the space at the proverbial table to discuss issues that are of great importance to them. This indicates that culturally we must shift the dynamic of the discourse surrounding Caucasian American Muslim women from one of distrust and fear to one of understanding and acceptance. As academics, policy makers, and activists, we must work toward allowing the voices of these women to come forward so that we are speaking *with* them, rather than *about* them.

In better understanding the experiences of Caucasian female Americans who have converted to Islam in post-9/11 America, we have explored the ways in which conflict is experienced by these women in a twofold manner. This study shows the way that these women experience the phenomena of prejudice and discrimination as they shift from majority to minority in terms of social status, and how they experience both expressive and instrumental conflict that results from the societal acceptance of Islamophobia. This study is significant to the field of conflict analysis and resolution because it highlights the experiences of the women in this target demographic and personifies them. Because many American Muslims are reporting that they have been subjected to classification, symbolization, dehumanization, organization, polarization (which are the first five stages of the eight recognized stages in genocide studies[45]), it is paramount that we intervene and work to offset the hatred intrinsic in Islamophobic discourse before we progress toward a societal belief that preparation, extermination, and denial are reasonable outcomes.

NOTES

1. Karin van Nieuwkerk, Introduction to *Women Embracing Islam*.
2. Willy Jansen, "Two Contested Concepts," p. IX.
3. Yvonne Yazbeck Haddad, "The Quest for Peace in Submission."
4. Yvonne Yazbeck Haddad, Jane I. Smith, and Kathleen M. Moore, *Muslim Women in North America*.
5. Anne Sofie Roald, "The Shaping of a Scandinavian 'Islam.'"
6. Deepa Kumar, *Islamophobia and the Politics of Empire*.
7. Katherine Bullock, *Rethinking Muslim Women*.
8. Ibid.
9. Lori Peek, *Behind the Backlash*.
10. Aaron W. Hughes, *Muslim Identities*.
11. Najwa Raouda, *The Feminine Voice of Islam*.
12. Ben K. Beiten and Katherine R. Allen, "Relisiance in Arab American Couples," p. 263.
13. Maria M. Ebrahimji, "In Search of Fatima and Taqwa."
14. Katherine Bullock, *Rethinking Muslim Women*, p. xxiv.
15. Juliane Hammer, "Center Stage," p. 116.
16. Deepa Kumar, *Islamophobia and the Politics of Empire*.
17. Katherine Bullock, *Rethinking Muslim Women*.
18. Stephen Sheehi, *Islamophobia: The Ideological Campaign*.
19. Yvonne Yazbeck Haddad, Jane I. Smith, and Kathleen M. Moore, *Muslim Women in North America*.
20. Saleemah Abdul-Ghafur, Introduction to *Living Islam Outloud*.
21. Katherine Bullock, *Rethinking Muslim Women*.
22. Nousheen Yousuf-Sadiq, "Half and Half."
23. Maria M. Ebrahimji and Zahra T. Suratwala, Introduction to *I Speak for Myself*.

24. Gordon W. Allport, *The Nature of Prejudice.*
25. Dina M. Eletreby, "Conversion Experiences of Three White American Muslim Males: The Impact of Centering and De-centering Forces" (doctoral dissertation, Chapman University, 2010).
26. Ibid.p. 257.
27. Karin van Nieuwkerk, Introduction to *Women Embracing Islam,* p. 1.
28. Esra Özyürek, "German Converts to Islam."
29. Katherine Bullock, *Rethinking Muslim Women.*
30. Haifaa Jawad, "Female Conversion to Islam."
31. Jamillah Karim, *American Muslim Women.*
32. Geneive Abdo, *Mecca and the Main Street.*
33. Karin van Nieuwkerk, "Gender, Conversion, and Islam."
34. Brenda Major and S. Brooke Vick, "The Psychological Impact of Prejudice," p. 142.
35. Geneive Abdo, *Mecca and the Main Street.*
36. Carol L. Anway, *Daughters of Another Path,* p. 14.
37. Gordon W. Allport, *The Nature of Prejudice.*
38. Adriana Faur, "Analysis of Cultural Discrimination Stress."
39. Ibid., p. 110.
40. William W. Wilmot and Joyce L. Hocker, *Interpersonal Conflict,* p. 9.
41. David W. Augsburger, *Conflict Mediation Across Cultures.*
42. Ibid.
43. Tony Cox, *Brain Maturity Extends Well Beyond Teen Years,* National Public Radio, October 10, 2011, http://n.pr/18Bzqo9.; Tim Elmore, "The Marks of Maturity," *Psychology Today,* November 14, 2012, http://bit.ly/1oqrCr3.
44. Gordon W. Allport, *The Nature of Prejudice.*
45. Gregory H. Stanton, "The Eight Stages of Genocide."

INDIVIDUAL TEXTURAL DESCRIPTIONS

REILLY

Reilly is a 37-year-old woman from urban Pennsylvania who was raised in a Catholic home. When asked about her religious upbringing, Reilly spoke in sweeping terms about the religious identities of her family and her mother's role in her religious life, instead of her own identification with Catholicism. In her young years, Reilly was placed in a Catholic home for children for 2 years, and this exposure taught her how to practice the faith; however, she always questioned the teachings. Reilly identified as being a seeker of spirituality and religious grounding her entire life. "I was always a seeker" Reilly reported, "I searched, I think I read about just about every type of religion, including maybe non-religion if you want to include it or call it, like you know Atheism. Some people think that's a religion, some people don't. But I searched. I searched just about everything."

Reilly had never met any Muslims before she began working in an apartment complex when she was 30 years old. In her position at the apartment complex, she came into frequent contact with five Muslims who also worked with her. She began to engage in religious dialogue with them so that she could better understand their religious beliefs and practices, and their responses led her to begin a process of active inquiry into Islam as a personal decision for herself. Reilly indicated that when reading about Islam and learning more about Islam through interactions with her colleagues that the information "kind of clicked for me" and it "kind of made sense, kinda the principles I agreed with."

© The Author(s) 2017
A.M. Guimond, *Converting to Islam*,
DOI 10.1007/978-3-319-54250-8

Coming out as Muslim to her family was a somewhat natural process to Reilly. She indicated that her family was shocked, but that this shock wasn't negative as much as surprising. She indicated that conversations included "where did this come from? But not a bad shock like *oh my God, that's horrible*, so like kind of asking me a lot of questions, you know." In this role, Reilly served as an educator on Islam in helping her family to better understand the process that led to her conversion, as well as how Islam personally resonated with her. Reilly also reported that she felt that her family has been holding her to a higher standard since her conversion and subsequent adoption of hijab, and that her conversion has been used against her. She reported, "there's been arguments between me and my mother that have nothing to do with religion. But the religion will always be brought into it."

In terms of her relationships with friends, Reilly found herself having to explain and clarify her motives for her conversion but "they weren't vicious about it, they just had a lot of questions. So I had to explain myself over and over and over to everybody." Many of the questions have been surrounding the perception that she converted for a man or that she dresses with modesty because she is forced to, and this greatly saddens her. In her role with her friends, Reilly finds herself educating about the misconceptions of Islam, as well as defending her own choice for converting.

The experiences Reilly has had with the general community have been far less innocuous than that with her family or friends. Reilly reports that she has been stared at in public, mocked and laughed at, and been subjected to rude comments. Reilly explained that one time at Rite Aid with her young children, a Caucasian man in his 30s "turned around and he said *we don't wear towels in America*."

Reilly believes that the media plays a large role in shaping the attitudes of the general American public, and actively participates in the marginalization of Muslims. She reported, "Americans have that perception of Muslims because the media, television, radio, movies, whatever have you . . . that's the way they give off the impression. So naturally, that's what people are going to see. And they trust our government, and they trust the United States, and you know everything is hunky dorey, so that must be the truth."

Throughout the conversion process, Reilly has felt sadness, frustration, and isolation, but she attributes her coping strategies to her passion and love for Islam, using sarcastic or avoidant conflict resolution styles, and relying on her own personal toughness. In talking about how she responded to rude or disrespectful comments, Reilly said, "I pick and choose my battles, I guess. You know? I don't like go full-fledged and freak out on someone, but you know. If the comment is rude enough I'll say something back." She further indicated that if the rude or disrespectful comments happen in front of her children, she is less likely to ignore the situation.

When asked whether she would prefer a traditionally American pseudonym or a more Qur'anically based pseudonym, Reilly was very quick to choose an American one. She stated, "I would say American. Because I haven't, I haven't dropped my culture. I'm just following a religion that's different from some of my culture. But um, I would say American. The reason, and like I said, that reason is because I still identify myself [as American]."

NAWAL

Nawal is a 59-year-old woman from urban Minnesota who was raised in a Catholic home, and who ultimately suggested that she be given a Qur'anically based pseudonym. When asked about her religious upbringing, Nawal spoke in concise statements about her own belief system and her own religious understanding. When indicating that she and her family were Catholic, it was clear that for her, Catholicism was not only a religious identity but encompassed a larger cultural component as well. She indicated that she was also considered the most pious and modest member of her family, always seeking to have a good relationship with God. She left the Catholic Church after high school and subsequently moving away from home. After she was married, she and her husband engaged in a seeking process to find a church, and they explored Lutheran and Baptist denominations before finding their spiritual home in a Born-Again Baptist community. While involved in this Born-Again community, Nawal took on an active leadership role within the church, teaching Sunday school and vacation Bible school, and leading children's youth group. She indicated that at this church, she "did everything but sing in the choir."

Nawal indicated that she was exposed to Islam during two trips to Israel/Palestine. As she explained later, clarifying the story she told through her interview process, "Both [were] self-guided tours (rental car, GPS & a map) with another Sunday School teacher to tour the Holy Land. As I reflected on the people we interacted with on the first trip, the

Muslim business owners were the most polite and helpful during our travel. In fact, I later found it difficult to believe that they were the Muslims [that] I had been told were *the enemy to Jesus*. On the second trip we connected again with the [same] Muslim [man]... because we remembered his passion." With her experiences with this man, "there was like a depth of what he had to say about God. I was like wow, this is missing in my life, how – how? There was just like this depth in it that I was missing. It was after the second trip that my husband died and I returned to live in Minnesota. The trips to Palestine was my first contact with the Muslim world beyond the mainstream media, evangelical literature, and sermons."

When she returned home after her trips to the Middle East, Nawal began to engage in a process of active inquiry into Islam, she indicated that she spent an exhaustive amount of time reading and downloading texts online, and questioning everything she had been taught in her religious life prior to the trips. During the inquiry process, Nawal had to unpack her internalized Islamophobia and stated, "of course I had all that Islamophobia that I hadn't – that I had to get rid of so to speak, or to put in order." In the end, Islam appealed to Nawal's logic and resonated with her beliefs. She reported, "and when I realized that, I still get goosebumps. When I realized that, only God of Creations could have dictated that. That, being the timing of the five daily prayers. That was the straw that broke the camel's back – as my reading had explained the truth in the Islamic claim that the Christian Bible was not in its original form and not reliable as the infallible word of God. And no one in the desert could have realized that something like 1400 years ago. So right then and there, I realized that Islam was the truth and it frightened me. Because I thought, well what do I do now?"

Coming out as a Muslim to her family and friends was such a dread-filled process that Nawal chose to instead not share her religious conversion in order to keep the peace within these relationships. Nawal reported a story of her mother that highlighted the reason that she chose to keep her conversion private. She reported, "I was overseas for a little while, and when I was in Jordan. And if you didn't put some type of scarf on your head, whether its wrapped tight or casually, you were judged. You know, just like you know Muslims are judged here, without a scarf in Islamic countries, you are looked at... I just casually had it on my head, and it was cold so I had a scarf on. Anyway, my mom saw that picture and she said *'Oh My GOD!! You are wearing a scarf!'* And she just came unglued. And

I thought, well I'm not saying- I wasn't even a Muslim yet, and it's like *well I'm not saying nothing.*"

For the most part, Nawal has only recently chosen to wear hijab because she feels that she would be hypocritical if she only wore hijab part of the time. To keep the peace with her family, she does continue to remove it in front of immediate family and her 85-year-old mother whom she is the primary caregiver for. As she intimated, "when I need to go to her, I just take my scarf off before I get there." Nawal is still in the process of coming out and being perceived as Muslim by the surrounding community, and she indicated that she is fearful of judgment and fearful of prejudices. She later clarified, "I am finding most people very polite and even experienced a question about why wearing the scarf from a clerk at Target; and the manager at my apartment – who abides by my former Christian beliefs – recently referred to me as a *good friend* – this after knowing me 16 months without scarf and 3 months with scarf." She made it clear that covering is a personal choice, and that it represents "what I believe. And I wear it because I am obeying God."

The majority of Nawal's social circle is immigrant Muslims who she has met through the local college. She indicated that she serves to help not only her friends with navigating American cultures but also that her immigrant friends treat her with awe and respect. She explained the relationship with her immigrant friends by saying, "I don't want to say they're fascinated, but they're like *wow, we heard that there's American reverts, and now we know one . . .* and *you make me love my faith more.*"

Nawal believes that the media plays a large role in shaping the attitudes of the general American public, and actively participates in the marginalization of Muslims. She reported that her family's attitudes regarding Islam can be traced directly back to the media and that her mother and those like her could not believe, understand, or accept that the evening news and "The Church" could lie to her.

Throughout the conversion process, Nawal has felt isolation and loneliness, but she attributes her coping strategies to her passion and love for Islam. To cope with this isolation and loneliness, she uses the time alone to her advantage. She indicated, "I was very much alone. But that's OK because it allowed me to read and to really know what I believe and why. So um, I am thankful to Allah that I was alone and I would read what I wanted to and I wasn't you know, forced to go out and do anything. Even though I was lonely sometimes, that's OK. I wasn't influenced by people."

In the end, Nawal wants the opportunity to be seen and heard, rather than be spoken for. She reported quite vehemently, "America is so focused on the scarf and its like oh, for God's sake. Why not be concerned about what I believe and why? You know? Why don't you think about God? Why don't you go find out what it is I believe, instead of being angry or being whatever it is you're thinking because somebody else told you? It's like, I was in their shoes you know? Six years ago, I was just like them."

EMILY

Emily is a 44-year-old woman from suburban New Hampshire who was raised Christian. When asked about her religion of origin, Emily spoke specifically about her own place within her religious upbringing and within her family, rather than a general discussion of the role of religious life in her family. By the time she was 16 years old, her family had explored a variety of religious theologies including Lutheranism, Mormonism, and Presbyterianism. In her young-adult life, Emily strayed away from religion until she was about 25 years old, and she felt that she was drawn back toward Christianity. At her Christian church, she became active in a leadership role and headed the ministry of missions. As she was preparing for her missions trip, she believed she needed to better understand the religions in the region she was traveling to. Emily stated, "I started to think, OK so now I am gonna go to a different country, I have to speak against other religions, am I going to actually be able to know the difference?" And thus her inquiry into Islam began.

This research and inquiry into Islam coincided with a struggling relationship with her husband and feelings that she later interpreted were ostracism from the church. Emily indicated, "I was researching Islam to understand more about that as I was still leading the group and missions in the church. The church decided that they did not like me anymore because of the fact that I was having problems in my relationship, therefore I stopped going altogether. Kind of like – they kicked me out." Her research into Islam continued and she actively engaged in seeking knowledge, through books, articles, websites, and networking. Emily intimated that through her research, there was an appeal to logic and an overarching sense of peace with the idea of converting. Of her first time visiting a mosque, she reported, "I felt completely at peace, and that I – this was my home for the rest of my life."

Emily anticipated shunning and backlash from her friends and family when she revealed to them that she had converted. She shared, "I know that there is a good chance that I could lose everyone that I've ever known." Anticipating the fallout from friends and family proved to be stressful in itself, and Emily reported, "I was under so much stress that I ended up losing my hair and all that kind of stuff." Fortunately, the process of sharing with friends was better than she anticipated. Although she received isolated barbed comments from family, the experience from relatives has been overwhelmingly positive. She intimated that recently she had been to visit her brother in Florida and he "accepted me one hundred percent and that was fine. Of course, he was asking me all kinds of questions. And my other brother who is totally Christian, he's OK with me that way that I am, he doesn't have any problem with me. My mom is one hundred percent, she doesn't know anything about it [Islam] and she just wants to learn and understand. And my [kids], they are everything, and they don't care about anything because I'm just – I'm still mom." Her relationships with friends on the other hand were strained, and she was rejected. She remains connected through some supportive friendships in the online community though. Emily has indicated that throughout the process, her ex-husband has served as an advocate and a buffer as relationships were renegotiated and helped to educate their children about Emily's new religious identity.

Emily indicated that her experiences in public have been less than ideal after she adopted hijab. She reported, "I would walk out of my home, I always felt that I was being stared at. And I remember the first time I was driving with the hijab and I had another car driving by me, and she was pointing at me. Like there's two women in the car and she was pointing at me, and was laughing at me." Emily explained that, for the most part, her experiences in public have been kind but that it is "totally opposite of how I feel internally." She explained, "Everyone has been, if anything it has been – it's a really weird dynamic. I mean, when I have hijab, it's like so odd. More people open doors for me, and more people go out of their way to like, let me go by. But I don't know if it's because they're being like – but I know it's like, it's almost like *here let me actually let you go through first*. Like they are being so extra kind." Further, Emily recognizes that she previously took her status as a "white American Christian for granted.... Because when I converted, all of a sudden, I felt every single eye on me every time that I wanted out of my home.... And Muslim women, when they wear hijab, [people] see that. Just like they see the color of your skin.

And all of a sudden, I'm an outcast." Emily noted that while in public, people assume that she is a foreigner and will speak another language.

Emily believes that social media plays a large role in fostering negative attitudes of Muslims. She explained, "online it is a whole different world, and I can get attacked left and right." She blames this in part on news media who doesn't share enough about positive Muslims or situations in which Muslims are being maltreated throughout the world.

Emily noted that amongst the Muslim community, Caucasian American converts are "not represented anywhere, on any level." As she explained, "you don't ever see, even on the WhyIslam.org where they show this whole video thing, they don't even show a white woman in a hijab. At least they show a white man … but they didn't actually show it as a white woman in hijab. Well where am I in that picture?" Emily wants desperately to be represented, seen, and heard. And this underrepresentation is compounded by relationships with other members of her mosque. According to Emily, "you have the cliques, you know, like all – like a mosque may be all Turkish, you know, and I'll stand out because I'm an American." She indicates that it is difficult to navigate between culture and religion within the local Muslim community and explained how this has been highlighted during holidays. As Emily explained, "You know, during Ramadan everybody brings all their meals for – to celebrate Iftar, and I'm like, I'm – this will be my second full year at Ramadan – and I'm sitting here going *OK, well you're gonna be bringing Bosnian food, you're gonna bring all this, and do I bring like macaroni and cheese?*"

Throughout the conversion process, Emily has felt sadness, frustration and fear, isolation, confusion, stress, and subsequent physical manifestations of that stress. She uses the personal calmness that is provided through Islam as a coping strategy, and with people that she knows who make negative comments online, she will openly confront them. As she explains, Islam has provided her with the tools that she needs to deal with the negative impacts that her relationships have had in her life, and that although she says that"it's the most lonely existence ever," she also reports, "if I had to change anything over again, I would never change. It's just, because the reward is so much bigger than everything here." For Emily, the conversion process has been one of having to redefine herself and "trying to figure out: OK, now who is actually Emily? Emily the Muslim, who am I? And that's what I've been working on, trying to figure out where's the middle ground between this extreme Muslims that all that, to Emily who is all that? And I'm trying to figure out who I am in the middle."

When asked whether she would prefer a traditionally American pseudonym or a more Qur'anically based pseudonym, Emily was very quick to choose an American one stating that "you should use American." In her explanation for using an American name, she intimated "that's all that I've ever known my entire life, is that I'm an American. But an American is my history. . . . I don't know how to explain it. It's like yeah, my American part of me is who I am, who my past generations have been. They've been here, they came here years and years [ago] – like hundreds of years ago, and I can't deny my past."

SUMAYA

Sumaya is a 34-year-old woman who currently lives in urban Illinois and who was raised in a nonpracticing Southern Baptist home in a different (and much more conservative) state. She spoke about her religious upbringing in sweeping terms about how her family identified and practiced their faith, not how she herself practiced. She became a single mother at a young age and placed her children in the care of her parents while she was pursuing her education.

She identified as being a seeker of religious knowledge and was exposed to Islam through a college course she took on international relations. Sumaya indicated that she had to actively pursue knowledge of Islam and states that she "looked around for a Qur'an and I couldn't find one at the bookstore. I didn't think to look online, so I went on Skype and I found Saudi Arabia, and I found a friend there. And I asked him please send me books from – you know? And of the Qur'an, and about Islam." She indicated that the process of reading, learning, and networking was difficult for her as she had to unpack her own internalized Islamophobia, "I was really, I was kind of weary of the people because all I know was what I saw on TV, and all the bad negative images, and it was, I was scared of them." Ultimately, Sumaya found that Islam resonated with her and "I felt like that's what I already believed."

Telling her friends and family about her conversion was a painful process for Sumaya, which included consequences of harassment, rejection, trying to convert her back to Christianity, shunning, excommunication, and both threatening statements and behaviors. Sumaya reported, "my parents told me if I do my thing in their house, meaning praying, that they're gonna call the police. And that, they also said to me that I wasn't welcome in their house anymore."

According to Sumaya, she was completely estranged from her family, and the last time she had spoken to them was during the custody battle for her children. Her family used her status as a Muslim – and their own misconceptions of Islam – as justification for why she should not have her children returned to her care. As she stated, "my parents said that I needed supervised visits, ah the court appointed an attorney to my parents and the attorney was asking me if I believed Islam, if I believed in the Qur'an, if I believed in my husband having four wives, if I'm gonna force my kids to wear hijab. And also, they asked me if I support Israel. And I was like *I don't know what the hell this has to do with me being a mom.*" Ultimately, she lost the custody battle for her children and feels that she was victimized and marginalized by the courts.

Sumaya has also indicated that she has been marginalized and discriminated against at multiple places of employment. "I faced struggles in employment" she stated, "I did get harassed at work, at more than one job. Because I am white, and I'm a convert to Islam. I would wear hijab and I would have people make direct comments to me, or they would go behind me and harass me, like cause problems for me at work, trying to sabotage my performance or make me look bad. I had people play jokes on me."

Not only did Sumaya feel alienated and excluded from the general public after her conversion, but she also noted that she was alienated and excluded from the Muslim community. In her new Muslim community, there has been an active process of surveillance by the FBI and finds that she is frequently suspected as being an undercover officer. As she explained, "Another woman started telling people that I worked for the government, and so being a white convert and being a white Muslim convert, I'm being alienated. Or I feel like I'm being alienated from the Muslim community here. Cuz I'm white and a convert, and it gives people – most people – [the impression] that I work for the government. Which is not true." Sumaya has also been exploited by the immigrant community in many ways. She stated, "I have been exploited. I feel like I have had people try to take advantage of me. It's like the [immigrant Muslim] lady who I came here [to help], her intent and purpose for me being here was for me to take over her organization, that's what she told me. And also to try to get me to marry somebody for a green-card. And um, her intention was to put me in trouble. To get me in trouble so she could cover [her money laundering]. Or help her friend or whatever. And from my point of view she's, I feel like she's trying to sell me."

Throughout the conversion process, Sumaya has felt sadness, frustration and isolation, loneliness, confusion, grief, denial, anxiety and panic, and physical manifestations of stress. She has had a series of health-related issues that have been attributed to the stress she has faced through the conversion experience. As she explained, "all of it has to do with the situation. I was very healthy before and all of a sudden, my health started deteriorating and I'm somebody who seems to cope with stress, but it was coming out in my health. And my last doctor said the reason why I'm having all these problems is because of the stress." Not all of her doctors have been this helpful though, and Sumaya intimated that in the early stages of seeking help, she felt that they were trying to diagnose her hijab and her conversion. As she explained, "I know I just needed to talk about it, and I thought I could go to the doctors to talk about it and they would right away ask me why I would wear the hijab, like changed my religion. They would diagnose me changing my identity, and you know act like there's something wrong. Like you can't change your religion without it being something wrong."

Although she has experienced great marginalization and significant health impact due to stress, Sumaya still considered herself an incredibly strong woman. She attributed that strength to her love of God and her increased Muslim faith. Of all her experiences combined, she reported, "I feel that this is definitely a touch from God you know, I feel like it makes me a stronger person, it makes me realize that the only thing that's there for you is God. Because the way I make it through life is through Him." Though she wished that she had a stronger support system and was actively seeking a support group for women who were facing the difficulties she had faced, she took comfort in Islam, and had a passion for the faith and all the benefits this had on her life.

When asked whether she would prefer a traditionally American pseudonym or a more Qur'anically based pseudonym, Sumaya was quick to choose not only a Qur'anically based one but specifically the name Sumaya. This name resonated with her on a personal level, as she explained, "It's a Muslim name that I like. And the reason why I like that name is because the very first Muslim convert in the history of Islam, her name was Sumaya. She was the first martyr in Islam. She was killed for her faith. And the people tried to force her to worship an idol called Uhud, and because she wouldn't, they killed her. Yeah, so even when she was being tortured, she was saying *no, there's only one God, there's only one God.* And yeah, so I identify with the name because of that reason. Because of the things that I've gone through."

AMY MARIE

Amy Marie is a 45-year-old woman from suburban Ohio who was raised in a Catholic home. When asked about her religious upbringing, Amy Marie spoke about her own experiences and her own active participation in religious life, which was halted after her parents were divorced because attending services and practicing the faith became too difficult. She spoke about always wanting a relationship with God and being a seeker of that relationship, saying, "I would go along with friends from school, um whatever religion. I know I went to Baptist church, went to the Nazarene church, and other churches. So I – I always wanted to have you know, God in my life. So after the divorce, and not being able to go to the Catholic Church, I just started searching, I guess." Her sister converted to Pentecostal, and this paved the way for her to explore Islam by reading Islamic materials and networking. Overall, Amy Marie's family was supportive of her conversion to Islam, although one of her sisters was concerned with her safety.

Amy Marie indicated that her biggest struggles since converting have been in her home life, with both her relationship and unpacking culture from religion. Amy Marie married a man from Morocco and though their marriage, her husband was able to secure papers to immigrate to the United States. She later learned that her marriage was not for love, but rather to secure his green card, amongst other things. As she reported, "his intent was never to have a marriage with me. That was never the intent. He came here and took everything from me including my daughter, my child, my home, all of my possessions, all of them, my car, my savings, everything is gone." Further, only after they married and he moved to the United States, did Amy Marie understand the extent of his depravity. Soon, the FBI was knocking at her door inquiring about their marriage, which ultimately led to her husband revealing that the FBI was also investigating him for predatory online sexual behavior with a young American girl and for engaging in the consumption of child pornography. Amy Marie and her husband are currently estranged.

Amy Marie explained that she felt victimized and marginalized by law enforcement who investigated her husband's behavior. She reported, "they made a deal with him that he would search for terrorists online, do fake things in chat-rooms and stuff like that to try and find terrorist cells... instead of doing the right thing – which is what every other

American would have happen to them – he would have gone to prison and he would have been kicked out of the country." Further, Amy Marie reported that after her husband beat her for the first (and only) time, and after she began to experience significant physical manifestations of her stress, a friend who was a police officer approached the FBI in an unofficial capacity to seek assistance in protecting her. The FBI didn't handle the situation appropriately, which left her feeling further victimized. As she explained, "Instead of calling me when he's at work, or talk to me in private or whatever, saying what's going on Amy Marie, you can talk to me, stuff like that. No, he brought [my husband and I] in the office and confronted me about it." She explained further, "instead of like confiding in this contact person with the FBI, he like pulled it out with a spotlight on in front of him [the husband]. Do you know what that felt like? It felt like – well this is my attacker, my abuser, and instead of helping me, you're like telling that I'm having someone call to try and protect me."

Amy Marie didn't talk about her relationships with friends, but she did indicate that she felt that she was isolated from the surrounding American community, which she attributes in part to the role of the media, reporting "they tell us what they want us to hear, they teach us what they want us to learn and to think." Amy Marie believes that the media actively perpetuates Islamophobia in the way that they report stories, and she intimated, "when do we in America attach a religion to these criminals? We don't. We don't say the Baptist rapist, the Christian murderer, or whatever it is, you know? But it's very convenient to attach to these criminals the – the Muslim faith."

Compounding the issue of isolation, she explained that there was a cliquishness to the Muslim community and that frequently left her feeling as an outsider. She reported, "there are the converts from America, white people, mostly women. Then there's the women who are from Iraq or wherever the Muslim countries, and the feeling is like, they're judgmental. They're – They're better than you. And so it's not very welcoming. It's not like I can go to the mosque, at least the ones in my area. I can't go there and find a sister who will you know, take me under her wing and be my buddy, and help me with everything that I want to learn and know."

Although Amy Marie spoke a lot about her victimization and marginalization as a female white convert, she also spoke a lot about hope. She had a strong desire to be seen and heard, and help other women within this demographic. She aimed to assist others who are isolated after their conversion to Islam and/or targeted by immigrants with nefarious intent.

At the time of the interviews, Amy Marie was currently working with a victims assistance program and believed that the greater community needs to be aware that these women are completely unrepresented. As she explained, "I'm gonna talk to my congressman. I – that is one place where I want my advocate to go with me, to talk to the congressman ... the women that you're reaching, I know I've met some myself. They've – they want their voices heard. I'm not the only one who's talking." Further, Amy Marie had great concern that by allowing her estranged husband to flip for antiterrorism initiatives, the FBI and other law enforcement agencies were actually compromising the integrity of the United States and allowing these women to become casualties of these antiterrorism initiatives. As she reported, "Not only is this person laughing at me, he is laughing at our country, our government, the FBI, Homeland Security this, Immigration that. All these men, not just the one that I married, all of them are laughing at all of us. Because nobody is protecting us. They're taking advantage of us, they're abusing us, hitting us, taking everything from us, and you know what? And they know that the authorities don't give a crap and aren't going to do anything. So do you know what? Our government, our authority here, are giving them the power to do whatever they want, and they know it. And they're laughing at all of us. We are the fools. Because [the government doesn't] do nothing. They let them abuse and do whatever."

Throughout the conversion process, Amy Marie has felt sadness, frustration, isolation, devalued, loneliness, stress, and anxiety and has suffered health complications from this stress and anxiety. But takes comfort in her love of Islam.

When asked whether she would prefer a traditionally American pseudonym or a more Qur'anically based pseudonym, Amy Marie was quick to state that she was personally attached to her own name because that's where her roots are; however, there was a strong need to shield her identity because the situation with her estranged husband had yet to be resolved and she indicated suffering great abuses at his hand. She chose the name Amy Marie instead stating, "if I had another daughter I wanted Amy Marie." This statement indicates the great amount of hope that Amy Marie had toward a better future. As she explained earlier in the interview, "when you look into your future you can see your children. My children were stolen from me, you know? It – he could have left me alone, someone – someone with a true heart could have fallen in love with me and had a family, more children." As she stated at the time of the interview, Amy Marie still had time for that kind of life, and she was hopeful about the potential for love, a better husband, and more children in the future.

LYNN

Lynn is a 39-year-old woman from rural Maine who was raised in a Catholic home. At the time of the interviews, she had very recently left the United States to stay with her in-laws in the Middle East because she essentially lost everything after her conversion to Islam. She still identified as American in every way and believed that just because she had recently left the United States, she was able to provide perspective on the experiences of what it means to be a white female American convert to Islam in post-9/11 America. When speaking about the religion of her upbringing, she spoke mostly about her own role in religious life and how she sought a relationship with God as depicted through Abrahamic films like *The Ten Commandments* and *Ben Hur*. To her, this helped answer some of her questions about religion. As she reported, "so I would watch them every Easter, Christmas. I would feel guilty and put them in, you know? But in my adult – like I look going back – I still had questions. I was one of those children who always asked why."

When she dated her now ex-husband, Lynn found that they were actively seeking a spiritual home and they began "shopping for churches." After her former marriage became emotionally abusive, Lynn returned to watching movies as a way to alleviate guilt, but she also began a process of seeking attention from men through what she described as questionable behavior. It was during this self-described acting-out phase that she came into contact with a Muslim man and began comparing religious teachings. He encouraged her to actively pursue religious knowledge on her own, by reading, thinking, and interpreting various texts. She explained, "I went into it just to learn because I'm curious. I want to know what it says about it, not that I wanted to change religions . . . people, my parents, everyone that found out that I was doing this and talking to a Muslim man come up into a conversation, say you're not gonna change" and then she laughed off their concerns saying "no, no, there's no way I'm gonna become a Muslim, no."

But over time, her curiosity led to revelations about Islam, and a realization that there was a deep resonation between what she was learning during her inquiry and what she previously believed. Lynn further reported that although she later married the Muslim man who guided her on the path to understanding Islam, "I can honestly say that I accepted Islam on my own. Not because someone told me something and I believe it. I did the research myself. What hurts me even more is from my family, they believe it's because of him, and that I've been brainwashed. Everyone knew me as a hard headed stubborn independent person, and then as soon as I converted, *oh, she must have been brainwashed by some guy.* What an insult to me. I mean, come on, give me a break. You really think that low of me that I can't make up my own mind?"

In her friendships post-conversion, Lynn found that she was often misunderstood, that she was being rejected, and was being avoided by those who didn't share the same views on religion. In her home life, Lynn reported that her family had a certain amount of embarrassment by her new appearance as a hijabi. This made family situations uncomfortable, and these relationships were difficult to renegotiate as she set new boundaries. This led to estrangement, isolation, and rejection. Lynn's conversion was the topic of family gossip, and the family chose to ignore the opportunity to get her conversion narrative from Lynn herself. Instead, Lynn intimated that her family just avoided all topics regarding her newfound faith in Islam. As Lynn reported, "at one point, I did go to my mother and sat her down, and told her that this is – *I've become a Muslim, do you have any questions?* But by then, the gossip and the assumption and the speculation had already gone so far into her own mind that she was so upset with me that she couldn't talk to me. And in fact, she still is the same way today. I tried to talk to her about it, she starts crying *I don't want to talk about it.* It doesn't get talked about, and she – she says that her daughter died. You know, I'm right here." This was indicative of Lynn's strong desire to be seen and heard, as well as validated.

Lynn's ex-husband used her religion to harass and threaten her. According to Lynn, "all of the anti-Islamic stuff my ex was posting on Facebook, all of the hate phone calls and voice-mails he would leave me, um there's this song about open season on Muslims, he would call my home and play it on my answering machine, so when I came home. . . ." Although her ex-husband had a track record with victimizing her, suffering mental health issues, struggling with serious addictions, and more, she felt victimized by the court system because "all this stuff, I could not submit as evidence." She wound up losing custody of her daughters at the end of the custody proceedings. Lynn's attorney and domestic abuse counselor were both surprised by the outcome. When asked how she felt this all played into the larger purpose of understanding marginalization of Muslim converts, and whether discrimination was at play, she explained, "absolutely, that's why I said there was discrimination. I thought if I showed up to trial in a hijab...I never even had a speeding ticket. I've never broken the law. I went to – in college, my major was [pertaining to law].... I have no record. I've never done anything wrong."

Since custody of her children was granted to her ex-husband, her children were used as a tool to harm her. Her ex-husband actively engaged in indoctrinating the children in Islamophobic rhetoric. Lynn reported, "now he has fed them so much Islamophobic stuff. You know anti-Islam anti-Muslim hate stuff that you know – my oldest daughter stopped talking to me. My younger daughter, she's just trying to avoid me so it is hurtful. My youngest daughter, we chat through a game. You know, we can text each other, send messages through this game, talk to each other here and there. You know, I'll Skype when I can, if I see she's online, I'll call. But usually she's only – see, he's always there. When he's not there, they'll talk to me no problem. When he's there – my oldest daughter, she tends to seek his approval or show off, do crazy things. Like take a piece of bacon and then eat it in front of me and say *oh this is so good*."

Lynn indicated that media, including social media, play a large role in shaping the perceptions of the general public. As she explained, "the Christian drunk driver killed a family of four, they don't put Christian in there. But if it's a Muslim man, regardless of you know, it would be in the news. When most everyone is Christian, and you look at the police blotter in the newspaper, almost all of them are Christian, but they don't make the headlines, you know, sell papers. So I mean, even molesting priests don't even make the news anymore. It's all kept hush, hush. So it, again, yeah it's the media. But I think the biggest one is social media – the internet." Lynn witnessed social media being used as a tool to propagate Islamophobic discourse, and combined with what she witnessed through print and television media, she adopted a certain amount of distrust. She said this distrust is incongruent with Muslim philosophy, but she admitted that she has become so concerned about the portrayal of Muslims that she even questioned the motives behind the request for her to participate in this study. She reported, "That's something Islam teaches. To expect the best in everyone. Not – you're not supposed to think the worst. But even with you, I was cautious. This could go the wrong way, but you gotta have – you gotta give the benefit of the doubt as much as possible."

Throughout the conversion process, Lynn had felt fearful to come out, had been scared of the consequences of coming out, and had been fearful at the thought of covering because it would change her minority status to one that is outwardly identifiable. Through it all, she also indicated feeling immense sadness, frustration, isolation (including self-imposed isolation), loneliness, confusion, and great emotional turmoil. Although she has experienced great difficulties, she spoke with hope. She believed that her ability to cope could be attributed to her faith and love for Islam, which also helped rebuild her sense of self-worth and allowed her to remain strong. As Lynn reported, "if it wasn't for my faith, I would be, I think, suffering from severe depression. Absolutely. I am 100% sure of it. The only thing that seems to keep me together is my faith. Because I've seen people lose it for less. No, and who could have done this? I've gone from full-time mother 13 years, I can't imagine any woman having their children taken away like that wouldn't be devastated. And yeah it hurts, yeah I was upset, but I knew that it would get better at some point. Trust that God loves us, he doesn't allow bad things to happen to us without a purpose. I know that something in the end, waiting, he should be waiting for us. It should be great."

Lynn made it clear that she wanted to be seen and heard in her entirety as both American and Muslim. As she stated, "It's just that I am an American. And I happen to be Muslim, you know? Its – because I wear something on my head, does that make me any different than if I wear a baseball cap? Or I dyed my hair purple? Or a mohawk? Or pierced my nose? Or you know, anything that American women do, you know? Just because we're not...whatever, doesn't mean that they're hated and different than who they are. I am who I am. You know? I'm still me."

JESSICA

Jessica is a 33-year-old woman from Urban Louisiana who was raised in a Catholic home. When asked about her religious upbringing, Jessica spoke about the religious identities of her family and how she devoutly followed the religion of her mother until she hit a rebellious period during her teenage years. She spoke about Catholicism as both a religion and a cultural identity, stating "I considered myself a Catholic you know, everybody's a Catholic, you're never not a Catholic." But during her rebellious period, she began to identify as more of a seeker. She questioned everything and began to search for answers on her own. She realized that she was going through the motions of Catholicism because Catholicism was the religion of her mother. When she realized that Catholicism was not necessarily what she identified with, she "apostated." She was introduced to Islam while in college, when she and her roommate had long existential conversations about religion, which sparked them both to read about Islam and seek different religious perspectives. Jessica's roommate converted to Islam before she did.

Jessica continued to explore various religions and to unpack Arab culture from Islam, admitting that it was a difficult process of accepting that Islam truly resonated with her personal philosophy on spirituality. As she explained, "it took me a long time to really recognize in myself that I wanted – to admit to myself that I believed in Islam. Because even before 9/11, this was well before 9/11 (from '98 on), to grapple with the stereotypes culture taught me, and it was hard to disentangle the two. OK, and once I did, it was just a completely different experience. And I don't have to be Arab. There's nothing to do with Arabs, and so on and so forth. So it was a process, it took from 98, well into November 2001 [which] was when I converted, when I took the faith. And it um, it was a wild ride."

Jessica indicate that she had a difficult process of renegotiating some of her friendships, and that she was a fairly shy person without a lot of deep friendships to begin with. Her best friend (her roommate) had previously converted to Islam, so in that respect, she already had someone she could share the experience with. This was helpful to her during the conversion process. Jessica lamented the 11-year hiatus of a friendship with someone who was unable to unpack the cultural practices from religious practices but indicated that the relationship was on the path of restoration. Jessica viewed her friendships optimistically and normalized the adjustment period where relationships had to be renegotiated with friends after her conversion.

Sharing her religious conversion with her family was one rife with conflict. Jessica's parents had previously passed away, and she and her siblings were each going to different geographical locations, so Jessica acknowledged that interaction with family was already somewhat limited by distance. When they did communicate, Jessica felt that she was misunderstood and marginalized. As she explained, "I think they felt like I was just being influenced by my Muslim friends and that I had no thought in the matter. You know? Like most people will say, especially if a woman marries a man, that she was brainwashed. And it's – it's still to this day, hard to show people how much of a process it was, how much kicking and screaming I did. But you know, they did not like it. Especially when I'm living out here, they were like *what are you doing? Do you want to be a terrorist? What do you want this for?*" The relationships had gotten better after some of her siblings moved back to Louisiana, but she did talk about the upheaval with family during the early stages of the conversion process. As she explained, "the treatment was like Jessica is not here, she's an alien . . . so that was hard to deal with. Um just proving to them that I'm still myself. That I haven't become the death by some alien life forms, that was difficult." Proving who she truly was had been a long process that took an emotional toll on Jessica. She felt isolated and estranged, but Jessica recognized and understood that renegotiation of relationships is not an immediate process.

Jessica experienced great hardship and significant marginalization, as well as violence as she moved through American society and to different geographic locations. She noted that in Louisiana, for the most part, she was able to peacefully live her life free of fear and harassment, but in the other places she lived, her experiences were markedly different. After Jessica converted, she married a fellow Caucasian American convert to Islam and they relocated to Georgia for his work. While there, she attended – and was a member of – the Islamic Center of Savannah when on August 24, 2003, it was burned down in a hate-related arson, just days after it had been shot at. Jessica reported that the treatment of Muslims was awful in Savannah, where "people would come up to me and scream at me, and just the vilest things. Walking down the street, people would roll down their window and *F this.*"

Her treatment in Alabama was better, though she explained that it was still a very intolerant community. It was on her first night living in Mobile that Jessica was assaulted by someone who threw an egg at her within feet of the front door of her new apartment. Although she experienced this assault, she indicated that her experiences were less physical and more subtle. As she explained, "you really do fear being lynched at every moment. You know, anywhere you go, there are stares, deathly stares. And I'm just smiling and trying to like, make people feel at ease. Just going into public and having to be Islam's representative, having to be the person that – kind of like the ambassador to, feelings of good will." She went on further to explain, "people just come up to you and take pictures of you for no reason. They don't want to speak to you. People assuming you don't speak English, people assuming you're an Arab. Um all the comments *where are you from? Where are you really from.*"

Jessica attributed much of the current discourse on Muslims in America to the media, indicating that many Muslims want to speak about the stereotypes and educate on why the dominant discourse is incorrect. As she reported, "Two percent of the Muslim population are creating such problems for the world. For Americans and American Muslims. They have terrorized us as well. And the media just ignoring, Ignoring the Sheiks and Imams – the people who say this isn't right, this isn't Islam. Just ignoring that and coming to say *where are the voices? Where are the Muslims?* saying that. We're here, we're trying, you won't let us. I felt betrayed in that I thought that I had freedom of religion, but I did not." She further questioned the motives behind the media's representation of Muslims, stating "how are you gonna describe a quarter of the population in such sweeping terms? And such deroga – not derogatory, but the connotation is there. Absolutely. To lead people to think that we're all like this. That we're all enemies of the United States. And it's such a political conundrum." If given the platform to be represented in the media, Jessica stated "I am an American. I never had to give that up to be a Muslims, and I never did give that up. I love my country, I love – I love the American people because there are so many good, even though I have seen a lot of bad. I know that there is good, you know? And I can't blame people who have been convinced to hate me, because they don't know. You know? And I am not a threat to you. I'm not. There's no reason to be frightened of me."

Throughout the conversion process, Jessica felt sadness, hurt, anger, and isolation and was fearful for her personal safety. Although she has experienced great marginalization and victimization, Jessica spoke about hope as she reported, "This is the thing people, we can be American and Muslim . . . I've had an indication that things are getting better. I'm not sure. I think they will get better whether or not people convert just because we're fighting for our space to say what we need to say. And I'm hoping people listen." Jessica attributed her coping strategies to her love and passion for Islam, and the comfort she received through her faith. As she reported, people are faced with a choice with how to cope, "they either become more withdrawn or they learn how to deal. And I think my faith has been a tool. And being a Muslim, a visible Muslim has helped me."

When asked whether she would prefer a traditionally American pseudonym or a more Qur'anically based pseudonym, Jessica was very quick to choose an American one. As she explained, "I really would prefer an American name. I've written on this topic, that I don't have to have an Arab name. I'm not an Arab. If Jessica is my name, then Jessica is a normal name. Ah, I think I would really like an American name because it brings about cultural awareness. Like oh, somebody with that name can be a Muslim."

Jena

Jena is a 26-year-old woman from urban New Jersey who was raised in a Catholic home. When asked about her religious upbringing, Jena explained that religion was less a search for truth and more of a guide. As she explained, "my mom likes to think of herself as a bit of a hippie. So she was more of a like – those coexist type of ladies. It was always thought of as, I think more of a grounds for teaching you things like morals. Instead of a literal interpretation and God on Earth as many Catholics believe, it was more of just a framework for their own moral interpretation."

She grew up in a community where there were a number of Muslims, and she learned about Islam through them and through her own process of active inquiry. In college, Jena's roommate was an international student from Saudi Arabia, and she began attending the mosque with her to experience the social aspects of that religious community. As she explained, "I felt a peace there, and I don't know – even now, if I can truly say that I'm having this phenomenon that God is all around us or a tinkerer, but it gives me a peace." After that, she felt that she was ready to convert. It was through her visits to the mosque that she met a man from a Palestinian family, whom she fell in love with and later married.

Jena attributed her family's acceptance of her conversion to their open-minded attitudes about religion. It wasn't always a linear process of acceptance, but they approached acceptance as a process of learning and understanding. According to Jena, "it's funny, I think my family were so trying to make me feel like they were OK with it, you know? In the back of their minds you could see the hesitation, but they were so trying to be gung-ho, and if that's what you want … it was about five months until I started wearing hijab, and that's when all of a like *oh, you're a Muslim. You're wearing that thing on your head*. Even now, it's been four years and my father, my father is the most accepting." Her extended family was less than accepting, and she attributed that to the closed-minded values that they had developed throughout life. She took many opportunities to educate her family and to ensure that they could successfully unpack culture from religion. She attributed these misconceptions in part to the media's perpetuation of negativity and caricature-like representations of Muslims.

Although her close friends were very understanding and very supportive, acquaintances from her childhood proved to have difficulty with accepting her new faith. Jena explained, "I remember walking into stores and they stare at me, and it's just very odd that they thought – I guess my biggest problem was – I was always one of those staunch feminist types, you know? So many people have this impression now that I was wearing this because I had a Muslim husband, you know? And I was being oppressed, and wearing this is – how much I have changed to allow that to happen to myself. And for me, it was like a big problem. People thought I wasn't who I was anymore. That I was just a silent partner. And even, I have found acquaintances from high school, and I see them out and about town, and they won't approach me anymore, you know? They're very standoffish."

Jena explained that as a Muslim woman wearing hijab, she was personally responsible for the maltreatment that she received. Although she doesn't drink, Jena has attended parties where other people have been consuming alcohol. She explained that the alcohol can make people say things that they wouldn't normally say "and they tell me *then why don't you just take off the hijab, wouldn't that just make things easier if we didn't all have to have this?* And I told them *I don't know why I have to do it, it's not gonna change who I am, its not going to change my heart as a person,* you know? I don't expect them to take off a cross, I never have and I never would. I never went to a young Jewish man and been like *take off that yarmulke,* you know like that's – I don't know. And I don't think those same people that tell me I should take this off would have the nerve to go up to a Jewish man and say *why are you wearing this, and this is what's separating us,* you know? Or to a Jewish woman and say it, it's just really open secret that we're allowed to pick on certain people." This revelation that she was to blame for her maltreatment because she chooses an outward identifier of her faith was eerily reminiscent of the way that rape victims are often held responsible for the violence committed against them if they drank or wore revealing clothing prior to their assault.

With the larger community, Jena stated that she had some difficulties as well. Jena became emotional when she explained that she had been assaulted on the bus (although she didn't recognize it as an assault); yet, this was also an opportunity to strengthen and share her joy of Islam. In her own words, "I had a man on the bus try to rip off my hijab. And I cried for weeks after it, you know? I just want to – I never thought it would happen, it makes me so much sadder at times, but you know? But, we say we pray for those people for peace, so they don't have to hurt anyone else. Because I have my peace. It's sad." For the most part though, the experiences in the community with marginalization have been much more subtle. She has had people mock her in public, look at her funny, and talk about her behind her back. But again, she also finds that there are people who stand up for her, defending her against rude behavior or comments. This strengthens her faith in the American public. As she explained, "it just happened so many times to me that people make snide comments and strangers behind me will tell them to shut up."

Jena spoke about being marginalized and rejected through the cliquishness of the local Muslim community. She explained, "I have to honestly say, more of the feedback that I get that is hurtful is from other Muslimahs, like other – especially Arab Muslimahs. Like they look at me almost in that cultural phenomenon of African American women that look at black men and white women, there's a stigma against it. I find it's also very alive and well in the Arab American community. Like *what she's doing marrying an Arab boy?* You know, *wearing hijab?*"

Although Jena has approached a number of women in the local Muslim community, she feels as if she has been rejected. She reported, "It's hard because you feel this distance all of a sudden from your own culture because you're publicly displaying something that isn't – and the culture that you thought was going to be that community that brings you – for the most part saying *oh no, that was nice of you to try, but this is our thing.*" She spoke about her rejection from the local community with sadness saying, "do I think there's a place for me in the Palestinian American community as a Muslim here? I don't know that there is much of a place for me. I don't think that I'm ever gonna really be part of their community. I think I'm always gonna be married to a part of their community and be on the outside of that circle."

Throughout the conversion process, Jena felt sadness, frustration, isolation, and loneliness, but she explained that Islam provided her with the tools to cope. Islam provided her with peace and fulfillment, her love and passion for Islam comforted her, and she was able to cope though a personal attitude of patience and love. This peace helped her to maintain a heightened level of personal strength. As she explained, "I don't think everyone in this world has to be Muslim, but I think everyone should always be searching for what makes them a better version of themselves. And I am so thankful that I found that within Islam, within Allah, within my relationship with my husband. And I just hope that everyone else can come to a point where they're happy with where they are, that we don't have to be picking on each other, you know? For the differences we have, and we can just be happy with the peace we find within our hearts, you know? And that's – to me, that's important. I just hope that everyone around me, even if you're not young and you're on your death bed, that you can get to the point where you're happy with what's inside of you."

References

Abdo, Geneive. *Mecca and the Main Street*. New York, NY: Oxford University Press, 2006.

Abdul-Ghafur, Saleemah. Introduction to *Living Islam Outloud: American Muslim Women Speak*, edited by Saleemah Abdul-Ghafur. Boston, MA: Beacon Press, 2005.

Ahluwalia, Muninder K., and Laura Pellettiere. "Sikh Men Post-9/11: Misidentification, Discrimination, and Coping." *Asian American Journal of Psychology* 1, no 4 (2010): 303–314.

Ahmad, Sara J. *Evaluating the Framing of Islam and Muslims Pre- and Post-9/11: A Contextual Analysis of Articles Published by the New York Times*. Saarbrucken, Germany: VDM Verlag Dr. Muller, 2008.

Ahmed, Parvez. "Prejudice is Real and Exacts a Heavy Toll." In *Islamophobia and Anti-Americanism: Causes and Remedies*, edited by Mohamed Nimer, 15–20. Beltsville, MD: Amana Publications, 2007.

Alan Cooperman, Besheer Mohamed, Jessica Martinez, Becka Alper, Elizabeth Sciupac, Claire Gecewicz, Conrad Hackett, and Juan Carlos Esparza Ochoa. "America's Changing Religious Landscape," *Pew Research Center*. May 12, 2015. http://pewrsr.ch/1FhDslC.

Alexander, Scott C. "We Should Deconstruct our Supremacist Master Narratives." In *Islamophobia and Anti-Americanism: Causes and Remedies*, edited by Mohamed Nimer, 41–53. Beltsville, MD: Amana Publications, 2007.

Alldred, Pam, and Val Gillies. "Eliciting Research Accounts: Re/producing Modern Subjects?" In *Ethics in Qualitative Research*, edited by Melanie Mauthner, Maxine Birch, Julie Jessop, and Tina Miller, 53–69. London: SAGE Publications, 2002.

© The Author(s) 2017
A.M. Guimond, *Converting to Islam*,
DOI 10.1007/978-3-319-54250-8

Allen, Chris. *Islamophobia*. Surrey, England: Ashgate Publishing Limited, 2010.

Allievi, Stefano. "The Shifting Significance of the Halal/Haram Frontier: Narratives on the Hijab and Other Issues." In *Women Embracing Islam: Gender and Conversion in the West*, edited by Karin van Nieuwkerk, 120–149. Austin, TX: University of Texas Press, 2006.

Allison, Clinton B. "Okie Narratives: Agency and Whiteness." In *White Reign: Deploying Whiteness in America*, edited by Joe L. Kincheloe, Shirley R. Steinberg, Nelson M. Rodriguez, and Ronald E. Chennault, 229–244. New York, NY: St. Martin's Press, 1998.

Allport, Gordon W. *The Individual and His Religion*. London: Constable and Company, Ltd., 1950.

Allport, Gordon W. *The Nature of Prejudice*. Cambridge, MA: Addison-Wesley Publishing Co., 1954.

Andrew Kohut. "Muslim Americans: Middle Class and Mostly Mainstream," *Pew Research Center*. May 22, 2007. http://pewrsr.ch/2aLExGR.

Anway, Carol L. *Daughters of Another Path*. Lee's Summit, MO: Yawna Publications, 1996.

Apple, Michael W. Forward to *White Reign: Deploying Whiteness in America*, edited by Joe L. Kincheloe, Shirley R. Steinberg, Nelson M. Rodriguez, and Ronald E. Chennault. New York, NY: St. Martin's Press, 1998.

Augoustinos, Martha, and Katherine J. Reynolds. "Prejudice, Racism and Social Psychology." In *Understanding Prejudice, Racism and Social Conflict*, edited by Martha Augoustinos, and Katherine J. Reynolds, 1–23. London: SAGE Publications Ltd., 2001.

Augsburger, David W. *Conflict Mediation Across Cultures*. Louisville, KY: Westminster John Knox Press, 1992.

Baker, Abdul Haqq. *Extremists in Our Midst: Confronting Terror*. London: Palgrave Macmillan, 2011.

Batelaan, Peter. "Intercultural Education in Europe: A Recent History of Dealing with Diversity and Learning to Live Together." In *Confronting Islamophobia in Educational Practice*, edited by Barry van Driel, 53–62. Staffordshire, England: Trentham Books Limited, 2004.

Baumeister, Roy F. *Evil: Inside Human Violence and Cruelty*. New York: Holt Paperbacks, 1999.

Baumeister, Roy F., and David A. Butz. "Roots of Hate, Violence and Evil." In *The Psychology of Hate*, edited by Robert J. Sternberg, 87–102. Washington, D. C.: American Psychological Association, 2005.

Beiten, Ben K., and Katherine R. Allen. "Resilience in Arab American Couples After September 11, 2001: A Systems Perspective." *Journal of Marital and Family Therapy* 31, no 3 (2005): 251–267.

Berkowitz, Leonard. "On Hate and its Determinants: Some Affective and Cognitive Influences." In *The Psychology of Hate*, edited by Robert J. Sternberg, 155–184. Washington, D.C.: American Psychological Association, 2005.

Birch, Maxine, and Tina Miller. "Encouraging Participation: Ethics and Responsibilities." In *Ethics in Qualitative Research*, edited by Melanie Mauthner, Maxine Birch, Julie Jessop, and Tina Miller, 91–106. London: SAGE Publications, 2002.

Breakey, William R. "Psychiatry, Spirituality and Religion." In *Religion in Politics and Society*, edited by Michael Kelly and Lynn M. Messina, 18–27. New York: H. W. Wilson, 2002.

Brian J. Grim, and Mehtab S. Karim. "Future of the Global Muslim Population," *Pew Research Center*. January 27, 2011, http://pewrsr.ch/1hUQ1qG.

Bullock, Katherine. *Rethinking Muslim Women and the Veil: Challenging Historical and Modern Stereotypes*. London: International Institute of Islamic Thought, 2007.

Carter, Vicki K. "Computer-assisted Racism: Toward an Understanding of 'Cyberwhiteness.'" In *White Reign: Deploying Whiteness in America*, edited by Joe L. Kincheloe, Shirley R. Steinberg, Nelson M. Rodriguez, and Ronald E. Chennault, 269–284. New York, NY: St. Martin's Press, 1998.

Chaudhry, Kashif N. "Hirsi Ali: Telling a Critic From an Islamophobe." *The Huffington Post*, April 30, 2014. http://huff.to/2aJjUy3.

Council on American-Islamic Relations (CAIR). "Louisiana Teacher Removed After Hijab Incident." *CAIR-Council on American Islamic Relations*. July 13, 2012. http://bit.ly/2aD1VGN.

Cox, Tony. *Brain Maturity Extends Well Beyond Teen Years*. National Public Radio, October 10, 2011. http://n.pr/18Bzqo9.

Creswell, John W. *Qualitative Inquiry and Research Design: Choosing Among Five Approaches*. Thousand Oaks, CA: SAGE, 2007.

Curtis, Edward E., IV. "The Black Muslim Scare of the Twentieth Century: The History of State Islamophobia and its Post-9/11 Variations" In *Islamophobia in America: The Anatomy of Intolerance*, edited by Carl W. Ernst, 75–106. New York, NY: Palgrave Macmillan, 2013.

Denny, Frederick M. "Islam and Peacebuilding: Continuities and Transitions." In *Religion and Peacebuilding*, edited by Harold Coward and Gordon S. Smith, 129–146. Albany, NY: State University of New York Press, 2004.

Dewan, Shaila K. "Muslim Girl Punched in Face: Boy is Arrested." *New York Times*, September 17, 2003. http://nyti.ms/2aoM95G.

Dirks, Debra L. "Introduction: America and Islam in the 21st Century: Welcome to the Sisterhood." In *Islam Our Choice: Portraits of Modern American Muslim Women*, edited by Debra L. Dirks, and Stephanie Parlove, 1–16. Beltsville, MD: Amana Publications, 2003.

Dovidio, John F., Samuel L. Gaertner, and Adam R. Pearson. "On the Nature of Prejudice: The Psychological Foundations of Hate." In *The Psychology of Hate*, edited by Robert J. Sternberg, 211–234. Washington, D.C.: American Psychological Association, 2005.

Duncombe, Jean, and Julie Jessop. "'Doing Rapport' and the Ethics of 'Faking Friendship.'" In *Ethics in Qualitative Research*, edited by Melanie Mauthner, Maxine Birch, Julie Jessop, and Tina Miller, 91–106. London: SAGE Publications, 2002.

Dweck, Carol. S., and Joyce Ehrlinger. "Implicit Theories and Conflict Resolution." In *The Handbook of Conflict Resolution: Theory and Practice (2nd ed.)*, edited by Morton Deutsch, Peter T. Coleman, and Eric C. Marcus, 317–330. San Francisco, CA: Jossey-Bass, 2006.

Dyer, Richard. "The Matter of Whiteness." In *White Privilege: Essential Readings on the Other Side of Racism*, edited by Paula S. Rothenberg, 9–14. New York: Worth Publishers, 2008.

Eagly, Alice H., and Amanda B. Diekman. "What is the Problem? Prejudice as an Attitude-in-context." In *On the Nature of Prejudice: Fifty Years After Allport*, edited by John F. Dovidio, Peter Glick, and Laurie A. Rudman, 19–35. Malden, MA: Blackwell Publishing, 2005.

Ebrahimji, Maria M. "In Search of Fatima and Taqwa." In *I Speak for Myself: American Women on Being Muslim*, edited by Maria M. Ebrahimji and Zahra T. Suratwala, 23–28. Ashland, Oregon: White Cloud Press, 2011.

Ebrahimji, Maria M., and Zahra T. Suratwala. Introduction to *I Speak for Myself: American Women on Being Muslim*, edited by Maria M. Ebrahimji and Zahra T. Suratwala, XV–XVI. Ashland, Oregon: White Cloud Press, 2011.

Edwards, Rosalind, and Melanie Mauthner. "Ethics and Feminist Research: Theory and Practice." In *Ethics in Qualitative Research*, edited by Melanie Mauthner, Maxine Birch, Julie Jessop, and Tina Miller, 14–31. London: SAGE Publications, 2002.

Ehrlich, Howard J. *Hate Crimes and Ethnoviolence: The History, Current Affairs, and Future of Discrimination in America*. Boulder: Westview Press, 2009.

Eletreby, Dina M. "Conversion Experiences of Three White American Muslim Males: The Impact of Centering and De-centering Forces." Doctoral dissertation, Chapman University, 2010.

Elmore, Tim. "The Marks of Maturity." *Psychology Today*, November 14, 2012. http://bit.ly/1oqrCr3.

Ernst, Carl W. Introduction to *Islamophobia in America: The Anatomy of Intolerance*, edited by Carl W. Ernst, 1–19. New York, NY: Palgrave Macmillan, 2013.

Faur, Adriana. "A Qualitative Analysis of Cultural Discrimination Stress." Doctoral dissertation, The University of Toledo, 2008.

Finkelstein, Beth. "Practical Educational Programming that Confronts Islamophobia." In *Confronting Islamophobia in Educational Practice*, edited by Barry van Driel, 77–93. Staffordshire, England: Trentham Books Limited, 2004.

Gaertner, Samuel L., and John F. Dovidio. "Categorization, Recategorization and Intergroup Bias." In *On the Nature of Prejudice: Fifty Years After Allport*, edited by John F. Dovidio, Peter Glick, and Laurie A. Rudman, 71–88. Malden, MA: Blackwell Publishing, 2005.

Gaskew, Tony. "Confronting Political Islam: An Ethnographic Representation of Muslim Americans in the Aftermath of 9/11" Doctoral dissertation, Nova Southeastern University, 2007.

Gaylin, Willard. *Hatred: The Psychological Descent into Violence.* New York: Public Affairs, 2003.

GhaneaBassiri, Kambiz. "Islamophobia in American History: Religious Stereotyping and Out-grouping of Muslims in the United States." In *Islamophobia in America: The Anatomy of Intolerance*, edited by Carl W. Ernst, 53–74. New York, NY: Palgrave Macmillan, 2013.

Gillies, Val, and Pam Alldred. "The Ethics of Intention: Research as a Political Tool." In *Ethics in Qualitative Research*, edited by Melanie Mauthner, Maxine Birch, Julie Jessop, and Tina Miller, 32–52. London: SAGE Publications, 2002.

Gottschalk, Peter, and Gabriel Greenberg. *Islamophobia: Making Muslims the Enemy.* Lanham, MD: Rowman and Littlefield Publishers, Inc., 2008.

Greene, Joshua. *Moral Tribes: Emotion, Reason, and the Gap between Us and Them.* New York, NY: The Penguin Press, 2013.

Haddad, Yvonne Yazbeck. "The Quest for Peace in Submission: Reflections on the Journey of American Women Converts to Islam." In *Women Embracing Islam: Gender and Conversion in the West*, edited by Karin van Nieuwkerk, 19–47. Austin, TX: University of Texas Press, 2006.

Haddad, Yvonne Yazbeck, Jane I. Smith, and Kathleen M. Moore. *Muslim Women in North America: The Challenge of Islamic Identity Today.* New York, NY: Oxford University Press, 2006.

Hague, Amber. "Islamophobia in North America: Confronting the Menace." In *Confronting Islamophobia in Educational Practice*, edited by Barry van Driel, 1–18. Staffordshire, England: Trentham Books Limited, 2004.

Hammer, Juliane. *American Muslim Women, Religious Authority, and Activism.* Austin, TX: University of Texas Press, 2012.

Hammer, Juliane. "Center Stage: Gendered Islamophobia and Muslim Women." In *Islamophobia in America: The Anatomy of Intolerance*, edited by Carl W. Ernst, 107–144. New York, NY: Palgrave Macmillan, 2013.

Hasan, Asma Gull. *American Muslims: The New Generation.* New York: Continuum, 2000.

Hasan, Asma Gull. *Why I am a Muslim: An American Odyssey.* London: Element, 2004.

Heriot, Kirk. *Understanding Each Other After 9–11: What Everyone Should Know about the Religions of the World.* Fort Bragg, CA: Lost Coast Press, 2012.

Hirsi Ali, Ayaan. *Infidel.* New York, NY: Atria, 2008.

Huddy, Leonie, Stanley Feldman, Gallya Lahav, and Charles Taber. "Fear and Terrorism: Psychological Reactions to 9/11." In *Framing Terrorism: The News Media, the Government and the Public*, edited by Pippa Norris, Montague Kern, and Marion Just, 255–278. New York: Routledge, 2003.

Hughes, Aaron W. *Muslim Identities: An Introduction to Islam.* New York: Columbia University Press, 2013.

Huntington, Samuel P. *The Clash of Civilization and Remaking of the World Order.* New York: Touchstone, 1996.

Jansen, Willy. "Conversion and Gender, Two Contested Concepts." In *Women Embracing Islam: Gender and Conversion in the West*, edited by Karin van Nieuwkerk, IX–XII. Austin, TX: University of Texas Press, 2006.

Jawad, Haifaa. "Female Conversion to Islam, the Sufi Paradigm." In *Women Embracing Islam: Gender and Conversion in the West*, edited by Karin van Nieuwkerk, 153–171. Austin, TX: University of Texas Press, 2006.

Johnson, Allan G. "Privilege as Paradox." In *White Privilege: Essential Readings on the Other Side of Racism*, edited by Paula S. Rothenberg, 117–121. New York: Worth Publishers, 2008.

Karim, Jamillah. *American Muslim Women: Negotiating Race, Class, and Gender within the Ummah.* New York: New York University Press, 2009.

Katz, Neil H., Marcia Kopplman Sweedler, and John W. Lawyer. *Communication and Conflict Resolution Skills (2nd ed.).* Dubuque, IA: Kendall Hunt Publishing Company, 2010.

Khalidi, Omar. "Living as a Muslim in a Pluralistic Society and State: Theory and Experience." In *Muslims' Place in the American Public Square: Hope, Fears and Aspirations*, edited by Zahid. H. Bukhari, Sulayman S. Nyang, Mumtaz Ahmad, and John L. Esposito, 38–72. Walnut Creek, CA: AltaMira Press, 2004.

Kincheloe, Joe L., and Shirley R. Steinberg. "Addressing the Crisis of Whiteness: Reconfiguring White Identity in a Pedagogy of Whiteness." In *White Reign: Deploying Whiteness in America*, edited by Joe L. Kincheloe, Shirley R. Steinberg, Nelson M. Rodriguez, and Ronald E. Chennault, 3–30. New York, NY: St. Martin's Press, 1998.

Kincheloe, Joe. L., and Shirley R. Steinberg. "Why Teach Against Islamophobia? Striking the Empire Back." In *Teaching Against Islamophobia*, edited by Joe. L. Kincheloe, Shirley R. Steinberg, and Christopher D. Stonebanks, 3–27. New York, NY: Peter Lang Publishing, Inc., 2010.

Kincheloe, Joe L., Shirley R. Steinberg, and Christopher D. Stonebanks. "Re-educating Against Miseducation." In *Teaching Against Islamophobia*, edited by

Joe. L. Kincheloe, Shirley R. Steinberg, and Christopher D. Stonebanks, ix–xii. New York, NY: Peter Lang Publishing, Inc., 2010.

Kumar, Deepa. *Islamophobia and the Politics of Empire*. Chicago: Haymarket Books, 2012.

Lean, Nathan. *The Islamophobia Industry: How the Right Manufactures Fear of Muslims*. London: Pluto Books, 2012.

Lee, Rebekah. "Conversion and its Consequences: Africans and Islam in Cape Town." In *Can Faith Make Peace? Holy Wars and the Resolution of Religious Conflicts*, edited by Philip Broadhead and Damien Keown, 124–133. New York: I. B. Tauris & Co. Ltd., 2007.

Liese, J'lein. "The Subtleties of Prejudice: How Schools Unwittingly Facilitate Islamophobia and How to Remedy this." In *Confronting Islamophobia in Educational Practice*, edited by Barry van Driel, 63–76. Staffordshire, England: Trentham Books Limited, 2004.

Lipsitz, George. "The Possessive Investment in Whiteness." In *White Privilege: Essential Readings on the Other Side of Racism*, edited by Paula S. Rothenberg, 67–90. New York: Worth Publishers, 2008.

Major, Brenda, and S. Brooke Vick. "The Psychological Impact of Prejudice." In *On the Nature of Prejudice: Fifty Years After Allport*, edited by John F. Dovidio, Peter Glick, and Laurie A. Rudman, 139–154. Malden, MA: Blackwell Publishing, 2005.

Malhotra, Priya. "Islam's Female Converts." In *Religion in Politics and Society*, edited by Michael Kelly and Lynn M. Messina, 172–175. New York: H. W. Wilson, 2002.

Massoumi, Narzanin. "Beyond Personal Belief? The Role of Religious Identities Among Muslim Women Respect Activists." In *Women and Islam*, edited by Zayn R. Kassam, 63–92. Santa Barbara, CA: Praeger, 2010.

McCloud, Aminah. B. "Conceptual Discourse: Living as a Muslim in a Pluralistic Society." In *Muslims' Place in the American Public Square: Hope, Fears and Aspirations*, edited by Zahid. H. Bukhari, Sulayman S. Nyang, Mumtaz Ahmad, and John L. Esposito, 73–83. Walnut Creek, CA: AltaMira Press, 2004.

Mian, Hassan. A. "What is Islam? A Conversation with the Magisterial Intellectuals of the Past." In *Teaching Against Islamophobia*, edited by Joe. L. Kincheloe, Shirley R. Steinberg, and Christopher D. Stonebanks, 65–76. New York, NY: Peter Lang Publishing, Inc., 2010.

Miller, Tina, and Linda Bell. "Consenting to What? Issues of Access, Gate-keeping and 'Informed Consent.'" In *Ethics in Qualitative Research*, edited by Melanie Mauthner, Maxine Birch, Julie Jessop, and Tina Miller, 53–69. London: SAGE Publications, 2002.

Mirza, Khurrum, and Naved Bakali. "Islam: The Fundamentals Every Teacher Should Know." In *Teaching Against Islamophobia*, edited by Joe. L. Kincheloe,

Shirley R. Steinberg, and Christopher D. Stonebanks, 49–64. New York, NY: Peter Lang Publishing, Inc., 2010.

Monahan, Brian A. *The Shock of the News: Media Coverage and the Making of 9/11.* New York: New York University Press, 2010.

Moore, Peter. "Divide on Muslim Neighborhood Patrols but Majority Now Back Muslim Travel Ban." *You Gov.* March 16, 2016. http://bit.ly/1VTHqIN.

Morey, Peter, and Amina Yaqin. *Framing Muslims: Stereotyping and Representation after 9/11.* Cambridge, MA: Harvard University Press, 2011.

Mourchid, Younes. "The Dialectics of Islamophobia and Homophobia in the Lives of Gay Muslims in the United States." In *Teaching Against Islamophobia*, edited by Joe. L. Kincheloe, Shirley R. Steinberg, and Christopher D. Stonebanks, 187–203. New York, NY: Peter Lang Publishing, Inc., 2010.

Moustakas, Clark. *Phenomenological Research Methods.* London: SAGE Publications, 1994.

Muhammad, Precious R. "To be Young, Gifted, Black, American, Muslim, and Woman." In *Living Islam Outloud: American Muslim Women Speak*, edited by Saleemah Abdul-Ghafur, 36–49. Boston, MA: Beacon Press, 2005.

Murphy, Elizabeth, and Robert Dingwall. "The Ethics of Ethnography." In *Handbook of Ethnography*, edited by Paul Atkinson, Amanda Coffey, Sara Delamont, John Lofland, and Lyn Lofland, 339–351. London: SAGE Publications, 2001.

Nacos, Brigitte L., and Oscar Torres-Reyna. "Framing Muslim-Americans Before and After 9/11." In *Framing Terrorism: The News Media, the Government and the Public*, edited by Pippa Norris, Montague Kern, and Marion Just, 133–157. New York: Routledge, 2003.

Nesdale, Drew. "The Development of Prejudice in Children." In *Understanding Prejudice, Racism and Social Conflict*, edited by Martha Augoustinos, and Katherine J. Reynolds, 57–72. London: SAGE Publications Ltd., 2001.

Nimer, Mohamed. Introduction to *Islamophobia and Anti-Americanism: Causes and Remedies*, edited by Mohamed Nimer. Beltsville, MD: Amana Publications, 2007.

Nimer, Mohammed. "Muslims in the American Body Politic." In *Muslims' Place in the American Public Square: Hope, Fears and Aspirations*, edited by Zahid H. Bukhari, Sulayman S. Nyang, Mumtaz Ahmad, and John L. Esposito, 145–164. Walnut Creek, CA: AltaMira Press, 2004.

Norris, Pippa, Montague Kern, and Marion Just. "Framing Terrorism." In *Framing Terrorism: The News Media, the Government and the Public*, edited by Pippa Norris, Montague Kern, and Marion Just, 3–23. New York: Routledge, 2003.

Oakes, Penelope J., and S. Alexander Haslam. "Categorization on Trial for Inciting Intergroup Hatred." In *Understanding Prejudice, Racism and Social*

Conflict, edited by Martha Augoustinos, and Katherine J. Reynolds, 179–194. London: SAGE Publications Ltd., 2001.

Opotow, Susan. "Hate, Conflict and Moral Exclusion." In *The Psychology of Hate*, edited by Robert J. Sternberg, 121–154. Washington, D.C.: American Psychological Association, 2005.

Özyürek, Esra. "German Converts to Islam and their Ambivalent Reactions with Immigrant Muslims." In *Islamophobia/Islamophilia: Beyond the Politics of Enemy and Friend*, edited by Andrew Shryock, 172–192. Bloomington, IN: Indiana University Press, 2010.

Peek, Lori. *Behind the Backlash: Muslim Americans after 9/11*. Philadelphia, PA: Temple University Press, 2011.

Plummer, Ken. "The Call of Life Stories in Ethnographic Research." In *Handbook of Ethnography*, edited by Paul Atkinson, Amanda Coffey, Sara Delamont, John Lofland, and Lyn Lofland, 395–406. London: SAGE Publications, 2001.

Pollio, Howard R., Tracy B. Henley, and Craig J. Thompson. *The Phenomenology of Everyday Life*. Cambridge: Cambridge University Press, 1997.

Raouda, Najwa. *The Feminine Voice of Islam: Muslim Women in America*. South Bend, IN: The Victoria Press, 2008.

Roald, Anne Sofie. "The Shaping of a Scandinavian 'Islam': Converts and Gender Equal Opportunity." In *Women Embracing Islam: Gender and Conversion in the West*, edited by Karin van Nieuwkerk, 48–70. Austin, TX: University of Texas Press, 2006.

Rodriguez, Nelson M. "Emptying the Content of Whiteness: Toward an Understanding of the Relation Between Whiteness and Pedagogy." In *White Reign: Deploying Whiteness in America*, edited by Joe L. Kincheloe, Shirley R. Steinberg, Nelson M. Rodriguez, and Ronald E. Chennault, 31–62. New York, NY: St. Martin's Press, 1998.

Rothenberg, Paula S. Introduction to *White Privilege: Essential Readings on the Other Side of Racism*, edited by Paula S. Rothenberg, 1–5. New York: Worth Publishers, 2008.

Royzman, Edward B., Clark McCauley, and Paul Rozin. "From Plato to Putnam: Four Ways to Think About Hate." In *The Psychology of Hate*, edited by Robert J. Sternberg, 3–36. Washington, D.C.: American Psychological Association, 2005.

Sabir, Nadirah Z. "The Adventures of a Muslim Woman in Atlanta." In *Shattering the Stereotypes: Muslim Women Speak Out*, edited by Fawzia Afzal-Khan, 127–141. Northampton, MA: Olive Branch Press, 2005.

Safi, Louay. "Truth and Vanity Shape Anti-Americanism and Islamophobia." In *Islamophobia and Anti-Americanism: Causes and Remedies*, edited by Mohamed Nimer, 21–26. Beltsville, MD: Amana Publications, 2007.

Salhani, Claude. *Islam Without a Veil*. Washington, D. C.: Potomac Books, Inc., 2011.

Salhani, Claude. "The Problem is Knee-jerk Reactions and Counter-reactions." In *Islamophobia and Anti-Americanism: Causes and Remedies*, edited by Mohamed Nimer, 93–97. Beltsville, MD: Amana Publications, 2007.

Shaheen, Jack G. *Guilty: Hollywood's Verdict on Arabs After 9/11*. Northampton, MA: Olive Branch Press, 2012.

Shaheen, Jack G. *Reel Bad Arabs: How Hollywood Vilifies a People*. New York: Olive Branch Press, 2003.

Sheehi, Stephen. *Islamophobia: The Ideological Campaign against Muslims*. Atlanta, GA: Clarity Press, 2011.

Sheridan, Lorraine. "Islamophobia Before and After September 11th 2001" In *Confronting Islamophobia in Educational Practice*, edited by Barry van Driel, 163–176. Staffordshire, England: Trentham Books Limited, 2004.

Shryock, Andrew. "Introduction: Islam as an Object of Fear and Affection." In *Islamophobia/Islamophilia: Beyond the Politics of Enemy and Friend*, edited by Andrew Shryock, 1–25. Bloomington, IN: Indiana University Press, 2010.

Stack, Liam. "American Muslims Under Attack," *The New York Times*, February 15, 2016. http://nyti.ms/28PT2vo.

Stanton, Gregory H. "The Eight Stages of Genocide." *Genocide Watch*. March 16, 2016. http://bit.ly/1jEhWKd.

Staub, Ervin. "The Origins and Evolution of Hate, With Notes on Prevention." In *The Psychology of Hate*, edited by Robert J. Sternberg, 51–66. Washington, D. C.: American Psychological Association, 2005.

Sternberg, Robert J. "Understanding and Combating Hate." In *The Psychology of Hate*, edited by Robert J. Sternberg, 37–50. Washington, D.C.: American Psychological Association, 2005.

Sternberg, Robert J., and Karin Sternberg. *The Nature of Hate*. Cambridge, NY: Cambridge University Press, 2008.

Uddin, Asma T. "Conquering Veils: Gender and Islams." In *I Speak for Myself: American Women on Being Muslim*, edited by Maria M. Ebrahimji, and Zahra T. Suratwala, 36–41. Ashland, Oregon: White Cloud Press, 2011.

van Driel, Barry. Introduction to *Confronting Islamophobia in Educational Practice*, edited by Barry van Driel. Staffordshire, England: Trentham Books Limited, 2004.

Van Nieuwkerk, Karin. "Gender, Conversion, and Islam: A Comparison of Online and Offline Conversion Narratives." In *Women embracing Islam: Gender and Conversion in the West*, edited by Karin van Nieuwkerk, 95–119. Austin, TX: University of Texas Press, 2006.

Van Nieuwkerk, Karin. Introduction to *Women Embracing Islam: Gender and Conversion in the West*, edited by Karin van Nieuwkerk, 1–16. Austin, TX: University of Texas Press, 2006.

Wander, Philip C., Judith N. Martin, and Thomas K. Nakayama. "The Roots of Racial Classification." In *White Privilege: Essential Readings on the Other Side of*

Racism, edited by Paula S. Rothenberg, 29–34. New York: Worth Publishers, 2008.

Williams, Linda Faye. "The Construction of Race: American Social Policy at the Dawn of the New Century." In *White Privilege: Essential Readings on the Other Side of Racism*, edited by Paula S. Rothenberg, 91–95. New York: Worth Publishers, 2008.

Willis, Jerry W., Muktha Jost, and Rema Nilakanta. *Foundations of Qualitative Research: Interpretive and Critical Approaches*. London: Sage Publications, 2007.

Wilmot, William W., and Joyce L. Hocker. *Interpersonal Conflict (7th ed.)*. New York, NY: McGraw-Hill, 2007.

Wilson, Reid. "The Second Largest Religion in Each State," *The Washington Post*, June 4, 2014. http://wapo.st/UcWdB5.

Wohlrab-Sahr, Monkia. "Symbolizing Distance: Conversion to Islam in Germany and the United States." In *Women Embracing Islam: Gender and Conversion in the West*, edited by Karin van Nieuwkerk, 71–92. Austin, TX: University of Texas Press, 2006.

Yousuf-Sadiq, Nousheen. "Half and Half." In *I Speak for Myself: American Women on Being Muslim*, edited by Maria M. Ebrahimji and Zahra T. Suratwala, 18–22. Ashland, Oregon: White Cloud Press, 2011.

INDEX

© The Author(s) 2017   193
A.M. Guimond, *Converting to Islam*,
DOI 10.1007/978-3-319-54250-8

Printed in the United States
By Bookmasters